PEOPLE, MARKETS, GOODS:
ECONOMIES AND SOCIETIES IN HISTORY
Volume 2

Child Workers and Industrial Health in Britain, 1780–1850

PEOPLE, MARKETS, GOODS:
ECONOMIES AND SOCIETIES IN HISTORY

ISSN: 2051–7467

Series editors
Barry Doyle – University of Huddersfield
Nigel R. Goose – University of Hertfordshire
Steve Hindle – The Huntington Library
Jane Humphries – University of Oxford
Kevin O'Rourke – University of Oxford

The interactions of economy and society, people and goods, transactions and actions are at the root of most human behaviours. Economic and social historians are participants in the same conversation about how markets have developed historically and how they have been constituted by economic actors and agencies in various social, institutional and geographical contexts. New debates now underpin much research in economic and social, cultural, demographic, urban and political history. Their themes have enduring resonance – financial stability and instability, the costs of health and welfare, the implications of poverty and riches, flows of trade and the centrality of communications. This new paperback series aims to attract historians interested in economics and economists with an interest in history by publishing high-quality, cutting-edge academic research in the broad field of economic and social history from the late medieval/early modern period to the present day. It encourages the interaction of qualitative and quantitative methods through both excellent monographs and collections offering path-breaking overviews of key research concerns. Taking as its benchmark international relevance and excellence it is open to scholars and subjects of any geographical areas from the case study to the multi-nation comparison.

PREVIOUS TITLES

1. *Landlords and Tenants in Britain, 1440–1660: Tawney's* Agrarian Problem *Revisited*, edited by Jane Whittle, 2013

Child Workers and Industrial Health in Britain, 1780–1850

Peter Kirby

THE BOYDELL PRESS

First published 2013
The Boydell Press, Woodbridge

ISBN 978 1 84383 884 5

The Boydell Press is an imprint of Boydell & Brewer Ltd
PO Box 9, Woodbridge, Suffolk IP12 3DF, UK
and of Boydell & Brewer Inc.
668 Mt Hope Avenue, Rochester, NY 14620–2731, USA
website: www.boydellandbrewer.com

A catalogue record for this book is available
from the British Library

The publisher has no responsibility for the continued existence or accuracy of URLs for
external or third-party internet websites referred to in this book, and does not guarantee
that any content on such websites is, or will remain, accurate or appropriate.

Papers used by Boydell & Brewer Ltd are natural, recyclable products
made from wood grown in sustainable forests

Typeset by BBR, Sheffield
Printed and bound in Great Britain by CPI Group (UK) Ltd, Croydon, CR0 4YY

To Carmel, Rose, Theo, Ruth, Calum, Hannah and Lily

Contents

Figures

Tables

Acknowledgements

The research for this book was made easier with the advice of friends and colleagues past and present, including Joseph Bergin, Laurence Brockliss, Romola Davenport, Douglas Farnie, Nigel Goose, Peter Hennock, Katrina Honeyman, Jane Humphries, Joanna Innes, Samantha Lane, Jack Langton, Anne Laurence, Alysa Levene, John Lyons, Don MacRaild, David Martin, Ashley Mathisen, Peter Maw, Linda McDowell, Roger Middleton, Beatrice Moring, Norris Nash, Deborah Oxley, Margaret Pelling, John Pickstone, Steve Rigby, Leonard Schwarz, Leigh Shaw-Taylor, John Stewart, Geoff Timmins, Katherine Venables and Bob Woods. Any errors or misconceptions in the text remain entirely the responsibility of the author.

The author wishes to thank the President and fellows of St John's College, Oxford, for a Visiting Research Associateship which allowed the completion of the typescript in an atmosphere of friendly and collegial support. I am also particularly grateful to the participants in the 'Children, Work and Welfare in Historical Perspective' symposium held at the College in November 2011 and to the Centre for the History of Childhood at Magdalen College, Oxford, for further helpful comments. Final revisions to the text were performed during a visiting scholarship at the Department of History in Fudan University, Shanghai, supported by the department and the Guanghua Humanities Foundation.

I also wish to thank staff at the libraries and archives visited during the course of the research including: Patricia Collins of the Manchester Central Reference Library; James Peters of John Rylands Library Special Collections (University of Manchester); Elaine Simpson, Curator of Official Publications at the National Library of Scotland; the staff of the International Cotton Association; Hannah Chandler, Official Papers Librarian at the Bodleian Law Library; the staff of Nuffield College Library, Oxford and the Wellcome Trust Library and Archives, London.

Finally, I wish to extend my gratitude to the Board of Trustees of the British Cotton Growing Association: Work People's Collection Fund without whose generous financial support the book would not have been completed, to Amanda Thompson for meticulous copyediting and typesetting services, and to Michael Middeke and the staff at Boydell & Brewer for their outstanding assistance in the editorial and publication phases.

Introduction

Locating Children's Industrial Health

In recent decades, economic and social historians have produced a growing number of monographical studies exploring the complex problem of child labour during the Industrial Revolution.[1] Historical demographers and medical historians, meanwhile, have offered increasingly detailed investigations of child health and welfare in early urban and industrial society.[2] The subject of children's occupational health, however, has attracted little serious analysis. Indeed, the poor health and ill-treatment of child labourers in mills and factories has long remained a seemingly incontrovertible feature

---

1   P. Bolin-Hort, *Work, Family and the State: Child Labour and the Organisation of Production in the British Cotton Industry, 1780–1920* (Lund: Lund University Press, 1989); H. Cunningham, 'The Employment and Unemployment of Children in England c.1680–1851', *Past & Present*, 126 (1990), 115–50; K. Honeyman, *Child Workers in England, 1780–1820: Parish Apprentices and the Making of the Early Industrial Labour Force* (Aldershot: Ashgate, 2007); S. Horrell and J. Humphries, '"The Exploitation of Little Children": Child Labor and the Family Economy in the Industrial Revolution', *Explorations in Economic History*, 32 (1995), 485–516; J. Humphries, *Childhood and Child Labour in the British Industrial Revolution* (Cambridge: Cambridge University Press, 2010); P. Kirby, 'The Historic Viability of Child Labour and the Mines Act of 1842', in *A Thing of the Past? Child Labour in Britain in the Nineteenth and Twentieth Centuries*, ed. M. Lavalette (Liverpool: Liverpool University Press, 1999), pp. 101–17; P. Kirby, *Child Labour in Britain, 1750–1870* (Basingstoke: Palgrave, 2003); P. Kirby, 'How many Children were "Unemployed" in Eighteenth- and Nineteenth-Century England?', *Past & Present*, 187 (May 2005), 187–202; P. Kirby, 'A Brief Statistical Sketch of the Child Labour Market in Mid-Nineteenth Century London', *Continuity and Change*, 20 (2005), 229–45; P. Kirby, 'The Transition to Working Life in Eighteenth and Nineteenth-Century England and Wales', in *Child Labour's Global Past: 1650–2000*, ed. K. Lieten and E. van Nederveen Meerkerk (Amsterdam: International Institute for Social History, 2011), pp. 119–36.
2   P. Huck, 'Infant Mortality and Living Standards of English Workers during the Industrial Revolution', *Journal of Economic History*, 55 (1995), 528–50; J. Brown, 'The Condition of England and the Standard of Living: Cotton Textiles in the Northwest, 1806–1850', *Journal of Economic History*, 50 (1990), 591–614; M. Pelling, 'Child Health as a Social Value in Early Modern England', *Social History of Medicine*, 1 (1988), 135–64;

of the historiography of British industrialisation.[3] Child industrial workers are popularly represented as marginal figures, creeping along narrow coal seams, clambering up chimneys or suffering beatings at the hands of cruel factory overseers. Such imagery has become emblematic of the panoply of social problems that accompanied early industrial capitalism. Early labour historians such as the Hammonds argued passionately that poor working conditions, ill-health and violence were commonplace in large factories and mines and that such privations increased in intensity alongside the growth of modern industry.[4] The weight of opinion over the health of child industrial workers has for more than a century been profoundly pessimistic. Children are portrayed as victims of avaricious employers and an inherently brutal system of production. Rarely have they been recognised as viable workers and earners in their own right. Such uncomplicated assumptions were rarely challenged in the twentieth century and few attempts have been

M. Pelling, 'Apprenticeship, Health and Social Cohesion in Early Modern London', *History Workshop*, 37, 1 (1994), 33–56; F. B. Smith, *The People's Health, 1830–1910* (London: Weidenfeld & Nicholson, 1979); R. Gray, 'Medical Men, Industrial Labour and the State in Britain, 1830–50', *Social History*, 16 (January 1991), 19–43; R. Gray, 'The Languages of Factory Reform in Britain, c.1830–1860', in *The Historical Meanings of Work*, ed. P. Joyce (Cambridge: Cambridge University Press, 1987), pp. 143–79; A. Levene, *Childcare, Health and Mortality at the London Foundling Hospital, 1741–1800: 'Left to the Mercy of the World'* (Manchester: Manchester University Press, 2007); A. Levene, *The Childhood of the Poor: Welfare in Eighteenth-Century London* (Basingstoke: Palgrave, 2012); H. Newton, *The Sick Child in Early-Modern England, 1580–1720* (Oxford: Oxford University Press, 2012); C. Hamlin, *Public Health and Social Justice in the Age of Chadwick: Britain, 1800–1854* (Cambridge: Cambridge University Press, 1998); B. A. Hanawalt, 'Childrearing among the Lower Classes of Late Medieval England', *Journal of Interdisciplinary History*, 8 (1977), 1–22; B. A. Hanawalt, *The Ties that Bound: Peasant Families in Medieval England* (Oxford: Oxford University Press, 1986) (particularly chapters 10 and 11 which examine child deaths from coroners' rolls).

3　There has been little development of the subject since the early twentieth century. See B. L. Hutchins and S. Harrison, *A History of Factory Legislation* (London: P. S. King & Son, 1903; 3rd edn, 1926); M. W. Thomas, *The Early Factory Legislation: A Study in Legislative and Administrative Evolution* (Leigh-on-Sea: Thames Bank Publishing, 1948); J. T. Ward, *The Factory Movement, 1830–1855* (London: Macmillan, 1962). Urban and industrial causes of child ill-health have often been seen as interchangeable: see, for example, M. Cruickshank, *Children and Industry: Child Health and Welfare in North-West Textile Towns during the Nineteenth Century* (Manchester: Manchester University Press, 1981).

4　J. L. Hammond and B. Hammond, *The Town Labourer, 1760–1832: The New Civilisation* (1917; London: Longmans, Green & Company, 1966); see also Humphries, *Childhood and Child Labour*.

made to explore the nature and causes of ill-health and poor treatment amongst working children.[5] Indeed, scepticism has been expressed about the quality of evidence available for a critical study of health amongst early industrial child workers. The present author argued a decade ago that the relative scarcity of sources prior to 1850 'prevents the historian from developing anything more than an impressionistic view of the effects of occupations upon children's health.'[6] The lack of any major monographical study of child industrial health provides the justification for the present volume. The chronology of the research is also self-defining. In 1780, child industrial health was hardly recognised as a topic for discussion by governments and social commentators but by the mid-nineteenth century changes in social attitudes, structural transformations in the workplace and new forms of social investigation had resulted in a much greater social awareness of the plight of working children in large industrial enterprises. By 1850, the first attempts at protective legislation had been introduced as well as the first reasonably effective government inspectorates. This book therefore concentrates primarily upon the emergence of health as a central element in debates over the industrial employment of children during a crucial period of economic, social and epidemiological transition. The emergence of larger and more regulated factories, mills and mines forms a major subject of the inquiry, though at the core of the study lies the complex and often diffuse relationship between children's occupational health and the changing urban manufacturing environment.

Quite what constituted a specifically child-centred occupational disease or injury in the past raises complex questions of evidence and causation

5   A few economic historians have dissented from the popular view that mills and factories caused a relative deterioration in the intensity of work. Dorothy George argued that the typical hand-loom weaver of the eighteenth century achieved 'mass-production by dint of unremitting bodily effort': cited in I. Pinchbeck and M. Hewitt, *Children in English Society, vol. 2, From the eighteenth century to the Children Act 1948* (London: Routledge, 1973), pp. 398–9. See also R. M. Hartwell, 'Children as Slaves', in *The Industrial Revolution and Economic Growth* (London: Methuen, 1971), pp. 390–408; W. H. Hutt, 'The Factory System of the Early Nineteenth Century', in *Capitalism and the Historians*, ed. F. A. Hayek (Chicago: University of Chicago Press, 1954), pp. 160–88; C. Nardinelli, *Child Labor and the Industrial Revolution* (Bloomington and Indianapolis: Indiana University Press, 1990).

6   Kirby, *Child Labour in Britain*, pp. 15–16. This view appears to have been shared by other historians of child employment who have mostly avoided any detailed discussion of the health of child labourers: Honeyman, *Child Workers*; Humphries, *Childhood and Child Labour*.

which become increasingly challenging the further back one looks.[7] Early authors of occupational health literature were not particularly concerned about the health and welfare effects of children's employment. Ramazzini's late seventeenth-century *Treatise of the Diseases of Tradesmen* (generally unknown in Britain before the late 1740s) largely failed to discuss the ailments of child workers. Moreover, most of the later eighteenth-century investigators of occupational health tended to focus narrowly on the effects of specifically harmful materials in a small number of skilled or semi-skilled adult trades.[8] Pioneering studies in the late eighteenth century, such as Pryce's commentary on metal mines, Lind's *Treatise on the Scurvy*, or Pott's discovery of sweeps' cancer, similarly, failed to develop any more general or integrated interest in occupational health as a discipline worthy of study.[9] Moreover, the emergence of seemingly new work-related health

---

7   Thomas Oliver reflected in 1902 that the long-term relationship between industrial health and economic growth has been 'a process of evolution wherein each succeeding stage of industrial development has been attended by labour problems, social difficulties, and diseases particularly its own': T. Oliver, 'Introduction', in *The Dangerous Trades: the Historical, Social and Legal Aspects of Industrial Occupations as Affecting Health*, ed. T. Oliver (London: John Murray, 1902), pp. 1–23 (p. 1).

8   B. Ramazzini, *Treatise of the Diseases of Tradesmen* (English edn, London: Andrew Bell, 1705); J. Rule, *The Experience of Labour in Eighteenth-Century Industry* (London: Croom Helm, 1981), p. 92, n. 3. Early studies include the effects of lead poisoning amongst ceruse makers, for example, or the paralytic poisoning of quicksilver miners: see P. Vernati, 'The Method of Making Cerusse', *The Philosophical Transactions of the Royal Society of London* (1672–83; abridged, London: C. & R. Baldwin, 1809), vol. 2, pp. 421–2; W. Pope, 'On the mines of mercury in Friuli', *The Philosophical Transactions of the Royal Society of London* (1672–83; abridged, London: C. & R. Baldwin, 1809), vol. 1, pp. 10–12; E. Brown, 'On the quicksilver mines in Friuli', *The Philosophical Transactions of the Royal Society of London* (1672–83; abridged, London: C. & R. Baldwin, 1809), vol. 1, pp. 407–9.

9   W. Pryce, *Mineralogia Cornubiensis* (London: J. Phillips, 1778); J. Lind, *A Treatise on the Scurvy* (Edinburgh: A. Millar, 1753). Percivall Pott's discovery in 1775 of the link between chimney soot and scrotal cancer in sweeps was probably the first occasion upon which a malignant disease was linked with a specific occupation: P. Pott, *Chirurgical Observations Relative to the Cataract, the Polypus of the Nose, the Cancer of the Scrotum, the Different Kinds of Ruptures, and the Mortification of the Toes and Feet*, vol. 3 (London: T. J. Carnegy, 1775), pp. 177–83; H. A. Waldron, 'A Brief History of Scrotal Cancer', *British Journal of Industrial Medicine*, 40 (1983), 390–401. Howlett complained in 1792 of the 'catalogue of our fellow creatures suffocated in mines and pits, or gradually poisoned by the noxious effluvia of metals, oils, powders, spirits &c. used in their work': J. Howlett, 'Defence of his Pamphlet on Population', *Gentleman's Magazine*, 52 (1792), 525–6 (p. 526).

challenges in the new manufacturing districts of the late eighteenth and early nineteenth centuries appeared contemporaneously against a more general backdrop of rapidly deteriorating urban public health. This created enormous problems for contemporary medical men in the diagnosis and aetiology of child occupational ailments. Many early nineteenth-century theories about the origins of worker ill-health were positively misleading. The 'expert' medical witnesses who appeared before the early nineteenth-century parliamentary committees of inquiry, for example, almost always had no experience of factory work or of life in manufacturing towns. As a result, many diseases, deformities and disabilities were attributed to the workplace when their origins clearly lay beyond the factory gate.[10] One of the major difficulties in understanding child industrial health in the century prior to 1850, therefore, lies in the relative absence of informed or impartial accounts of children's working conditions.

More recent occupational health histories offer few insights to the health and welfare of industrial children. Studies of early occupational health, such as the pioneering work of Sigerist, Rosen and Teleky in the 1930s and 1940s, promised a view of workers' healthiness that was grounded in very broad social questions. These early scholars cautioned against restricting the study of workplace health to isolated trades or transient medical theory and emphasised the intrinsic relationship between the workplace and the wider economic environment.[11] Much subsequent research in the field during the 1950s, 60s and 70s, however, tended to focus increasingly on the

---

10   Hutt, p. 167; PP 1831–2 (706), p. 514; R. B. Hope, 'Dr Thomas Percival, a Medical Pioneer and Social Reformer, 1740–1804' (MA thesis, University of Manchester, 1947), p. 114; Kirby, *Child Labour in Britain*, p. 15. Charles Thackrah, for example, framed his evidence to the Sadler Committee broadly within a framework of constitutional effects reflecting a wide set of environmental and epidemiological influences. Thackrah's opinions about factory work were, in fact, quite theoretical. He stated to the Committee that his view that excessive labour shortened the lives of workers had been arrived at it not as a result of personal observation but from 'medical reading': PP 1831–2 (706), pp. 512, 517.

11   H. E. Sigerist, 'Historical Background of Industrial and Occupational Diseases', *Bulletin of the New York Academy of Medicine*, 12 (1936), 597–609; G. Rosen, 'On the Historical Investigation of Occupational Diseases: An Aperçu', *Bulletin of the History of Medicine*, 5 (1937), 941–6; G. Rosen, *The History of Miners' Diseases: A Medical and Social Interpretation* (New York: Schuman's, 1943); L. Teleky, *History of Factory and Mine Hygiene* (New York: Columbia University Press, 1948). Hunter's monumental *Diseases of Occupations* contains a lengthy (though Whiggish) historical discussion: D. Hunter, *The Diseases of Occupations* (1955; London: Hodder & Stoughton, 1978), pp. 1–141. The importance of treating industrial diseases as part of a wider social context has more recently been emphasised in J. Greenlees, '"Stop Kissing and Steaming!":

discrete occupational conditions of adults and on trades that were particularly harmful. Meanwhile, the history of occupational medicine itself as a discipline remained largely the preserve of occupational health doctors themselves together with a small band of pioneering northern social historians.[12] It was not until the 1980s that interest in the broader economic and social context of workers' health was revived with the publication of Wohl's *Endangered Lives*, Weindling's *Social History of Occupational Health* and Rule's *Experience of Labour in Eighteenth-Century Britain*, each of which sought to locate the health of workers within a framework of social change.[13] Meanwhile, increasingly detailed studies emerged of diseases such as mule spinners' cancer, byssinosis, asbestosis, miners' lung, silicosis, plumbism, textiles workers' tuberculosis, and the causes and contexts of workplace injuries.[14] Industrial legislation and inspection also became more

Tuberculosis and the Occupational Health Movement in Massachusetts and Lancashire, 1870–1918', *Urban History*, 32 (2005), 223–46 (p. 224).

12 N. Ware, *The Industrial Worker, 1840–1860* (1924; Chicago: Quadrangle Books, 1964); W. R. Lee, 'Emergence of Occupational Medicine in Victorian Times', *British Journal of Industrial Medicine*, 30 (1973), 118–24; W. R. Lee, 'Robert Baker: the First Doctor in the Factory Department, Part 1. 1803–1858', *British Journal of Industrial Medicine*, 21 (1964), 85–93; A. Meiklejohn, 'Outbreak of Fever in Cotton Mills at Radcliffe, 1784', *British Journal of Industrial Medicine*, 16, 1 (1959), 68–70; A. Meiklejohn, 'Industrial Health – Meeting the Challenge', *British Journal of Industrial Medicine*, 16, 1 (1959), 1–10; M. E. Rose, 'The Doctor in the Industrial Revolution', *British Journal of Industrial Medicine*, 28 (1971), 22–6; J. V. Pickstone, 'Ferriar's Fever to Kay's Cholera: Disease and Social Structure in Cottonopolis', *History of Science*, 22 (1984), 401–19. See also T. Carter, 'British Occupational Hygiene Practice, 1720–1920', *Annals of Occupational Hygiene*, 48 (2004), 299–307; L. J. Goldwater, 'The History of Occupational Medicine', *Clinics in Podiatric Medicine and Surgery*, 4 (1987), 523–7; H. K. Abrams, 'A Short History of Occupational Health', *Journal of Public Health Policy*, 22 (2001), 34–80.

13 A. S. Wohl, Chapter 10, 'The Canker of Industrial Diseases', in *Endangered Lives: Public Health in Victorian Britain* (1983; London: Methuen, 1984), pp. 257–84; P. Weindling, 'Linking Self Help and Medical Science: The Social History of Occupational Health', in *The Social History of Occupational Health*, ed. P. Weindling (London: Croom Helm, 1985), pp. 2–31 (p. 2); Rule, pp. 74–94. Rule's chapter remains one of the most vivid discussions of workplace hazards faced by eighteenth-century workers.

14 T. Wyke, 'Mule Spinners' Cancer', in *The Barefoot Aristocrats: A History of the Amalgamated Association of Operative Cotton Spinners*, ed. A. Fowler and T. Wyke (Littleborough: George Kelsall, 1987), pp. 184–96; S. Bowden and G. Tweedale, 'Mondays without Dread: The Trade Union Response to Byssinosis in the Lancashire Cotton Industry in the Twentieth Century', *Social History of Medicine*, 16, 1 (2003), 79–95; S. Bowden and G. Tweedale, 'Poisoned by the Fluff: Compensation and Litigation for Byssinosis in the Lancashire Cotton Industry', *Journal of Law and Society*, 29, 4 (2002), 560–79; A. McIvor, *Lethal Work: A History of the Asbestos Tragedy in Scotland* (Glasgow: Tuckwell, 2000);

carefully located within an analysis of medical and socio-legal change whilst studies of the ecological and cultural contexts of industrial health sought to contrast the body as a biological entity alongside the spread of machine production, whose pace and regularity in new industrial centres dominated most aspects of manufacturing life.[15] The profile of occupational health history has been raised further in recent monographs by Mills (on aspects of mines safety), Bronstein (on nineteenth-century industrial

G. Tweedale, *Magic Mineral to Killer Dust: Turner & Newall and the Asbestos Hazard* (2nd edn; Oxford: Oxford University Press, 2001); A. McIvor and R. Johnston, *Miners' Lung: A History of Dust Disease in British Coal Mining* (Aldershot: Ashgate, 2007); C. Holdsworth, 'Dr John Thomas Arlidge and Victorian Occupational Medicine', *Medical History*, 42 (1998), 458–75; C. Holdsworth, 'Potters' Rot and Plumbism: Occupational Health in the North Staffordshire Pottery Industry' (Ph.D. thesis, University of Liverpool, 1995); Greenlees, 'Stop Kissing and Steaming!'; J. Greenlees, *Female Labour Power: women workers' influence on business practices in the British and American cotton industries, 1780–1860* (Aldershot: Ashgate, 2007); M. W. Dupree, *Family structure in the Staffordshire potteries, 1840–1880* (Oxford: Clarendon Press, 1995); R. Cooter and W. Luckin (eds.), *Accidents in History* (Atlanta: Rodopi, 1997).

15 P. W. J. Bartrip, 'British Government Inspection, 1832–1875: Some Observations', *Historical Journal*, 25 (1982), 605–26; P. W. J. Bartrip, 'Success or Failure? The Prosecution of the Early Factory Acts', *Economic History Review*, 38 (1985), 423–7; P. W. J. Bartrip and P. T. Fenn, 'The Administration of Safety: the Enforcement of the Early Factory Inspectorate, 1844–1864', *Public Administration*, 58 (1980), 87–107; P. W. J. Bartrip and P. T. Fenn, 'The Conventionalization of Early Factory Crime: A Re-assessment', *International Journal of the Sociology of Law*, 8 (1980), 175–86; P. W. J. Bartrip and P. T. Fenn, 'The Evolution of Regulatory Style in the Nineteenth-Century British Factory Inspectorate', *Journal of Law and Society*, 10 (1983), 201–22; Bolin-Hort, *Work, Family and the State*; W. G. Carson, 'White-Collar Crime and the Enforcement of Factory Legislation', *British Journal of Criminology*, 10 (1970), 383–98; W. G. Carson, 'The Conventionalization of Early Factory Crime', *International Journal of the Sociology of Law*, 7 (1979), 37–60; Hutchins and Harrison, *History of Factory Legislation*; Kirby, 'Historic Viability of Child Labour'; Kirby, *Child Labour in Britain*, pp. 105–10; B. Martin, 'Leonard Horner: a Portrait of an Inspector of Factories', *International Review of Social History*, 14 (1969), 412–43; H. P. Marvel, 'Factory Regulation: A Reinterpretation of Early English Experience', *Journal of Law and Economics*, 20 (1977), 379–402; C. Mills, *Regulating Health and Safety in the British Mining Industries, 1800–1914* (Aldershot: Ashgate, 2010); C. Nardinelli, 'Child Labor and the Factory Acts', *Journal of Economic History*, 40 (1980), 739–55; C. Nardinelli, 'The Successful Prosecution of the Factory Acts: A Suggested Explanation', *Economic History Review*, 38 (1985), 428–30; A. E. Peacock, 'The Justices of the Peace and the Prosecution of the Factory Acts, 1833–1855' (D.Phil. thesis, University of York, 1982); A. E. Peacock, 'The Successful Prosecution of the Factory Acts, 1833–55', *Economic History Review*, 37 (1984), 197–210; A. F. McEvoy, 'Working Environments: an Ecological Approach to Industrial Health and Safety', in *Accidents in History*, ed. R. Cooter and W. Luckin (Atlanta: Rodopi, 1997), pp. 59–89.

injuries) and Long (on the political economy of twentieth-century factory inspection).[16] Despite such advances in occupational health history, the vast majority of research has remained focused on developments from about the mid-nineteenth century from which point the coverage of the 'dangerous trades' in state reports, popular periodicals and newspapers became increasingly detailed.[17] By contrast, the study of occupational health during the 'classic' Industrial Revolution period remains hindered by a general lack of consistent evidence and the health of workers between 1780 and 1850 remains a dark and polemical area of historical research.[18] Weindling's complaint of nearly three decades ago that '[o]nly a fraction of the historical literature on industry, the labour movement and medicine is concerned with occupational health' still remains relevant to the century prior to 1850. Joyce, too, lamented the lack of historical understanding of 'the material nature of work ... What was the level of noise, dirt and disease, and how were workers affected outside work by ... deafness or hereditary and perhaps caste-like occupational ailments and sensibilities?'[19] Such questions remain largely unanswered in published research. The most relevant and detailed studies of child health in urban and industrial situations have been largely confined to unpublished graduate dissertations, of which the most valuable include Huzzard's institutional history of the factory surgeon, Paterson's study of late eighteenth-century mill fever and Van Manen's research into the political campaigns surrounding the employment of climbing boys.[20] By contrast, the enduring preoccupation

16   Mills, *Regulating Health and Safety*; J. L. Bronstein, *Caught in the Machinery: Workplace Accidents and Injured Workers in Nineteenth-Century Britain* (Stanford: Stanford University Press, 2008); V. Long, *The Rise and Fall of the Healthy Factory: The Politics of Industrial Health in Britain, 1914–60* (Basingstoke: Palgrave, 2010).

17   This is an area in which some outstanding research has been produced. For example, see P. W. J. Bartrip, *The Home Office and the Dangerous Trades: Regulating Occupational Disease in Victorian and Edwardian Britain* (Amsterdam: Rodopi, 2002), and P. W. J. Bartrip and S. B. Burman, *The Wounded Soldiers of Industry: Industrial Compensation Policy, 1833–1897* (Oxford: Oxford University Press, 1983).

18   On this see, for example, Hartwell, 'Children as Slaves'.

19   Weindling, p. 2; P. Joyce, 'Work', in *Cambridge Social History of Britain*, ed. F. M. L. Thompson (Cambridge: Cambridge University Press, 1990), vol. 2, pp. 131–94 (p. 173), cited in A. McIvor, 'Health and Safety in the Cotton Industry: A Literature Survey', *Manchester Region History Review*, 9 (1995), 50–7 (p. 51).

20   S. Huzzard, 'The Role of the Certifying Factory Surgeon in the State Regulation of Child Labour and Industrial Health' (MA thesis, University of Manchester, 1976); C. S. Paterson, 'From Fever to Digestive Disease: Approaches to the Problem of Factory Ill-Health in Britain, 1784–1833' (Ph.D. thesis, University of British Columbia, 1995);

amongst political and social historians with parliamentary debates, the achievement of industrial regulation and the morality of child labour offers surprisingly few insights into the health of children in the workplace.[21]

The burgeoning literature on the children of the labouring poor provides rich contextual material for the historian of child health. In *Children of the Poor* (1991), Cunningham offered a vivid insight into attitudes towards children in poverty in eighteenth and nineteenth-century society and highlighted the development in the minds of philanthropists and legislators of a concept of rights that might be applied to those who were too young to protect themselves.[22] Levene, meanwhile, has investigated the plight of poor children and families dependent upon welfare and charitable institutions. She has focused chiefly upon those groups of children for whom there was little available work, either because they were too young (i.e.

N. Van Manen, 'The Climbing Boy Campaigns in Britain, *c*.1770–1840: Cultures of Reform, Languages of Health and Experiences of Childhood' (Ph.D. thesis, University of York, 2010). See also Hope, 'Dr Thomas Percival'; J. E. M. Walker, 'John Ferriar of Manchester. M.D.: His Life and Work' (MSc thesis, University of Manchester, 1973); J. Mottram, 'The Life and Work of John Roberton (1797–1876) of Manchester, Obstetrician and Social Reformer' (MSc thesis, University of Manchester, 1986).

21 Hutchins and Harrison, *History of Factory Legislation*; Thomas, *Early Factory Legislation*; A. J. Heesom, 'The Coal Mines Act of 1842, Social Reform, and Social Control', *Historical Journal*, 24 (1981), 69–88; A. J. Heesom, 'The Northern Coal-Owners and the Opposition to the Coal Mines Act of 1842', *International Review of Social History*, 25 (1980), 236–71; O. MacDonagh, *Early Victorian Government* (London: Weidenfeld & Nicolson, 1977); A. M. Anderson, 'Historical Sketch of the Development of Legislation for Injurious and Dangerous Industries in England', in *The Dangerous Trades: the Historical, Social and Legal Aspects of Industrial Occupations as Affecting Health*, ed. T. Oliver (London: John Murray, 1902), pp. 24–43; T. Djang, *Factory Inspection in Great Britain* (London: Allen & Unwin, 1942). Similarly, the attention of most scholars working on earlier periods has, of necessity, been concentrated upon more fragmentary sources and discrete features of the child labour scene such as apprenticeship, aspects of social policy or medical theory: Pelling, 'Child Health'; Pelling, 'Apprenticeship, Health and Social Cohesion'; Smith, Chapter 3, 'Childhood and Youth', in *People's Health*, pp. 136–94; Hamlin, *Public Health and Social Justice*; M. B. Rose, 'Social Policy and Business: Parish Apprenticeship and the Early Factory System, 1750–1834', *Business History*, 31 (1989), 5–32; Gray, 'Medical Men'.

22 Cunningham, 'Employment and Unemployment'; H. Cunningham, *The Children of the Poor: Representations of Childhood since the Seventeenth Century* (Oxford: Blackwell, 1991). Mathisen's important recent thesis on the medical treatment of poor children in eighteenth-century London, notably, contains virtually no coverage of the health of working children: A. Mathisen, 'Treating the Children of the Poor: Institutions and the Construction of Medical Authority in Eighteenth-Century London' (D.Phil. thesis, Oxford University, 2011); Kirby, 'Brief Statistical Sketch'.

London foundlings or the substantial numbers of young children under metropolitan Poor Law care) or because they lived in dense urban centres where demand for child labour was considerably lower in comparison with agricultural, proto-industrial or industrial regions. Such research provides a highly detailed picture of urban welfare, disease and mortality and Levene's models of pauper childhood in the later eighteenth century offer valuable insights to the family and workhouse settings from which parish children were often bound out to employers.[23] Further detailed research on the lives of pauper apprentices has been conducted by Honeyman who has explored their position within the early textiles industry of the eighteenth and early nineteenth centuries. Honeyman sought to highlight the importance of agency amongst early pauper factory apprentices, arguing that they were not merely passive victims of Poor Law officials and factory masters. The study of the resourcefulness of early parish apprentices has informed more recent research by Peers on pauper children employed by the Gregs' mill at Styal.[24] Despite the valuable research on child destitution and the plight of parish apprentices, however, this literature hardly ever discusses the effects of work processes upon the health of children. Indeed, the issue almost always appears more implied than evaluated.

The relative absence of primary statistical evidence prior to the 1850s presents further difficulties to any quantitative analysis of child occupational health. There were no properly constituted systems of reporting workplace ill-health during the 'classic' Industrial Revolution period. Indeed, the collection of statistics on machinery injuries in factories did not become systematic until well into the 1840s (later in coalmines) and it was not until the 1860s that the state became involved in investigating the major hazardous trades such as Lucifer match-making, percussion cap and cartridge manufacture, fustian cutting and earthenware manufacture.[25]

---

23 Levene, *Childcare, Health and Mortality*; Levene, *Childhood of the Poor*.

24 Honeyman, *Child Workers*, p. 264; S. Peers, 'Power, Paternalism, Panopticism and Protest: Geographies of Power and Resistance in a Cotton Mill Community, Quarry Bank Mill, Styal, Cheshire, 1784–1860' (D.Phil. thesis, Oxford University, 2008). Numerous authors have discussed pauper apprentices: see S. D. Chapman, *The Early Factory Masters: the Transition to the Factory System in the Midlands Textile Industry* (Newton Abbot: David & Charles, 1967); J. Innes, 'Origins of the Factory Acts: the Health and Morals of Apprentices Act, 1802', in *Law, Crime and English Society, 1660–1830*, ed. N. Landau (Cambridge: Cambridge University Press, 2002), pp. 230–55; Rose, 'Social Policy and Business'. However, only Paterson has sought to explore the health of factory workers in any depth (on this see Chapter 2 below): Paterson, 'Factory Ill-Health'.

25 W. R. Lee, 'Occupational Medicine', in *Medicine and Science in the 1860s:*

Similarly, byssinosis (a major pulmonary disease of textiles workers) was only formally identified as a work-related illness in the 1860s and no usable statistics of such factory diseases were gathered.[26] From 1837, the General Register Office began to collect evidence of age-specific mortality but there were few attempts to provide statistics linking occupations with ill-health or death. By 1851, an awareness of the harmful effects of workplace materials was evident in the earliest national census classification of occupations, which grouped workers in specific jobs according to the raw materials with which they came into contact, and the Registrar General's decennial occupational mortality supplements from 1851 also began to provide limited statistics on work-related deaths.[27] Early statistics can be misleading, however, because they often lacked any comparative analysis of risk and frequently omitted workers who had left their main employment on account of disability to take up lighter employments prior to death. Other traditional sources of information on causes of death present similarly intractable problems for the historian of child health. Coroner's inquests, for example, frequently recorded work-related deaths as merely 'accidental' and often attributed causes to the negligence of workers themselves. In some traditionally dangerous trades, fatalities were so common as not to warrant the involvement of the Coroner. Few inquests were held on coalminers killed in English mines in the eighteenth century, for example, though surviving reports from mining communities suggest that around 40 per cent of all recorded fatal accidents occurred in or around the workplace.[28] The testimony of workers about their own

proceedings of the sixth British Congress on the History of Medicine, University of Sussex, 6–9 September, 1967, ed. F. N. L. Poynter (London: Wellcome Institute of the History of Medicine, 1968), pp. 151–81 (p. 173); Bartrip, *Home Office and the Dangerous Trades*.

26   J. A. Smiley, 'Background to Byssinosis in Ulster', *British Journal of Industrial Medicine*, 18, 1 (1961), 1–9 (p. 2); Bowden and Tweedale, 'Poisoned by the Fluff', p. 561.

27   In the census, cotton workers were classed alongside processors of vegetable products whilst woollen workers were grouped along with those working with materials of animal origin: E. Higgs, 'Disease, Febrile Poisons, and Statistics: the Census as a Medical Survey, 1841–1911', *Social History of Medicine*, 4 (1991), 465–78 (pp. 469–73). See also PP 1863 [3221], pp. 225–32; Hunter, p. 97.

28   Reports from the mining community of Prescot between 1746 and 1789 also show that deaths of males accounted for 90 per cent of workplace mortality: F. A. Bailey, 'Coroner's Inquests held in the Manor of Prescot, 1746–89', *Transactions of the Historic Society of Lancashire and Cheshire*, 86 (1934), 21–39, pp. 21–39; P. A. Sambrook, 'Childhood and Sudden Death in Staffordshire, 1851 and 1860', in *Staffordshire Histories: Essays in Honour of Michael Greenslade*, ed. P. Morgan and A. D. M. Phillips (Stafford:

health and that of their children can also be deceptive. Many employees were stoical in the face of industrial diseases and injuries which were often assumed to form part of the price of labour in the relatively new and better-remunerated industrial occupations. Employees often feared that improvements in workplace safety might result in a slowing-down in production, the imposition of time-consuming safety procedures and a consequent fall in wages.

An additional obstacle is that only a minority of illnesses or injuries proved fatal. Few sources provide any useful evidence of the incidence of non-fatal diseases or accidents amongst early nineteenth-century workers. Consequently, the experiences of the majority of workers who survived such experiences have rarely been explored. Ground-breaking research by Riley on the morbidity of adult workers and by Hardy on the relationship between fatal and non-fatal diseases amongst children has prepared the ground for future explorations of the effects of ill-health and disability upon productivity and attendance. Knowledge about the effects of chronic and debilitating conditions for both child and adult workers, however, remains extremely sketchy.[29] Perhaps more importantly, little evidence survives prior to the late 1840s of the extent of injuries to the upper limbs of factory children – almost certainly the most common industrial injury – or how such physical insults and disabilities affected their future employment prospects. The effect of the disease environment of early manufacturing towns complicates matters still further. Survivors of infantile and early childhood diseases would have borne various disabilities and complications into their early working lives, rendering it extremely difficult, even for the most astute of contemporary observers, to distinguish pre-existing conditions from those caused specifically by the work process. Other potential indicators of the effects of labour on child health remain largely uncharted by economic and social historians. The burgeoning literature on the history of human stature and nutritional status, for example, which seeks ostensibly to measure the effects of non-fatal disease

Staffordshire Record Society, 1999), pp. 216–52 (p. 227); Anon., 'Fatal Accident', *Blackburn Standard*, 11 December 1839, p. 2.

29   J. C. Riley, *Sick, Not Dead: the Health of British Workingmen during the Mortality Decline* (Baltimore: Johns Hopkins University Press, 1997); A. Hardy, 'Rickets and the Rest: Child-care, Diet and the Infectious Children's Diseases, 1850–1914', *Social History of Medicine*, 5 (1992), 389–412; see also B. Harris, M. Gorsky, M. Guntupalli and A. Hinde, 'Long-term Changes in Sickness and Health: Further Evidence from the Hampshire Friendly Society', *Economic History Review*, 65 (2012), 719–45.

Table 1: The physical condition of 534 male children in different occupations, 1841

	Mines (%)	Farms (%)	Potteries (%)	Worsted (%)
Below par	3.83	5.05	70.66	46.05
At par	24.40	27.27	29.33	52.63
Muscular	33.49	42.42	0.00	0.00
Very muscular	38.28	25.25	0.00	0.00
No. of children	209	99	150	76

Source: PP 1842 [382], App. A, pp. 77–86, tabs. 1–5.
Note: The 'very muscular' children included 'those whose fibres were extremely prominent and well-defined' whilst those 'below par' were said to be 'lax, slender, and feeble'.

and dietary influences in early life, has paid scant attention to influences such as child employment. This is all the more surprising since the near-universal transition from dependency to independent economic activity amongst young people in the past was normally achieved contemporaneously with the completion of the growth cycle at the close of the second decade of life. The effects of child and adolescent labour upon growth should therefore receive more serious attention from anthropometric historians. Studies of the stature of children in different occupations have demonstrated conclusively that significant variations existed in the pace of children's growth which seem to have been connected in complex ways with different work environments.[30] Surviving ordinal evidence certainly suggests that the physical condition of child workers varied a great deal according to occupation (Table 1).

30   P. Kirby, 'Causes of Short Stature among Coalmining Children, 1823–1850', *Economic History Review*, 48 (1995), 687–99; J. Humphries, 'Short Stature among Coalmining Children: A Comment', *Economic History Review*, 50 (1997), 531–7; P. Kirby, 'Short Stature among Coalmining Children: A Rejoinder', *Economic History Review*, 50 (1997), 538–42; J. Humphries and T. Leunig, 'Cities, Market Integration and Going to Sea: Stunting and the Standard of Living in Early Nineteenth-Century England and Wales', *Economic History Review*, 62 (2009), 458–78. See also the commentary in R. H. Steckel, 'Heights and Human Welfare: Recent Developments and New Directions', *Explorations in Economic History*, 46 (2009), 1–23 (p. 4) and Kirby, 'Transition to Working Life'. The most recent major contribution to the debate has virtually nothing to say about the influence of child occupations: see R. Floud, R. W. Fogel, B. Harris and S. C. Hong, *The Changing Body: Health, Nutrition, and Human Development in the Western World since 1700* (Cambridge: Cambridge University Press, 2011).

Early nineteenth-century government surveys provide rare insights to contemporary thinking about the effects of labour processes on the bodies of young workers. The Children's Employment Commission of 1842 stressed the importance of the unique physiology of the working child during growth and development:

> Childhood is essentially the period of activity of the nutritive processes necessary to the growth and maturity of the body ... if at this period the kind and quantity of food necessary to afford the material for these processes be not supplied – if, instead of the pure air which is indispensable to convert the aliment into nutriment, the air which is constantly respired be loaded with noxious matters, – if, the comparatively tender and feeble frame be now taxed by toil beyond its strength, and at unseasonable and unnatural periods ... the organs will not be developed, their functions will be enfeebled and disordered, and the whole system will sustain an injury which cannot be repaired at any subsequent stage of human life.[31]

Changing body sizes and capabilities meant that children were affected by the work environment in fundamentally different ways from adult workers. For example, occupational diseases amongst adults usually involved a deterioration in health over many years whereas child workers were at greater risk of more immediate hazards such as machinery accidents or the effects of pathogens or contaminants in raw materials. Children also lacked the critical knowledge or authority to identify or make decisions about such hazardous situations or dangerous substances. It is also striking how many of the hazards which confronted children in early British industry are parallelled in today's developing economies where it has been observed that age, sex, fatigue, length of the working day and pre-existing health conditions all contribute in varying degrees to the risks facing working children.[32] The World Health Organisation has observed how the developmental characteristics of children 'such as the higher percentage of water in their organs, tissues and the body as a whole, higher metabolic rate and oxygen consumption, greater energy and

---

31   PP 1842 (380), p. 268.
32   Economic disadvantage and geographical and environmental factors remain major determinants of workplace accidents to children today, though injuries arise primarily from presence in high-risk environments: R. Reading, 'Poverty and the Health of Children and Adolescents', *Archives of Disease in Childhood*, 76 (1997), 463–7 (p. 464).

fluid requirements per unity body weight and larger body surface area in relation to weight when compared to adults, can affect their absorption of chemicals, dust and vapours and their ability to excrete ... Their rapid growth can also make them more susceptible to toxic agents and ergonomic hazards.'[33] The influence of occupation upon the stages of child development must also have been intensified by the tendency towards later physical maturity amongst children in the past. In the 1820s, children reached maturity about two years later than twenty-first century children and this would have exposed them to child-specific occupational risks over an extended period.[34] A further major complaint common to both past and present industrial child labour has been the impact and monotony of repetitive industrial tasks carried out over long periods, together with the associated lack of sleep amongst children in industrial jobs. Historically, this was thought to result in permanent psychological harm, insensitivity to stimuli and learning difficulties. As Mrs Tonna remarked of mill children, 'they are a community of automata. Nothing seems to animate them. The cold listlessness of their looks sends a chill to the heart of the spectator, who, if he feel rightly, must feel it a degradation to his species to be chained, as it were, to a parcel of senseless machinery, confused by its din, and forced to obey its movements with scarcely an interval for thought or repose.'[35] Early nineteenth-century social commentators also feared the effects of long hours upon the moral and educational growth of child workers. An awareness of the complex effects of labour processes upon the stages of child physical and psychological development is therefore crucial to any study of child occupational health.

The early factory inquiries

The earliest commentaries on the health of child workers emerged in the 1780s and were focused almost exclusively upon the control of

33   G. Eijkemans and A. G. Fassa, 'An Introduction to the Topic', *Global Occupational Health Network Newsletter* (Child Labour and Adolescent Workers), 9 (Summer 2005), 1–3 (pp. 2–3).
34   Kirby, *Child Labour in Britain*, p. 10; Kirby, 'Transition to Working Life'; Pelling, 'Child Health'.
35   Quoted in I. Kovačević and S. B. Kanner, 'Blue Book into Novel: The Forgotten Industrial Fiction of Charlotte Elizabeth Tonna', *Nineteenth Century Fiction*, 25 (1970), 152–73 (p. 168).

contagious diseases in early manufacturing districts. Outbreaks of fever in northern English cotton mills at Radcliffe during 1782–84 and 1789, and Ashton-under-Lyne and Dukinfield in 1796, were said to have been caused or aggravated by the close confinement of workers in cotton spinning mills. The outbreaks prompted an investigation by a committee led by the pioneering Manchester occupational health doctor, Thomas Percival.[36] However, the relationship between fever and mill work was little understood at the time and doctors offered contending causal explanations. Most early investigations focused as much on the state of workers' homes and their migratory habits as they did on actual working conditions in mills. In 1790, Sir William Clerke blamed factory fevers upon the unwholesomeness of food, overcrowding, lack of cleanliness and 'the fluctuation of the families of the manufacturers removing from one town to another'.[37] He identified the need for a large-scale and more integrated approach to the control of contagion in manufacturing districts:

> whoever is at all acquainted with the numberless means by which the infection of fever may be conveyed, will immediately see that the partial attention of any particular district to render this disorder less formidable, will, at best, but impart a temporary relief; sufficient, indeed, to enliven their hopes, and stimulate their endeavours, but totally insufficient to prevent a frequent visitation of this fatal disorder.[38]

Transmission was thought to occur through short to medium-distance labour migration and the regular movement of workers between home and the mill.[39] John Ferriar noted that 'infectious diseases have been conveyed

---

36   Hope, pp. 37–8; Innes, 'Origins of the Factory Acts'.

37   W. Clerke, *Thoughts upon the Means of Preserving the Health of the Poor, by Prevention and Suppression of Epidemic Fevers, Addressed to the Inhabitants of Manchester* (London: J. Johnson, 1790), pp. 9, 16. Ferriar noted the impossibility of halting the progress of fevers in manufacturing towns except by the removal of infected persons to a house of recovery: T. Bernard, 'Extract from a further account of the House of Recovery at Manchester', *Reports of the Society for Bettering the Condition and Increasing the Comforts of the Poor*, 2 (1800), 158–64 (pp. 158–9); J. V. Pickstone, *Medicine and Industrial Society* (Manchester: Manchester University Press, 1985), pp. 26–7.

38   Clerke, p. 9.

39   Percival's 1784 committee on the mysterious fever in the Radcliffe mills could not ascertain whether it had originated there or had been 'imported into Radcliffe from some other parts of the county': Meiklejohn, 'Outbreak of Fever', p. 68.

from Manchester to neighbouring towns, and cotton-mills, by persons going from infected houses.'[40] Children themselves were believed to act as major agents of contagion and early prophylactic advice sought to reduce transmission between home and the workplace. Parents of factory children were enjoined to wash them 'head to foot with cold water, before you send them to work in the morning'.[41] Class preoccupations and impressionistic theories also dominated explanations of illnesses in industrial districts. Distinctions were drawn between 'genuine' contagious fevers that affected society generally and 'low' fevers that might result from insanitary living conditions and constitutional factors affecting the working poor. The poor were thought to be largely responsible for the poverty, filth and indigence that predisposed them to ill-health, and an outward manifestation of illness was frequently thought to belie a failure of personal, moral or household hygiene.[42] This even extended to explanations of occupational conditions ostensibly caused by harmful industrial materials. Josiah Wedgwood, for example, claimed that the poisoning of children by white lead glazes in his ceramics factory was due to their being 'careless in their method of living, and dirty'. Sweeps' cancer, similarly, was often attributed to a lack of personal hygiene.[43] As late as the 1870s, it was claimed that the general physical degeneration of the factory population was attributable not to conditions of work, but to poor diet, indulgence in stimulants, and excessive smoking which ensured that 'the constitutions of the parents are debilitated, and their children are born with feeble constitutions as a consequence.'[44] It was believed that disease could also

40   J. Ferriar, 'Advice to the Poor', in *Medical Histories and Reflections* (London: W. Bulmer & Co., 1810), vol. 3, p. 281, reproduced in Walker, Appendix V, p. 5.xx.
41   Pelling, 'Child Health', p. 140; Ferriar, 'Advice to the Poor', p. 281, reproduced in Walker, Appendix V, p. 5.xviii.
42   C. Hamlin, 'Predisposing Causes and Public Health in Early-Nineteenth-Century Medical Thought', *Social History of Medicine*, 5 (1992), 43–70 (pp. 46–7). Similar findings were arrived at by Willan in 1801 who found extremely filthy conditions amongst the domestic manufactures of London, where working and living spaces were virtually indistinguishable: R. Willan, *Reports on the Diseases in London* (London: Phillips, 1801), pp. 133–6. Such views would remain current amongst many medical and public health figures well into the nineteenth century: M. Pelling, *Cholera, Fever and English Medicine, 1825–1865* (Oxford: Oxford University Press, 1978), pp. 41–2.
43   M. W. Thomas, *Young People in Industry, 1750–1945* (London: T. Nelson, 1945), pp. 20–1; Van Manen, p. 321.
44   F. Ferguson, 'The Degeneracy of the Factory Population', *Sanitary Record*, 25 September 1875, 211–12 (p. 211); F. Ferguson, 'Factory Children', *Sanitary Record*, 24 July 1875, 52–7 (p. 53).

arise spontaneously from decomposing waste animal or vegetable matter or through the rebreathing of air in confined spaces.[45] Industrial diseases, meanwhile, were not fixed phenomena but could manifest themselves in radically different ways, sometimes transforming into apparently new conditions in the bodies of different individuals.[46] The *London Medical Gazette* claimed that the factory system reduced Man to little more than a 'producing animal' and that this might result in 'maladies hitherto unheard of'.[47] Workers' bodies, meanwhile, might transmit diseases through perspiration and exhalations. As John Ferriar wrote, 'It is now generally allowed that the effluvia of living persons, confined in close situations, produces the poison of fever'. Those treating the sick were advised to 'preserve yourselves from being infected, by tying a handkerchief across your face, just below the eyes, to prevent the exhalations from the bodies of the sick from entering your mouth and nostrils.'[48] The entire fabric of the working-class dwelling posed a risk. Ferriar warned that 'their clothes, and the woollen and cotton parts of their furniture become infected, retain the infection tenaciously, and are capable of communicating the disease for a long time'.[49] Families were advised to destroy the soiled clothes, beds and bedlinen of the sick, though many poor families were often unable to bear the cost of destroying or purifying infected clothing and furniture.[50] Susceptibility to disease was also believed to be intergenerational and heredity was cited widely in explanations of conditions such as tuberculosis, scrofula and rickets which were thought to affect the children of manufacturing workers in particular.

45 J. V. Pickstone, 'Dearth, Dirt and Fever Epidemics: Rewriting the History of British "Public Health", 1780–1850', in *Epidemics and Ideas: Essays in the Historical Perception of Pestilence*, ed. T. Ranger and P. Slack (Cambridge: Cambridge University Press, 1995), pp. 125–48 (p. 130); Peter Gaskell argued that the 'deoxygenised' air of the factory was a crucial factor: Huzzard, p. 7.
46 J. Ferriar, 'Origin of Contagious and New Diseases', in *Medical Histories and Reflections* (London: W. Bulmer & Co., 1810), vol. 1, 261–92 (pp. 278, 280).
47 Anon., 'The Ten Hours' Labour Bill', *London Medical Gazette*, 26 January 1833, pp. 562–6 (562–3).
48 Ferriar, 'Advice to the Poor', p. 281, reproduced in Walker, Appendix V, p. 5.xix. The inhalation of 'human miasma' was still cited as a cause of disease in the 1840s: Pickstone, 'Dearth, Dirt and Fever', p. 134.
49 Ferriar, 'Contagious and New Diseases', p. 287.
50 Clerke, p. 9. Environmental risks such as the inappropriate location of slaughter-houses, dung heaps and privies were also implicated as sites for the generation and transmission of fever.

Most doctors in early factory districts, therefore, believed that mill work acted as a focus for a much broader spectrum of urban contagion arising from domestic, hereditary, constitutional and urban environmental factors. Early efforts at prevention sought to transfer standards of good domestic hygiene to the mill. At the New Lanark mills, for example, care was taken to wash the mill floors and machinery each week with hot water and the mill itself was frequently lime-washed. This, it was claimed, resulted in an exceptionally low rate of sickness and mortality amongst children.[51] For early occupational health doctors such as Percival and Ferriar, workplace and domestic hygiene were interchangeable and early efforts to improve factory hygiene, such as the frequent advocacy of ventilation, fumigation and the lime-washing of the interior of mills, must be regarded as attempts to insulate the crowded industrial workplace from a wider and more harmful epidemiological environment.[52] The majority of Percival's recommendations in the wake of the Radcliffe fever outbreak, for example, consisted merely of normal domestic precautions against contagion.[53] In the 1780s and 90s, therefore, the factory was not considered primarily a progenitor of industrial diseases but rather a focus for wider contagion centred largely on the filthy living conditions of workers. Indeed, two of the doctors responsible for the 1784 report on the Radcliffe mills visited some of the nearby cottages inhabited by workers and declared the mill 'the paradise of the place.'[54]

The cost of maintaining the sick poor was also intimately connected with contemporary perceptions of occupational health. Early textiles mills tended to dismiss children when they reached the age of sixteen or seventeen and replace them with younger, cheaper, workers, thus placing upon the parish purse a further burden of sick, unskilled and unemployed

51   See the commentary on personal hygiene, ventilation and lime-washing of the mills at New Lanark in T. Bernard, 'Extract from an Account of Mr Dale's Cotton Mills at New Lanerk, in Scotland', *Reports of the Society for Bettering the Condition and Increasing the Comforts of the Poor*, 2 (1800), 250–7 (p. 251). Lime-washing was also recommended for the homes of the poor: Clerke, p. 13.
52   As Paterson has observed, 'the crowding of workers, the contaminating influences of physical and moral decay, and the length of time and portion of the day in which individuals were confined in the factory ... pertained more to the domiciliary capacity of the mill than to its productive purpose' (p. 56).
53   Hutchins and Harrison, p. 8.
54   Anon., 'The Putrid Fever at Robert Peel's Radcliffe Mills', *Notes and Queries*, January 1958, 26–35 (p. 28).

young adults.[55] Sickness and disability also reduced a child's earning capacity in later life. Early occupational health treatises such as Holland's study of metal grinders were careful to stress how the 'inability of the artisan to continue his occupation from disease, throws him, and, perhaps, a numerous family, upon the parish for support ... on his death, the same dependence, if not indeed in an aggravated form, becomes indispensable for years.'[56] Infectious diseases did not recognise class distinctions and medical activists such as Ferriar often sought to appeal to the self-interest of the wealthy, drawing attention to the danger of contagion which by 'secret avenues ... reaches the most opulent, and severely revenges their neglect, or insensibility to the wretchedness surrounding them ... the safety of the rich is intimately connected with the welfare of the poor ... a minute and constant attention to their wants, is not less an act of self-preservation than of virtue.'[57] Such appeals succeeded in encouraging worried middle-class poor-rate payers (upon whom the burden of maintaining the sick poor fell heaviest) to subscribe to the growing number of dispensaries for the sick poor.[58] Ferriar also advised self-help amongst workers to prevent contagion, suggesting that mill workers club together to support fever sufferers during their recovery to prevent them returning to work too early.[59]

Fears of contagion were further aggravated by the social origins of many of the child workers recruited to early manufactories. Occupations with particularly unfavourable conditions tended to recruit a higher proportion of orphan and destitute children who, through their vulnerable social status, were at greater risk of ill-treatment, deficient nutrition and poor health. This was particularly the case in the final quarter of the eighteenth century in the emergent (and still largely rural) silk, wool

55   Chapman, *Early Factory Masters*, pp. 202–3; Bernard, 'Mr Dale's Cotton Mills', p. 256. In some instances, such as chimney sweeping, this was because children had become physically too large to work in constrained spaces: T. Bernard, 'Extract from an Account of a Chimney Sweeper's Boy, with Observations and a Proposal for the Relief of Chimney Sweepers', *Reports of the Society for Bettering the Condition and Increasing the Comforts of the Poor*, 1 (1798), 108–14 (p. 109); Lee, 'Emergence of Occupational Medicine', p. 119.

56   G. C. Holland, *Diseases of the Lungs from Mechanical Causes* (London: John Churchill, 1843), p. vi; see also A. Knight, 'On the Grinders' Asthma', *North of England Medical and Surgical Journal*, 1 (1 August 1830), 85–91 and 2 (1 November 1830), 167–79.

57   Ferriar, 'Contagious and New Diseases', pp. 284, 289–90.

58   Pickstone, 'Dearth, Dirt and Fever', p. 131.

59   Ferriar, 'Advice to the Poor', p. 281, reproduced in Walker, Appendix V, p. 5.xx.

Figure 1: Robert Cruikshank, 'English Factory Slaves. Their daily
employment' (1832), in C. Singer, *A Short History of Medicine*
(Oxford: Oxford University Press, 1928), p. 191. Wellcome Library,
London, number L0010118. Slide number not given (available under
Creative Commons).

and cotton processing industries which came to rely heavily upon the
forced urban-to-rural migration of pauper children as a partial solution
to local labour supply difficulties.[60] The virtual legal 'ownership' of
pauper apprentices by early factory masters attracted comparisons with
slavery.[61] Indeed, Matthew Boulton admitted candidly in 1768 that his
firm employed 'Fatherless Children, Parish Apprentices, and Hospital
Boys, which are put to the most slavish part of our Business' whilst Jonas

---

60   The binding of workhouse children to northern textiles mills has featured promi-
nently in the literature on child employment in the early industry: Rose, 'Social Policy
and Business'; P. Horn, 'The Traffic in Children and the Textile Mills, 1780–1816',
Genealogists' Magazine, 24, 5 (March 1993), 177–85; Honeyman, *Child Workers*.
61   T. Wakley, 'The Factory-Slave Bill', *A Voice from the Commons*, 15 May 1836, 1–16
(p. 1).

Hanway, in his *Sentimental History of Chimney Sweepers* of 1785, also compared the position of apprenticed climbing boys with slaves.[62] In the early decades of the nineteenth century, debates over the abolition of slavery and the slave trade would overlap with the growing factory controversy and came to form a key support in broader efforts to regulate child industrial labour (Figure 1).[63] Evidence relating to the health and treatment of factory apprentices, however, is frequently contradictory and generally reflects the wide variation in masters and workplaces to which pauper children were bound. The isolated rural setting of many early water-powered textiles mills sometimes provided opportunities for the schemes of utopian industrialists such as Robert Owen and Samuel Greg. Such early industrial visionaries often attracted praise for removing poor children from the moral and spiritual degradation of urban life. Many early textiles mills were looked upon as charitable enterprises. The building of Lombe's silk works at Derby was commended as a

> great relief and advantage of the poor. The money given by strangers is put into a box which is opened the day after *Michaelmas*-day, and a feast is made; an ox is killed, liquor prepared, the windows are illuminated, and the men, women, and children, employed in the work, drest in their best array, enjoy in dancing and decent mirth a holiday, the expectation of which lightens the labor [*sic*] of the rest of the year.[64]

Robert Blincoe, who had himself experienced severe deprivation and brutality as a mill apprentice, worked briefly at Samuel Oldknow's mill at Mellor and recalled that the apprentices he saw there were 'cheerful and

---

62   J. H. Clapham, *An Economic History of Modern Britain: The Early Railway Age, 1820–1850* (1926; Cambridge: Cambridge University Press, 1950), p. 371; L. J. Jordanova, 'Conceptualising Childhood in the Eighteenth Century: The Problem of Child Labour', *British Journal for Eighteenth-Century Studies*, 10 (1987), 189–99 (p. 193). Though Jonas Hanway, the prominent campaigner in the cause of climbing-boys, believed apprenticeship to be a protective institution and sent out indenture forms to all the master sweeps of London exhorting them to bind their child-sweepers as apprentices (only a dozen complied): G. L. Phillips, *England's Climbing-Boys: a History of the Long Struggle to Abolish Child Labor in Chimney-Sweeping* (Boston, MA: Baker Library, 1949), p. 8.
63   Hartwell, 'Children as slaves'.
64   W. Bray, *Sketch of a Tour into Derbyshire and Yorkshire, including part of Buckingham, Warwick, Leicester, Nottingham, Northampton, Bedford* (London: B. White, 1778), p. 64. Samuel Greg referred to his community at Bollington as 'our little colony': S. Greg, *Two Letters to Leonard Horner Esq., on the Capabilities of the Factory System* (n.p., 1840), p. 5.

contented, and looked healthy and well [and] were fed with milk porridge and wheaten bread for breakfast, and that all their meals were good and sufficient.' When Frances Collier visited Mellor in the early 1920s, she met an eighty-year-old woman 'whose mother had been brought from Chelsea, by stage-coach, to work as a child apprentice for Oldknow' and remembered kindness and 'abundant food'.[65] Reports from Stockport around 1805 suggested that apprentices were 'generally improved in their Appearance after leaving London', whilst at New Lanark the mills housed a number of sick children who had no parents or relatives and who 'were comfortably cared for, and but moderately worked'.[66] Some parish apprentices also received medical inspections and treatments and factory owners such as Samuel Greg provided inoculations for their employed children. However, such schemes were probably exceptional and although some children no doubt benefited from sick clubs and other schemes set up by employers or operatives, little evidence remains of the types of treatments received by most working children. Few therapeutic treatments were available for supposed factory illnesses beyond the occasional administration of emetics and expectorants which were thought to counteract the inspiration or ingestion of cotton waste and dust.[67] In 1819, investigations by a local magistrate revealed the wide range of workplace conditions. In a single township near Bolton, he discovered in one mill 'By reason of excessive Labour and apparent slender Meals, the Children were generally squalid and in Rags; and the Mill does not admit of sufficient Air for

65   G. Unwin, *Samuel Oldknow and the Arkwrights: The Industrial Revolution at Stockport and Marple* (Manchester: Manchester University Press, 1924), p. 173; T. S. Ashton, 'Frances Collier, 1889–1962: A Memoir', in F. Collier, *The Family Economy of the Working Classes in the Cotton Industry, 1784–1833*, ed. R. S. Fitton (Manchester: Manchester University Press, 1964), pp. v–x (p. vii).

66   PP 1819 (24), p. 311; Paterson, p. 63. A Scottish mill owner noted, the youngest children could 'hardly be employed in any thing but learning for a Year or Two at first': PP 1818 (90), p. 68; R. D. Owen, *Threading my Way: An Autobiography* (New York: G. W. Carleton, 1874), p. 34. Owen reported to the Peel committee of 1816 that when he had purchased his mills in 1799, he had found the apprentice children 'well fed and clothed and lodged' (cited in Hutt, p. 163, n. 7). Kitty Wilkinson, apprenticed at the age of twelve to a mill at Caton, thought 'if ever there was a heaven on earth it was that apprentice-house, where we were brought up in such ignorance of evil, and where ... the manager of the mill, was a father to us all': W. R. Rathbone, *The Life of Kitty Wilkinson: A Lancashire Heroine* (Liverpool: H. Young, 1910), pp. 24–5.

67   PP 1816 (397), p. 121. The use of such methods continued into the second half of the century: for example see J. Leach, 'Surat Cotton, as It Bodily Affects Operatives in Cotton Mills', *The Lancet*, 2, 5 December 1863, 648–9 (p. 648).

Health' whilst in a neighbouring mill he discovered 'perfect Ventilation; all the Apprentices, and in fact all the Children, are healthy, happy, clean, and well clothed; proper and daily Attention is paid to their Instruction; and [they] regularly attend Divine Worship on Sundays.'[68] Many of the smaller, marginal, mills and workshops employing little capital and higher proportions of child workers were the least salubrious and were the least reported upon. The quality and provision of workplace food to pauper children was also often rudimentary. In 1810, visitors to a weaving shed in Ancoats Street, Manchester observed that 'The Potatoes for Dinner were boiling with the skins on, in a State of great Dirtiness, and Eight Cow Heads boiling in another Pot for Dinner; a great Portion of the Food … was of a liquid Nature'.[69] Similarly, industrial workplaces were often insanitary. Percival's advice that factory privies be washed daily and properly ventilated may have had some limited results (as early as 1789 some form of flushing lavatory was said to have been installed in Manchester mills), however the vast majority of workplace lavatory provision was rudimentary.[70] Visitors to a Manchester cotton-weaving factory in 1810 found that 'the Privies were too offensive to be approached by us'.[71] In the Kidderminster carpet district, meanwhile, 'open cess-pools and urine-tubs [were] met with in every workshop'.[72] Witnesses at the Kenyon Committee of 1819 also stressed the difference between dirty and clean mills – the latter having a 'less gaseous Influence in the Air, and infinitely less Effluvia from the bad Construction of the Privies.'[73] In

---

68   PP 1819 (24), pp. 280–1. A Stockport physician noticed that 'in the dirty Mills the proportion of Sick was much greater': PP 1819 (24), p. 260.

69   PP 1819 (108), Report of Ralph Wright and Thomas Beard, App. D1, p. 57.

70   Hope, p. 107; W. H. Chaloner, 'Robert Owen, Peter Drinkwater and the Early Factory System in Manchester, 1788–1800', Bulletin of the John Rylands Library Manchester, 37 (1954/5), 78–102 (pp. 89–90).

71   PP 1819 (108), Report of Ralph Wright and Thomas Beard, App. D1, p. 57.

72   The urine of workers was collected and used as a dyeing agent: PP 1843 [432], C25.

73   PP 1819 (24), p. 286. There was a general opinion that only the country mills required legislative involvement: PP 1819 (24), p. 283. In coalmining, meanwhile, disused underground workings were used as lavatories and 'eating, drinking, urinating and defecating all went on side by side': PP 1842 (380), p. 170; J. Benson, British Coalminers in the Nineteenth Century: A Social History (Dublin: Gill & Macmillan, 1980), p. 33. Warm underground temperatures attracted rats and flies, and diseases such as ankylostomiasis (hookworm) were blamed on miners' inattention to personal hygiene: PP 1842 (381), p. 479; PP 1842 (382), p. 62; Oliver, 'Introduction', pp. 16–17. Transmission of pathogens from underground workings to the home may also partly explain the stubbornly high levels of infant mortality which affected mining communities well into the twentieth

general, pauper children bound out by Poor Law authorities experienced much more danger and ill-health compared with other working children. Contemporary statistics provide a glimpse of the health risks suffered by such children. Of 2,026 pauper apprentices aged between eight and eighteen, bound from London parishes between 1802 and 1811 'to various persons in the country', about a third could not be accounted for in 1814 and around 4 per cent were returned as 'dead'. This was a rate around three times the expected level for that age-group.[74]

Eighteenth-century authorities were aware of the problem of poorer health and higher mortality amongst pauper apprentices and some magistrates in industrial towns attempted to impose restrictions on the binding of children during epidemics – some going so far as to prohibit the binding of apprentices to cotton mills altogether.[75] However, approaches to the welfare of factory apprentices remained piecemeal until the early nineteenth century when the first attempts were made to formalise implicit duties towards the welfare of apprentices encompassed by the Poor Law. The Health and Morals of Apprentices Act of 1802 affected cotton, woollen and other mills where 'three or more apprentices, or twenty or more other persons' were employed.[76] The Act introduced the principle of outside inspection by visitors (normally a clergyman and a justice of the peace), who were empowered to enter and inspect mills or factories and make written reports to the quarter sessions on the conditions of apprentices.[77] The regulations were rarely enforced, however, and more than decade after the Act was passed, most magistrates and operatives

century. Buchanan has suggested that high infant mortality in late nineteenth-century colliery communities was also associated with fly contamination: I. Buchanan, 'Infant Feeding, Sanitation and Diarrhoea in Colliery Communities, 1880–1911', in *Diet and Health in Modern Britain*, ed. D. J. Oddy and D. S. Miller (Beckenham: Croom Helm, 1985), pp. 148–77.

74 PP 1814–15 (304), V, *Select Committee on Parish Apprentices*, p. 4. The author is grateful for the comments and advice of the late Professor Bob Woods in this respect.

75 J. T. Ward, 'New Introduction', in J. Fielden, *The curse of the factory system* (1836), ed. J. T. Ward (London: Kelley, 1969), pp. v–xlix (pp. vii–ix); Paterson, pp. 94–7.

76 42 Geo. III, c. 73. On the early legislation see Innes, 'Origins of the Factory Acts'; J. Innes, 'Le parlément et la regulation du travail des enfants dans les fabriques en Grande-Bretagne 1783–1819', in *La société civile. Savoirs, enjeux et acteurs en France et en Grande-Bretagne 1780–1914*, ed. C. Charle and J. Vincent (Rennes: n.p., 2011).

77 Walker, Appendix V, p. 4.8. Periodic fumigation of workplaces with tobacco was also advocated: Paterson, pp. 86–7; Innes, 'Origins of the Factory Acts', pp. 231–2. The Irish factory bill of 1819 sought to place the entire responsibility for inspection on clergymen: PP 1819 (247). Such were the misunderstandings of the Act that the appointed inspectors

in the Manchester district remained unaware of its terms. By 1816 only thirty-six reports had been received from mill visitors, and most of these had been submitted within the first three years of the Act's operation.[78] The primary aim of the 1802 Act was to afford minimum standards of health for children who had no family and no protectors in the workplace and this meant that the regulations did not apply to the majority of unapprenticed 'free' children working in textiles.[79]

Despite the high profile given to parish apprentices in the early textiles industry, the system of binding pauper children to textiles mills which had come to such prominence in the later eighteenth century was to be short-lived. A progressive locational shift from rural water mills to urban steam mills resolved many of the labour-supply difficulties that had dogged the rural mill owners. Moreover, by the 1830s and 40s, Poor Law officials had become increasingly hostile to the principle of pauper apprenticeship, whilst the incentives offered by parishes to factory masters to take such children had been largely removed.[80] A Poor Law Commission report of 1841 noted 'the gradual disuse of the system of granting premiums with pauper apprentices, and the substitution of a contract for hiring and service, in lieu of an indenture of apprenticeship.'[81] Rising living standards and expectations coupled with the increasing scale of textiles enterprises also meant that the costs of caring for and accommodating factory apprentices in isolated rural locations rose considerably. At the

---

(or 'visitors') would sometimes extend their surveillance to the entire child labour force: *Hansard* (Lords), 25 February 1819, col. 656; Paterson, pp. 135–6.

78   PP 1816 (397), pp. 187, 316–7; PP 1819 (24), p. 59.

79   Hutchins and Harrison, p. 16; M. Blaug, 'The Classical Economists and the Factory Acts – a Re-Examination', *Quarterly Journal of Economics*, 72 (1958), 211–26 (p. 212). Between 1802 and 1811 around 430 boys and girls were apprenticed annually from London. Earlier estimates suggest that around 1790, more than 100,000 children were employed in cotton manufacture: Clapham, p. 374; Anon., *Case of the British cotton spinners and manufacturers of piece goods, similar to the importations from the East Indies* (London: P. Colquhoun, 1790), App., p. 7. Honeyman suggests that a significant number of pauper apprentices came from localities close to the factory districts (pp. 56–90).

80   Pressley suggests that labour shortages in late nineteenth-century mill villages, however, led to occasional requests to boards of guardians to bind poor children: J. Pressley, 'Childhood, Education and Labour: Moral Pressure and the end of the Half-Time System' (Ph.D. thesis, Lancaster University, 2000), p. 36. In the 1830s, attempts were made to ensure that indentures should not be permitted unless a child had lived in the home of the intended master for three months prior to binding: Anon., 'A Bill to Amend the Laws Relating to Parish Apprentices', *Bradford Observer*, 10 July 1834, p. 181.

81   PP 1841 (I), p. xi.

Gregs' rural factory at Styal in Cheshire, the costs of keeping live-in apprentices doubled between the 1820s and 1840s whereas larger urban mill owners were largely free from any obligation to clothe and house working children.[82] Accommodation problems were frequently cited as a reason for the decline in the apprentice system. Asked in 1818, 'What is your Reason for having given over employing Parish Apprentices?', the proprietor of a large Mansfield spinning mill explained, 'We find it so much Trouble having them in the House; we prefer having free Hands ... who live out of the House.'[83] The early factory legislation had therefore been successful in establishing the principle of national directives surrounding the employment of vulnerable children and had introduced the first national regulations on factory hygiene such as the limewashing of the interior of mills and improved ventilation (both of which had been key recommendations of Percival's earlier committee). However, the proportion of pauper apprentices in the factory workforce had become extremely small by the 1820s and the Health and Morals of Apprentices Act had largely lost its significance.[84] Nonetheless, the stereotype of the abused and overworked pauper apprentice continued to be employed in campaigns against industrial child labour until the middle of the nineteenth century.

The problem of medical evidence

Historical perceptions of child ill-health in early manufacturing industry have been shaped in large part by medical testimony to parliamentary inquiries. Such evidence is highly problematical because the early committees were mostly *ad hoc* affairs convened exclusively in London. Expert medical witnesses tended to be recruited chiefly from metropolitan teaching hospitals and the majority had little or no experience of northern manufacturing work. Only one in eight of the medical witnesses to Peel's Committee of 1816, for example, had any direct observational experience

---

82   Cruickshank, pp. 15–16; C. H. Lee, *A Cotton Enterprise, 1795–1840: a History of M'Connel and Kennedy, Fine Cotton Spinners* (Manchester: Manchester University Press, 1972), pp. 114–15.

83   PP 1818 (90), p. 200.

84   Rose, 'Social Policy and Business', pp. 23–5. An Act of 1816 altered the format of parish indentures and compelled magistrates to enquire about the distance over which an apprentice was to be bound and all such bindings were to be restricted to within forty miles of the home parish.

of textiles mills or the medical conditions associated with them. Most medical testimony amounted to little more than abstract notions.[85] The evidence of the distinguished London surgeon and anatomist Sir Astley Cooper exemplified the lack of industrial experience amongst London medical witnesses.

> Have you had any opportunities of witnessing the state of health of children employed in manufactories? – I have not, excepting as a visitor in some of the large towns in the North. I have occasionally looked into a manufactory, but I have no experience respecting it.
>
> Have you observed in the countenances of any such children, any appearances of want of health? – It is now too long since I had an opportunity of visiting a manufactory, for me to speak decidedly about it.
>
> Have you, in your intercourse with other practitioners, ever heard of any detriment, in point of health, being sustained by children employed in manufactories; or any diseases arising therefrom? – I cannot say positively that I can apply an answer to that question. I understand the question, but I have not had sufficient experience of children being brought directly from manufactories to state positively that the disease was the result of that employment.[86]

By contrast with the impressionistic Peel Committee, the subsequent committees of Lord Kenyon of 1818 and 1819 paid much closer attention to the first-hand evidence of operatives and medical men who actually

---

85   Matthew Baillie was compelled to admit, 'I am not really acquainted with the condition of children employed in such manufactories', recalling that he had only once visited a mill. He had been escorted by Robert Owen at New Lanark ('The only manufactory of that kind I ever saw'): PP 1816 (397), pp. 29, 30. To the question 'Have you any knowledge of the general state of health of the children in manufactories?' another answered 'None at all' (p. 35). Yet another stated 'I am not in the habit of attending any manufactory' (p. 43); another, that his only experience of textile manufacture had been twenty years before on a visit to the lace manufactories of Buckinghamshire (p. 45). See also Hutt, p. 167; PP 1816 (397), p. 99. Thomas was rightly sceptical of such evidence and confined his coverage of the 1816 committee to a few paragraphs. Thomas, *Early Factory Legislation*, pp. 20–22.

86   PP 1816 (397), p. 33. Cooper was almost certainly referring to a visit he had made as a nineteen-year-old in 1787 to the Staffordshire potteries (where he had been introduced to Josiah Wedgwood). He was subsequently taken to visit several factories in the Manchester district: B. B. Cooper, *The Life of Sir Astley Cooper, Bart: Interspersed with Sketches from his Note-Books of Distinguished Contemporary Characters*, vol. 2 (London: John W. Parker, 1843), p. 159.

lived and worked in mill districts. The Kenyon committees also produced the first useful statistics on the health of textiles workers.[87] The findings of the first committee (largely promoted by the leading Manchester mills owners) challenged much of the evidence of hardship and illness offered at the earlier inquiry. Large-scale physical examination of both child and adult workers in Manchester mills suggested that their health was comparable with those in other urban occupations (though there was a fairly consistent opinion amongst doctors that the health of children who did little or no work was better than those who were employed full time).[88] Several of the doctors who had conducted the survey declared themselves surprised by the findings, one noting, 'so extraordinary have the Facts appeared, that have come out of the Investigation of these Factories, that I begin to doubt many of the common-place Opinions that have been entertained upon the subject.'[89] The greater experience of the Manchester medical witnesses also permitted them to deal more effectively with the form of leading questions which had shaped the evidence of doctors at the earlier Peel inquiry. Repeated requests for hypothetical opinions about illnesses and deformities amongst child factory and mill workers were objected to by Manchester doctors on the ground that causation had never been adequately demonstrated. James Ainsworth, surgeon to the Manchester Infirmary, suggested that such questions were 'too absurd to demand an Answer' and accused counsel for the reform lobby of 'putting extreme Cases to me, which I believe never could occur' (his response followed a speculative question about injurious effects upon 'an Infant who might have been compelled to walk in an erect Position for Fifteen Hours, in a Temperature of Eighty').[90] Kenyon's second committee of 1819, meanwhile, took evidence from operatives' representatives and reform campaigners and drew on qualitatively different sources, concentrating chiefly on the smaller mills where conditions were poorer.[91]

---

87 The evidence to the Kenyon Committees contains a mass of first-hand testimony and tabular evidence on the physical condition of children in cotton spinning. Some of the statistics of factory ill-health collected by the committee have been analysed by H. Freudenberger, F. J. Mather and C. Nardinelli, 'A New Look at the Early Factory Labor Force', *Journal of Economic History*, 44 (1984), 1085–90.
88 The manufacturer and operative interests were each represented by counsel who were permitted to cross-examine medical witnesses prior to reports being received in evidence.
89 PP 1818 (90), pp. 22, 28.
90 PP 1818 (90), p. 149.
91 S. E. Finer, *The Life and Times of Sir Edwin Chadwick* (1952; London: Methuen, 1980), p. 68.

They reported long hours, severe beatings, crippling disabilities and excessive heat in factories. Medical men who supported the reform lobby, however, faced major difficulties in gaining admittance to mills due to the objections of both owners and operatives and many continued to rely heavily upon hearsay. The leading Manchester surgeon, Thomas Bellott, for example, claimed that deformities and consumption were greatest amongst child cotton workers though was compelled to admit that he had never been inside a mill.[92] Where reform-minded doctors managed to gain admittance to factories, their unfamiliarity with the workplace often precluded any meaningful reporting. Three doctors who visited a Manchester mill in 1819 found that they 'could not remain Ten Minutes in the Factory without gasping for Breath, and without being induced involuntarily to run out of the Factory with all the Swiftness we could make use of.'[93] The Kenyon inquiries led to the first factory legislation to include the majority of 'free' child workers. The Factory Act of 1819 excluded children below the age of nine from cotton mills and restricted the hours of work of those below sixteen to twelve hours. No further provision was made for the inspection of children's working conditions, however, and no adequate methods of enforcement were introduced. The question of who was actually responsible for the employment of children also remained in doubt. Parents and employers might be equally liable to prosecution for breaches of the Act. Prosecutions were therefore rare and although further laws were enacted in 1825, 1829 and 1831 (extending provisions on night work and hours) enforcement remained patchy and ineffectual.[94] Moreover, the 1819 Act contained no provisions to improve the health of child workers beyond the established biannual limewashing of mill ceilings (this stipulation was reduced to annual limewashing in the subsequent Act of 1825).[95]

The committee of 1831–2 chaired by Michael Sadler (an outspoken critic of child employment and the 'factory system') was openly hostile to the manufacturing interest. The committee was also the most inventive with regard to medical reports of factory maladies.[96] Sadler obtained testimony almost entirely from opponents of the factory system and

---

92   PP 1819 (24), p. 268.
93   PP 1819 (24), p. 273.
94   59 Geo. III, c. 66; 60 Geo. III, c. 5; Thomas, *Early Factory Legislation*, pp. 25–33.
95   6 Geo. IV, c. 63.
96   For an early critique of the medical evidence to the Sadler Committee see Hutt, pp. 160–88.

published his report without taking the views of the leading manufacturers. This led to widespread criticism of Sadler's methods, even amongst supporters of factory reform who saw such obvious bias as counterproductive to their cause. The exaggerated medical reports of deformities and illnesses led the *London Medical Gazette* (mostly sympathetic to the cause of reform) to note that Sadler's questions to doctors were 'in great part, what is technically called leading questions, not admitting of much range in the replies, and, when they did, eliciting answers remarkable for their sameness.'[97] Friedrich Engels described the report as 'emphatically partisan, composed by strong enemies of the factory system, for party ends ... [containing] the most distorted and erroneous statements'. The eminent Scottish chemist, Andrew Ure (the author of a number of major studies of textile technology), accused Sadler of 'medical mystification' with regard to claims about deformities.[98] Much of the evidence of children's working conditions was also highly anachronistic. Many operative witnesses were in their thirties or forties at the time of giving evidence to the Committee and their testimony was frequently based on childhood experiences from around the turn of the century when conditions had been indisputably worse. Notwithstanding such widespread defects with the Sadler inquiry, many early economic historians accepted the report as an example of 'objective' evidence. The Hammonds, for example, described the report as 'a classical document ... one of the main sources of knowledge of the conditions of factory life at the time. Its pages bring before the reader ... the kind of life that was led by the victims of the new system'. Hutchins and Harrison, too, regarded Sadler's report as 'one of the most valuable collections of evidence on industrial conditions that we possess.'[99] In common with the earlier Peel

97   Anon., 'Ten Hours' Labour Bill', pp. 564–5.
98   F. Engels, *The Condition of the Working Class in England in 1844* (1845; Oxford: Oxford University Press, 1993), p. 179; Hutt, pp. 161–2; A. Ure, *Philosophy of Manufactures: or, an exposition of the scientific, moral, and commercial economy of the Factory System of Great Britain* (London: Charles Knight, 1835), p. 374.
99   The Hammonds claimed that the Sadler report confirmed widespread deformity and disability amongst child cotton workers and more recent studies presented such evidence in a similarly uncritical manner: J. L. Hammond and B. Hammond, *Lord Shaftesbury* (London: Constable & Company, 1923), pp. 16, 18; Hutchins and Harrison, p. 34; E. P. Thompson, *The Making of the English Working Class* (1963; London: Penguin, 1980), pp. 328–9; S. Hobbs, J. McKechnie and M. Lavalette, *Child Labor: a World History Companion* (Santa Barbara: ABC-Clio, 1999), pp. 76–7; L. J. Davis, *Enforcing Normalcy: Disability, Deafness and the Body* (London: Verso, 1995), pp. 86–9. Lane described the

Committee, however, the majority of Sadler's medical witnesses had never visited a mill or factory and were unable to produce any evidence linking illnesses and deformity directly with the work process. The minority of medical witnesses who did have experience of the industrial workplace were sceptical of the thrust of the Sadler inquiry. It is notable that Charles Thackrah was careful in his evidence not to isolate specific harmful factors in the work processes but focused his analysis instead on the perceived tendency of factories to undermine the constitution and expose children to diseases in later life.[100]

Such was the obvious bias in the Sadler report that a further large inquiry was commissioned almost immediately, largely at the behest of the dissatisfied manufacturing lobby, with instructions to investigate the broad national picture of working conditions amongst factory children. The Factory Commission of 1833 re-examined a number of Sadler's witnesses and often came to different conclusions about the health effects of industrial work. The Commission noted, in particular, the often inferior health of children in smaller workshop-based industries such as handloom weaving, frame work knitting and a variety of other domestic manufactures.[101] Nonetheless, the larger and better funded inquiry continued to be dogged by the problem of hypothetical medical opinions. Attempts to collect statistical information were also thwarted by a lack of cooperation from general practitioners.[102] A widespread opposition amongst doctors

physical deformity of industrial workers as 'inevitable': J. Lane, *A Social History of Medicine: Health, Healing and Disease in England, 1750–1950* (London: Routledge, 2001), p. 6; J. P. Kay, by contrast, denounced the lack of rigour of the early state inquiries ('statistics are neglected ... information is obtained by means of committees of the Commons, whose labours are so multifarious, as to afford them time for little else than the investigation of general conclusions'): J. P. Kay, *The Moral and Physical Condition of the Working Classes Employed in the Cotton Manufacture in Manchester* (London: James Ridgway, 1832, p. 19.

100   PP 1831–2 (706), p. 514. Though Thackrah's identification of progressive respiratory disease amongst mill workers was of great importance.

101   Pinchbeck and Hewitt, pp. 403, 410.

102   When questionnaires were circulated to practitioners in factory districts in the hope of gathering quantitative information on workers' health, it was soon discovered that no remuneration was to be provided for completion of the forms: J. C. Williams, J. M. Phillips and J. Wilson, letters, 4–9 June 1833, *London Medical Gazette*, 2, 12 (1833), 365–6; PP 1833 (519), D3, p. 1. The main body of detailed reports from the medical commissioners was not published until 1834, a year after the Commission's main report and the enactment of the new Factory Act of 1833: PP 1834 (167); PP 1833 (519), C3, pp. 7–8; Hamlin, *Public Health and Social Justice*, pp. 98–100.

to providing medical opinions and statistics free of charge also meant that the commissioners' aim of placing the medical aspects of the inquiry upon a 'scientific' footing largely foundered. Thomas Wakley was later highly critical of the lack of statistical information gathered by the Commission:

> The functionaries were certainly either very ignorant of statistical calculation on a large scale, or very neglectful of their business ... They ought to have obtained returns from the Benefit Societies. They should have prosecuted an examination of the population in manufacturing and other districts. They should have distinguished the actually sick from the healthy at different ages. They did neither. In short, their neglect of *certain* means of ascertaining the amount of ill-health in the entire labouring population, was complete. The omission almost appears to have been designed.[103]

Despite the lack of systematic medical evidence, however, the resulting Commission report was much more extensive and better resourced than any that had preceded it. It was also innovative in the collection of evidence. A major new feature was the abandonment of the practice of summoning witnesses to London in favour of the recording of field evidence by assistant commissioners. The Commission was also successful in achieving effective protective legislation. The Factory Act of 1833 led to the exclusion of children below nine from factories and prohibited the employment of those aged ten to twelve unless they had obtained a certificate of education from a schoolmaster.[104] The Commission also recommended the appointment of inspectors who were to be assisted by superintendents and factory surgeons and whose later periodic reports would mark a major shift towards the collection of empirical data on tangible threats to child health such as industrial injuries. It was not until 1844, however, that legislation for the first time included clauses on machine safety.[105] Deference to medical opinion in state reports on child employment declined substantially from the early 1830s as a new

---

103   Wakley, p. 5. As Finer observed, the 1833 medical inquiry was 'a riot of jobbery', with doctors appointed as a result of personal contacts rather than any particular experience of manufacturing work (p. 52).
104   Kirby, *Child Labour in Britain*, pp. 104–5.
105   Inspectors appointed under the 1833 Act were empowered to order the keeping of registers of sickness absence, though there is little evidence that such provisions were ever implemented.

wave of public health inquirers emerged, stressing a broader range of epidemiological dangers associated with the urban and manufacturing environment. The increasingly critical stance towards the theories of medical men was led by activists such as Edwin Chadwick who highlighted the inability of most doctors to understand even the most basic of public or occupational health problems.[106] Chadwick was largely successful in demonstrating that ailments and deformities were no more typical of factory workers than the amongst the general population.[107]

The evidence of early nineteenth-century medical men is therefore a highly unreliable basis for any serious inquiry into the health of industrial children. Any such study must look beyond the largely partial and theoretical medical testimony elicited from metropolitan doctors by avowed opponents of the factory system. Such was the remoteness and inaccuracy of early medical commentary on the health of child workers that the evidence of *non-medical* observers almost always proves of much greater value with regard to the internal working environments of mills and spatial descriptions of incidents such as industrial accidents. This study, therefore, does not focus primarily upon medical commentary but upon evidence from a wider range of industrial contexts. The analysis employs findings of recent research in occupational medicine together with studies of the health of child workers in modern developing economies to produce insights to the possible medical conditions suffered by child workers in the past. The book commences with an examination of the broad environmental context of child health in manufacturing districts and develops a number of related case studies of specific hazards such as child deformity, the effects of raw materials, industrial injuries and ill-treatment. The investigation also examines the effects of work and environment on the physical growth of child industrial workers and draws inferences from significant differences in height and strength amongst

---

106   See Hamlin, *Public Health and Social Justice*. Even Thackrah's pioneering study of occupational health attempted in only a limited way to get at the causes of child health problems: C. T. Thackrah, *The Effects of Arts, Trades, and Professions ... on Health and Longevity* (London: Longman, Orme, Brown & Green, 1831; 1832); Holland, *Diseases of the Lungs*; J. P. Kay, 'Observations and Experience concerning Molecular Consumption and on Spinners' Phthisis', *North of England Medical and Surgical Journal*, 1 (August 1830–May 1831), 348–63. At the Mines Commission of 1842 only 2.3 per cent of the witnesses were drawn from a medical background: P. Kirby, *Evidence to the Children's Employment Commission, 1842* (database), UK Data Archive, University of Essex (2009), http://www.esds.ac.uk/findingData/snDescription.asp?sn=6128.

107   Hamlin, *Public Health and Social Justice*, pp. 39–40.

children working in different industrial occupations. The primary aim of the research is to produce a comprehensive overview of the factors bearing upon the health and industrial working conditions of children in the context of the major occupational and epidemiological transitions of the Industrial Revolution.

Child Health and the Manufacturing Environment

Almost every aspect of the health of late eighteenth and early nineteenth-century child workers was affected by the unprecedented urban and industrial growth of the period. A tripling of the population in the century after 1750 was dwarfed by a quadrupling in the size of the major industrial and trading centres between 1800 and 1850.[1] New forms of production in the industrial districts of the West Midlands, northern England and the central belt of Scotland drew increasing numbers of workers into growing manufacturing towns, exposing them to unfamiliar raw materials, industrial chemicals, pollution and an unfavourable urban disease environment. Technical innovations also brought new heavy industrial machinery which changed fundamentally the types of operations required in industrial jobs and resulted in new and more violent forms of industrial injury. Of all the industrial sectors, cotton textiles experienced by far the most substantial rates of growth.[2] Migrants to manufacturing towns were also attracted by new job opportunities and increasing industrial wages which rose by around 50 per cent over the first half of the nineteenth century. However, the overcrowding and poor sanitation which accompanied the growth of manufacturing centres meant that higher industrial wages did not normally translate into better health for urban families. Rapidly built housing of poor quality and the rudimentary sanitary infrastructure of towns such as Manchester and Leeds were swamped by the influx of migrant workers.[3] By the mid-1840s, for example, 80 per cent

1 R. Rodger, *Housing in Urban Britain, 1780–1914* (Cambridge: Cambridge University Press, 1995), p. 8; R. Lawton, 'Regional Population Trends in England and Wales, 1750–1971', in *Regional Demographic Development*, ed. J. Hobcraft and P. Rees (London: Croom Helm, 1977), pp. 29–70 (p. 36, tab. 2.3). See also P. J. Corfield, *The Impact of English Towns, 1700–1800* (Oxford: Oxford University Press, 1982), pp. 99–123.

2 N. F. R. Crafts, *British Economic Growth during the Industrial Revolution* (Oxford: Clarendon Press, 1985), p. 23, tab. 2.4.

3 P. Huck, 'Infant Mortality and Living Standards of English Workers during the Industrial Revolution', *Journal of Economic History*, 55 (1995), 528–50; E. A. Wrigley

of Preston houses still lacked sewerage and half had no piped water.[4] Urban and manufacturing districts also suffered rising rates of infant and child illness and mortality as a result of family migration to the poor health environment of early industrial towns (though the question of whether working-class migrant families consciously traded the health of their infants in return for higher urban and industrial wages remains unclear). There was no improvement in urban infant mortality during the high point of rural-to-urban migration between 1820 and 1850, and urban districts suffered the most significant falls in life expectancy over the same period.[5] Younger children were susceptible to urban pollution and environmental hazards and would be exposed to such influences long before they entered the industrial labour market.[6] Overcrowded and unplanned development ensured that domestic life and industrial production often took place in neighbouring premises. The simple requirement to live within walking distance of the workplace resulted in high levels of respiratory complaints amongst industrial populations through the inhalation of smoke, chemicals and particulates. The burning of coal for residential and industrial purposes, and the dense pall of urban smoke pollution in industrial towns, also drastically reduced the penetration of sunlight, contributing to vitamin D deficiencies amongst children and widespread rickets.[7] An increase in crowd dwelling led to a decrease in the travelling distances for disease vectors such as rodents and flies which played a major role in the transmission of pathogens in

and R. Schofield, *The Population History of England, 1541–1871* (Cambridge: Cambridge University Press, 1989), pp. 415–16; J. Brown, 'The Condition of England and the Standard of Living: Cotton Textiles in the Northwest, 1806–1850', *Journal of Economic History*, 50 (1990), 591–614; M. Harrison, *Disease and the Modern World: 1500 to the Present Day* (Cambridge: Polity Press, 2004), p. 91.

4 Brown, 'Condition of England', p. 596.

5 Wrigley and Schofield, p. 230, tab. 7.15; S. Szreter and G. Mooney, 'Urbanisation, Mortality, and the Standard of Living Debate: New Estimates of the Expectation of Life at Birth in Nineteenth-Century British Cities', *Economic History Review*, 51 (1998), 84–112 (p. 105, fig. 1); Huck, 'Infant Mortality'; A. Hardy, *The Epidemic Streets: Infectious disease and the rise of preventive medicine, 1856–1900* (Oxford: Clarendon Press, 1993), pp. 3–4.

6 A. G. Fassa, D. L. Parker and T. J. Scanlon, 'A Rights-Oriented, Public Health Model of Child Labour' in *Child Labour: A Public Health Perspective*, ed. A. G. Fassa, D. L. Lewis and T. J. Scanlon (Oxford: Oxford University Press, 2010), pp. 37–43 (p. 41).

7 R. A. Smith, 'On the Air and Rain of Manchester', *Memoirs of the Proceedings of the Manchester Literary and Philosophical Society*, 10 (1852), 207–17 (pp. 211–17). The natural antiseptic qualities of ultraviolet radiation upon pathogens present on exposed urban surfaces would also have been reduced.

food and drink. Infant mortality was highest among the offspring of unskilled industrial workers, miners and textile workers.[8] The health effects of living in manufacturing towns were also highly age-specific. Most child mortality in industrial and urban districts was concentrated amongst infants and very young children, whereas the vast majority of child workers commenced their engagement with the work process at ages between ten and fifteen, when they were less likely to have suffered from infectious diseases. On average, around one child in forty died between the ages of ten to fifteen compared with one in ten amongst those aged one to five.[9] Working children therefore entered the industrial labour market at possibly the safest period of life with regard to disease. It is therefore crucial to distinguish between the influence of the urban disease environment upon very young children and the discrete effects of occupations amongst children of working age. Moreover, many child entrants to work would have been survivors of earlier childhood illnesses and would certainly have carried with them into early employment the disabilities and complications of previous conditions.[10] This raises difficult questions about the accuracy of contemporary diagnoses of ill-health amongst child workers. To what extent did illnesses observed amongst child workers result from the work process and what part was played by the harmful epidemiology of the early industrial town?

8   I. Buchanan, 'Infant Feeding, Sanitation and Diarrhoea in Colliery Communities, 1880–1911', in *Diet and Health in Modern Britain*, ed. D. J. Oddy and D. S. Miller (Beckenham: Croom Helm, 1985), pp. 148–77 (pp. 160–77); Huck, p. 537; R. I. Woods, P. A. Watterson and J. H. Woodward, 'The Causes of Rapid Infant Mortality Decline in England and Wales, 1861–1921, Part I', *Population Studies*, 42 (1988), 343–66 (p. 353); P. A. Watterson, 'Infant Mortality by Father's Occupation from the 1911 Census of England and Wales', *Demography*, 25 (1988), 289–306 (p. 296, fig. 5, p. 300, fig. 8); Woods *et al.*, pp. 363–4.

9   E. A. Wrigley, R. S. Davies, J. E. Oeppen and R. S. Schofield, *English Population History from Family Reconstitution, 1580–1837* (Cambridge: Cambridge University Press, 1997), p. 249.

10   Wrigley *et al.*, p. 300, tab. 6.24; R. Scola, *Feeding the Victorian City: The Food Supply of Manchester, 1770–1870* (Manchester: Manchester University Press, 1992), p. 271; A. Hardy, 'Rickets and the Rest: Child-care, Diet and the Infectious Children's Diseases, 1850–1914', *Social History of Medicine*, 5 (1992), 389–412 (p. 393, tab. 4); A. S. Wohl, *Endangered Lives: Public Health in Victorian Britain* (1983; London: Methuen, 1984), p. 257.

Families, poverty and ill-health

Poverty was the overarching factor influencing the relative ill-health of children in urban and manufacturing districts. Studies show that where a disease has an equal prevalence across social classes, the chances of survival are profoundly affected by household circumstances such as unemployment or short-term fluctuations in earnings. Post-neonatal mortality, for example, is extremely sensitive to changes in the earnings of mothers in social classes IV and V, whereas amongst the more affluent classes it shows little change in response to income effects.[11] In the early nineteenth century, contemporaries also pointed to intergenerational effects on the nutrition of children. Infant marasmus was blamed on inadequate or non-existent breastfeeding by mothers who were themselves deficient in vitamins C and D and who were said to have placed their children at greater risk of scurvy and rickets.[12] Poorly nourished mothers gave birth to lower weight babies who were statistically more likely to suffer from poorer health throughout their lives.[13] Family size also exerted a powerful influence upon levels of infant death. Levene points out that the simple addition of a birth within a family raised the likelihood of families falling into pauperism.[14] Stevenson found that in the second half of the nineteenth century, infant mortality rose from 117 per thousand

11   R. Reading, 'Poverty and the Health of Children and Adolescents', *Archives of Disease in Childhood*, 76 (1997), 463–7 (p. 464). See also R. G. Wilkinson, 'Income and Mortality', in *Class and Health: Research and Longitudinal Data*, ed. R. G. Wilkinson (London: Tavistock, 1986), pp. 88–114.

12   C. Hamlin, 'Predisposing Causes and Public Health in Early-Nineteenth-Century Medical Thought', *Social History of Medicine*, 5 (1992), 43–70 (pp. 58–9); V. A. Fildes, 'The English Disease: Infantile Rickets and Scurvy in Pre-Industrial England', in *Child Care Through the Centuries: An Historical Survey from Papers Given at the Tenth British Congress on the History of Medicine*, ed. J. Cule and T. Turner (Cardiff: British Society for the Social History of Medicine, 1986), pp. 121–34 (p. 127).

13   R. Floud, R. W. Fogel, B. Harris and S. C. Hong, *The Changing Body: Health, Nutrition, and Human Development in the Western World since 1700* (Cambridge: Cambridge University Press, 2011), p. 15; S. De Sanjose and E. Roman, 'Low Birthweight, Preterm and Small for Gestational Age Babies in Scotland, 1981–1984', *Journal of Epidemiology and Community Health*, 45 (1991), 207–10; M. G. Marmot, M. J. Shipley and G. Rose, 'Inequalities in Death – Specific Explanations of a General Pattern', *Lancet*, 1 (1984), pp. 1003–6; D. J. P. Barker, 'The Foetal and Infant Origins of Inequalities in Health in Britain', *Journal of Public Health Medicine*, 13 (1991), 64–8.

14   A. Levene, *The Childhood of the Poor: Welfare in Eighteenth-Century London* (Basingstoke: Palgrave, 2012), p. 27.

for one-child families to 368 in families of twelve and 429 for those having more than twelve children.[15] In some districts the mortality rate of illegitimate infants was double that of legitimate births.[16] Poverty and child dependency was also locked into the structure of early nineteenth-century society. In 1821 nearly half the population was aged below twenty and nearly 40 per cent was under fifteen. Moreover, the growth of child dependency during the Industrial Revolution is thought broadly to have mirrored increases in the supply of children to the labour market. Families often relied upon the wages of their children and dependency could be exacerbated by acute industrial crises and falling demand for child workers. In the 1730s, a decline in the Wiltshire fine woollen trade led to idle children becoming 'a dead weight upon their parents' hands' and a fall in household incomes.[17] Children living in poverty were therefore more likely to be exposed to ill-health in early life and to be affected by the dire household poverty which forced them into labour at early ages.

The illnesses, infirmities and mortality of parents were crucial factors in the exposure of children to early work. Diseases such as cholera and typhus killed adult breadwinners leaving dependent children in reconstituted or otherwise unconventional families. When breadwinners died, or were unable to earn sufficient to support their families, children were almost always forced to enter employment at earlier ages.[18] Emotional deprivation

15   T. H. C. Stevenson, 'The Fertility of Various Social Classes in England and Wales from the Middle of the Nineteenth Century to 1911', *Journal of the Royal Statistical Society*, 83, 3 (1920), 401–44 (pp. 401–2).

16   J. Keating, 'Struggle for Identity: Issues Underlying the Enactment of the 1926 Adoption of Children Act', *University of Sussex Journal of Contemporary History*, 3 (2001), 1–9 (p. 3).

17   P. Kirby, *Child Labour in Britain, 1750–1870* (Basingstoke: Palgrave, 2003), pp. 26–8; T. Andrews, *The miseries of the miserable or, an essay towards laying open the decay of the fine woollen trade and the unhappy condition of the poor Wiltshire manufacturers* (n.p., 1739), p. 13.

18   O. Saito, 'Labour Supply Behaviour of the Poor in the English Industrial Revolution', *Journal of European Economic History*, 10 (1981), 633–52 (p. 645); Kirby, *Child Labour in Britain*, p. 28; E. V. Edmonds, 'Public Health in the Economics of Child Labour', in *Child Labour*, ed. Fassa, Lewis and Scanlon, pp. 45–54 (p. 45); J. V. Pickstone, 'Dearth, Dirt and Fever Epidemics: Rewriting the History of British "Public Health", 1780–1850', in *Epidemics and Ideas: Essays in the Historical Perception of Pestilence*, ed. T. Ranger and P. Slack (Cambridge: Cambridge University Press, 1995), pp. 125–48 (p. 137); P. A. Sambrook, 'Childhood and Sudden Death in Staffordshire, 1851 and 1860', in *Staffordshire Histories: Essays in Honour of Michael Greenslade*, ed. P. Morgan and A. D. M. Phillips (Stafford: Staffordshire Record Society, 1999), pp. 216–52 (pp. 239–40). As Pelling points

and psychological distress were widespread and the high frequency of parental death must have had a profound psychological impact upon vulnerable children, not least because the poverty that followed the death of a breadwinner almost invariably led to an earlier than expected entry to working life.[19] Some children and adolescents suffered extreme grief reactions. When asked by the Children's Employment Commission for her father's occupation, an eighteen-year-old colliery haulage worker replied, 'He was a collier, but he was killed in a coal-pit. I go past the place where he was killed many a time when I am at work, and sometimes I think I see something'.[20] Emotional deprivation and anxiety following the death of a parent would also have depressed endocrine processes such as the production of growth hormone resulting in relatively poorer physical growth.[21] Occupational mortality amongst adults contributed further to the exposure of children to risks. In some occupations, high workplace death rates were an ever-present danger. Miners in Staffordshire and south Wales in the mid-nineteenth century were more than six times as likely to die as a result of an accident than the average male. Even in the safer coal districts of Durham and Northumberland, the death rate from accidents for male coal miners was twice the national average.[22] The relatively

out, 'the conventional "dependent" roles of younger and older people can be drastically modified by economic and physical disability:' M. Pelling, 'Child Health as a Social Value in Early Modern England', *Social History of Medicine*, 1 (1988), 135–64 (pp. 141, 163).
19   Contemporary theories of 'demoralisation' implied that mental ill-health could exist as both cause and effect of bodily illness and that mental states such as anxiety, anger, or 'depression of spirits' could manifest themselves in physical disease – see for example J. Ferriar, 'Origin of Contagious and New Diseases', in *Medical Histories and Reflections* (London: W. Bulmer & Co., 1810), vol. 1, 261–92 (pp. 285–6 – though it was commonly held that mental conditions such as 'insanity' could not affect children before puberty: S. Brandon, 'The Early History of Psychiatric Care of Children', in *Child Care Through the Centuries*, ed. Cule and Turner, pp. 61–78 (p. 64).
20   PP 1842 (382), p. 231.
21   P. B. Eveleth and J. M. Tanner, *Worldwide Variations in Human Growth* (Cambridge: Cambridge University Press, 1976), p. 1. There are few studies of the mental health effects of children's employment. A recent study of modern child labour in Denmark found that high emotional demands, harassment, bullying, heat, use of maximum physical strength and repetitive monotonous work were major risk factors for poor health among working children: M. Labriola, T. Lund and J. Andersen, 'Work Environment, Health and Wellbeing among Children and Adolescents in Denmark: Results from a Study of 545 13–17 Year Olds', *Occupational and Environmental Medicine*, 68, Supplement 1 (2011), Abstract 24, p. A23.
22   P. E. H. Hair, 'Mortality from Violence in British Coalmines, 1800–50', *Economic History Review*, 21 (1968), 545–61 (p. 546).

higher mortality of fathers added further to the difficulties of children in lone-parent households because female-headed households tended to earn lower wages.[23] Families headed by women represented some 9 per cent of English and Welsh households during the Industrial Revolution and in some districts the proportion was as high as 29 per cent – indeed, the most common cause of poverty in some London parishes in the early nineteenth century was the death of a father.[24] Female-headed households also accounted for a disproportionately large number of applicants for poor relief, whilst rigid welfare policies often added to the problems facing poor families with children.[25] Outdoor poor relief to widows was often curtailed by parishes as soon as children reached the ages of nine or ten and this often placed intense pressure on poor parents to have their dependent children employed as soon as they were physically able to perform basic work functions.[26] In two-parent families, the earning capacity of married women tended to fall as the number of dependent children increased. This led to increased pressure on older children to start work as soon as possible.[27]

Under such conditions, the lower labour intensity of textiles mills and factories coupled with a lack of formal regulation such as apprenticeship (which had customarily governed the entry of children to work) offered new opportunities for poor families to have their children employed at

---

23   Kirby, *Child Labour in Britain*, p. 29.

24   Levene, *Childhood of the Poor*, p. 36, tab. 2.4.

25   S. Horrell, J. Humphries and H-J. Voth, 'Stature and Relative Deprivation: Fatherless Children in Early Industrial Britain', *Continuity and Change*, 13.1 (1998), 73–115 (pp. 75–8).

26   PP 1843 [431], p. 104; P. E. H. Hair, 'The Social History of British Coalminers' (D.Phil. thesis, University of Oxford, 1955), p. 53, n. 1; PP 1819 (24), p. 28. Children working in potteries workshops were also more likely than the average to have been the offspring of deprived families and less likely to have been the children of potters themselves: M. W. Dupree, *Family structure in the Staffordshire potteries, 1840–1880* (Oxford: Clarendon Press, 1995), pp. 153, 231–3, 228. The link between pauperism and early working ages was an international phenomenon. Saito points out that pauper children in proto-industrial areas of Japan commenced work nearly three years earlier than children generally: O. Saito, 'Children's Work, Industrialism, and the Family Economy in Japan, 1872–1926', in *Child Labour's Global Past, 1650–2000*, ed. K. Lieten and E. Van Nederveen Meerkerk (Bern: Peter Lang, 2011), pp. 457–78 (pp. 467–9).

27   I. Pinchbeck, *Women Workers and the Industrial Revolution, 1750–1850* (London: Routledge, 1930), p. 96; Kirby, *Child Labour in Britain*, pp. 32–7; J. Humphries, *Childhood and Child Labour in the British Industrial Revolution* (Cambridge: Cambridge University Press, 2010), pp. 191–6.

early ages. Indeed, it has been suggested that the increasing availability of work for children in spinning mills rendered family migration to cotton towns increasingly attractive to poor households, especially those employed in declining domestic trades.[28] Moreover, a child's capacity for work was commonly regarded as parental property and as such, parents often objected strongly to any interference by local authorities or the state in limiting the labour and earning capacity of their children.[29] J. S. Mill deplored the 'absolute and exclusive control' exercised by working-class parents over children: 'One would almost think that a man's children were supposed to be literally, and not metaphorically, a part of himself, so jealous is opinion of the smallest interference of law with his absolute and exclusive control over them'.[30] A Royal Statistical Society report suggested that part of the increased reproductive capacity of working-class families during the Industrial Revolution had been prompted specifically by the increasing availability of child work:

> Children in the lower strata became actual financial assets ... to their families, because they went to work when 12 or 13 years of age, and the family income was proportionately increased according to the number of children. One therefore saw that in the past there had been an actual inducement in the lowest classes of society to have large families.[31]

Many poor parents also believed that early exposure to hard work would promote habits of industry and a physical resilience that might ensure a future continuity of employment.[32]

---

28   J. Lyons, 'Family Response to Economic Decline: Handloom Weavers in Early Nineteenth-Century Lancashire', *Research in Economic History*, 12 (1989), 45–91.

29   In 1857, the Prince Consort remarked that 'the working man's children were not only his offspring ... but constituted part of his productive power': A. Davin, 'Child Labour, the Working-Class Family, and Domestic Ideology in Nineteenth-Century Britain', *Development and Change*, 13 (1982), 633–52 (p. 638).

30   J. S. Mill, *On Liberty* (1859), in *Utilitarianism and On Liberty*, ed. M. Warnock (Oxford: Blackwell, 2003), pp. 88–180 (p. 172).

31   Comment by Dr Reginald Dudfield in Stevenson, pp. 441–2.

32   Thackrah observed that parents often forced their children into factory work at too early an age (PP 1831–2 (706), p. 518). Locke thought that deliberate exposure to cold, fatigue and hardship during childhood and youth (the so-called 'hardening system') could equip a child's body for future insults to physical and mental well-being. Though, as Goldsmith pointed out, the privations of peasant societies did not lead to increasing longevity and probably had the effect of hardening many children out of the world: J. Locke, *Some Thoughts Concerning Education*, intro. and notes R. H. Quick

Working-class parents were frequently blamed for a lack of interest in the health and welfare of their children.[33] Mothers, in particular, were subject to claims of inadequate childcare and poor nursing practices. Struve's childcare treatise of 1802 observed that the 'physical treatment of children, during the first years of infancy, is unquestionably one of the most important of human pursuits; inasmuch as health or disease, nay, life or death, materially depend on the proper conduct of parents and guardians.'[34] Doctors frequently attributed the ill-health of children to the moral failings and degenerate habits of parents. Farrer noted in 1773 that rickets was 'most incident and fatal to children whose parents are of a lax, and weak constitution; who are addicted to idleness and effeminacy.'[35] Meanwhile, external commentators, such as the French doctor, Louis-René Villermé, blamed high urban mortality upon the effects of low wages, poverty, and industrial production as well as workers' drunkenness and debauchery.[36] Debates over factory reform regularly featured attempts to stigmatise married women who worked long hours outside the household. Early reports of the Registrar General suggested that the relatively high levels of infant mortality in manufacturing districts resulted from a neglect of breast-feeding, the use of artificial feeding technologies and the employment of childminders. During the Lancashire 'cotton famine' it was observed that whilst the death rate in manufacturing districts increased, the rate of infant mortality declined. This, it was said, was due to out-of-work female factory workers being forced

(Cambridge: Cambridge University Press, 1889), p. 205n; O. Goldsmith, Letter to *The Bee*, 10 November 1759, in *The Miscellaneous works of Oliver Goldsmith: with an Account of his Life and Writings*, ed. W. Irving (Philadelphia: J. Crissy & J. Grigg, 1830), pp. 454–8 (p. 455).

33   A. O'Malley, *The Making of the Modern Child: Children's Literature and Childhood in the Late Eighteenth Century* (London: Routledge, 2003), pp. 69–70; A. Mathisen, 'Treating the Children of the Poor: Institutions and the Construction of Medical Authority in Eighteenth-Century London' (D.Phil. thesis, Oxford University, 2011), pp. 102–13.

34   C. A. Struve, *A Familiar View of the Domestic Education of Children during the early period of their lives: being a compendium addressed to all mothers, who are seriously concerned for the welfare of their offspring* (London: Murray & Highley, 1802), pp. viii–ix.

35   W. Farrer, *A Particular Account of the Rickets in Children; and Remarks on its Analogy to the King's Evil* (London: J. Johnson, 1773), p. 3.

36   L. R. Villermé, *Sur la population de la Grande-Bretagne: considérée principalement et comparativement dans les districts agricoles, dans les districts manufacturiers et dans les grandes villes* (Paris: n.p., 1834); A. E. F. La Berge, *Mission and Method: The Early Nineteenth-Century French Public Health Movement* (Cambridge: Cambridge University Press, 2002), pp. 163–4, 169.

through circumstance to breastfeed their babies.[37] Anderson has suggested that mothers' work may have had less of an influence upon the mortality of infants than has been thought because only a small proportion of infants belonging to working mothers in Lancashire industrial districts (about 2 per cent) were left with paid childminders.[38] An extensive Local Government Board inquiry of 1913 also discovered that infant mortality was excessively high in mining communities where mothers were less likely to work outside the home.[39] However, it seems clear that long hours of work for mothers away from home must have reduced the quality of childcare and the time available for breast-feeding and therefore must have had some effect upon infant mortality.[40]

The work patterns of parents were also implicated in child neglect and domestic injuries. Engels thought that the 'employment of women ... breaks up the family; for when the wife spends twelve or thirteen hours every day in the mill, and the husband works the same length of time ... what becomes of the children? They grow up like wild weeds'.[41] The risk of domestic injury to young children was certainly increased where both parents worked outside the home. In 1836, the *Bolton Free Press* reported that in the space of seven weeks 'there were no less than 32 cases ... of children being burnt to death, and that 27 of the 32 were in consequence of the neglect of the parents in leaving them alone in the house.'[42] Of four hundred inquests held in the borough of Manchester during the year 1840, 27 per cent were occasioned by the burning or scalding of children in their own homes whilst in Staffordshire, in the 1850s and 60s, 32 per cent

---

37 H. J. Tennant, 'Infant Mortality and Factory Labour (I)', in *The Dangerous Trades: the Historical, Social and Legal Aspects of Industrial Occupations as Affecting Health*, ed. T. Oliver (London: John Murray, 1902), pp. 73–84 (p. 75).

38 M. Anderson, *Family Structure in Nineteenth-Century Lancashire* (Cambridge: Cambridge University Press, 1971), p. 74.

39 Wohl, *Endangered Lives*, p. 28.

40 P. Hudson, *The Industrial Revolution* (London: Edward Arnold, 1992), pp. 141–2; see also the recent discussion of infant mortality and women's work in a variety of trades in the later nineteenth century in C. Malone, *Women's Bodies and Dangerous Trades in England, 1880–1914* (Woodbridge: Boydell Press, 2003), pp. 105–24.

41 M. Hewitt, *Wives and Mothers in Victorian Industry* (London: Rockliff, 1958), pp. 99–122, 140; see also C. Dyhouse, 'Working-Class Mothers and Infant Mortality in England, 1895–1914', *Journal of Social History*, 12, 2 (1978), 248–67; F. Engels, *The Condition of the Working Class in England in 1844* (1845; Oxford: Oxford University Press, 1993), p. 152.

42 Anon., *Bolton Free Press*, 19 February 1836, p. 2.

of non-work-related sudden deaths among children aged below fifteen resulted from domestic immolation.[43] Children taken to a workplace under parental supervision therefore may have experienced a lower risk of injury and death than those left unattended at home.

The health of working-age children

Although child illness and mortality in manufacturing districts was frequently blamed on industrial work, explanations of causation were frequently couched in highly generalised terms which stressed general 'debility' rather than specific occupational causes. Charles Thackrah argued at the Sadler Committee that children working in mills suffered no more disease and mortality than other urban children, though he insisted that working from an early age weakened the constitution and rendered children liable to chronic diseases in later life (a somewhat difficult concept to test in the 1830s).[44] By contrast, rural workers were said to possess 'firm fibre and dense blood' which afforded them protection against inflammatory diseases.[45] Crucially, the vast majority of mortality amongst urban children was concentrated in infancy and early childhood. Physicians who lived and practised in factory districts pointed out frequently that the mortality of children at ages when they commenced work in mills and factories was little different from that existing amongst children of the same ages in rural environments. Research by Levine has also shown

43   PP 1843 [432], B17. The comparable figure for rural districts in Staffordshire was less than a quarter (Sambrook, p. 228, tab. 10.4). A Potteries surgeon observed in 1843 a 'frightfully great' incidence of immolation of children, caused by 'the absence of mothers in the manufactories' (PP 1843 [432], C14).

44   He claimed that 'the factory system reduces the nervous power, in other words, the vigour of the constitution, that it renders persons more feeble, more subject to suffer from attacks of disease'; a relative lack of muscular development was also noted (PP 1831–2 (706), pp. 512–14).

45   W. Falconer, *An Essay on the Preservation of the Health of Persons Employed in Agriculture* (Bath: n.p., 1789), p. 34. Though it was also argued that a mix of agrarian and domestic industrial pursuits was conducive to both health and wealth: C. S. Paterson, 'From Fever to Digestive Disease: Approaches to the Problem of Factory Ill-Health in Britain, 1784–1833' (Ph.D. thesis, University of British Columbia, 1995), pp. 78–9. A lack of individual self-discipline was also implicated in the production of constitutional weakness amongst industrial workers: see K. Figlio, 'Chlorosis and Chronic Disease in Nineteenth-Century Britain: The Social Constitution of Somatic Illness in a Capitalist Society', *Social History*, vol. 3 (1978), 167–97 (pp. 187–9).

that although proto-industrial districts harboured high rates of infant and early childhood mortality compared with surrounding rural districts, children of working age enjoyed relatively good health.[46] In the mid-1830s, the Manchester doctor John Roberton had shown that the death rate amongst children aged five to ten in urban manufacturing centres was roughly equal with those in agricultural districts and that in some rural districts mortality was actually higher.[47] The Bolton physician James Black observed:

> A person who has heard nothing of cotton mills and the trade, but of prisons for white slaves and infanticide, will be surprised to find, that of those employed in them, as few children die between the ages of seven and sixteen in Bolton, as in many rural parishes. I find the ratio of deaths in Bolton between the ages of ten and nineteen inclusive, to be to the whole deaths, during the year, as 5.4 to 100 ... while in all England, from the population returns, it is 6 per cent.[48]

The widespread failure to distinguish between high urban mortality amongst infants and very young children and the comparatively lower death rates amongst children of working age was also highlighted by the Preston factory surgeon, James Harrison, whose 1835 study of more than a thousand children working in cotton mills showed that they took no more than an average of four days sickness absence per year.[49] Edwin Chadwick was also highly sceptical about claims of poor health amongst child factory workers, observing in 1842 that 'opinion is erroneous which ascribes greater sickness and mortality to the children employed in factories than amongst the children who remain in the homes

46   D. Levine, *Family Formation in an Age of Nascent Capitalism* (New York: Academic Press, 1977), p. 68, tab. 5.7, p. 86, tab. 5.17.

47   J. Roberton, 'On Infant Mortality in Manchester and some other Parts of Lancashire', *London Medical Gazette: or, Journal of Practical Medicine*, 15 (12 February 1835), 733–5. For a comparison of mortality at different ages drawn from the later nineteenth century (when infant mortality remained extremely high) see Hardy, 'Rickets and the rest', pp. 390–1, tabs 2–3.

48   J. Black, 'A Medico-Topographical, Geological, and Statistical Sketch of Bolton and its Neighbourhood', *Transactions of the Provincial Medical and Surgical Association*, 5 (1837), 125–224 (p. 179).

49   J. Harrison, 'Extracts from the Report of the Inspectors of Factories, Illustrating the State of Health in the Different Factories', *Edinburgh Medical and Surgical Journal*, 44 (1835), 425–32 (p. 426).

as these towns afford to the labouring classes ... more than 57 per cent die before they attain five years of age; that is, before they can be engaged in factory labour, or in any other labour whatsoever'. Even Peter Gaskell, an avowed opponent of the manufacturing system, concluded that the physical degeneration of factory children tended to begin in early life.[50]

Although children generally commenced manufacturing work during the safest period of childhood with regard to fatal illnesses, this did not mean that they necessarily enjoyed good general health. Unfortunately, little evidence exists of survivors of disease. It is clear that a majority of sufferers did not die and case mortality from the major infectious diseases may have been in the region of 20–45 per cent.[51] Some economic historians and historical demographers have even suggested that, during the eighteenth century, childhood diseases may actually have increased in

---

50   E. Chadwick, *Report on the Sanitary Condition of the Labouring Population of Great Britain* (1842), ed. M. W. Flinn (Edinburgh: Edinburgh University Press, 1965), p. 223. Chadwick described the populations of burgeoning towns and cities as 'an encamped horde': cited in J. H. Clapham, *An Economic History of Modern Britain: The Early Railway Age, 1820–1850* (1926; Cambridge: Cambridge University Press, 1950), p. 537. Chadwick's estimate of the 0–5 mortality rate is comparable with the 50 per cent death rate for Manchester estimated by Percival half a century earlier: T. Percival, 'Observations on the State of Population in Manchester, and Other Adjacent Places', *Philosophical Transactions*, 64 (1774), 54–66 (pp. 59–60). Buer, too, agreed that factories were probably much more healthy places than the homes of workers: M. C. Buer, *Health, Wealth, and Population in the early days of the Industrial Revolution* (London: Routledge, 1926), pp. 251–2; W. H. Hutt, 'The Factory System of the Early Nineteenth Century', in *Capitalism and the Historians*, ed. F. A. Hayek (Chicago: University of Chicago Press, 1954), pp. 160–88 (p. 172). Nassau Senior also thought that physical appearance of Manchester operatives was attributable mainly to their domestic conditions: J. Mottram, 'The Life and Work of John Roberton (1797–1876) of Manchester, Obstetrician and Social Reformer' (MSc thesis, University of Manchester, 1986), p. 195.
51   Some studies of adolescent health have been conducted from parish register entries but provide little direct evidence on the health effects of occupations. See the interesting research by R. Davenport, L. Schwarz and J. Boulton, 'The Decline of Adult Smallpox in Eighteenth-Century London', *Economic History Review*, 64, 4 (2011), 1289–314. Nominal causes of deaths in the Registrar General's returns also changed continually in line with advances in medical knowledge: A. Mercer, *Death, Disease and Mortality in the Demographic Transition: Epidemiological-Demographic Change in England since the Eighteenth Century as part of a Global Phenomenon* (Leicester: Leicester University Press, 1993), p. 75. Floud *et al.* described historical knowledge of childhood morbidity as 'patchy and unsatisfactory' (p. 298); W. Luckin, 'Evaluating the Sanitary Revolution: Typhus and Typhoid in London', in *Urban Disease and Mortality in Nineteenth-Century England*, ed. R. I. Woods and J. H. Woodward (London: Batsford Academic, 1984), pp. 102–19 (p. 104).

their prevalence whilst becoming less fatal. In densely populated urban environments, fewer people achieved adulthood without having contracted infectious diseases as children. This meant that the overall mortality rate from infectious disease fell whilst individuals acquired an early immunity to future infections. It is possible, therefore, that the transition from high-fatality adult epidemic diseases to endemic childhood infections may have reduced disease mortality whilst increasing the prevalence of non-fatal diseases amongst children.[52] The relationship between non-fatal diseases and the incidence of other diseases is also highly complex. Many of the widespread disabling diseases of childhood such as rickets had exceptionally low mortality rates but almost certainly predisposed children to other diseases.[53]

Although quantitative evidence of worker morbidity is rare, that which survives suggests that sickness was common amongst manufacturing workers. Examinations of cotton workers in 1818–9 showed that a substantial proportion displayed evidence of illness (Table 2). Of the nearly half who were found to be sick, 44 per cent were said to be suffering from 'nonspecific' or constitutional ailments (including systemic conditions described variously as 'delicate', 'feeble constitution', 'underweight', 'debility', 'fever' and 'enlarged glands').[54] Pulmonary complaints were responsible for the second largest group of illnesses at 27.7 per cent whilst musculoskeletal conditions accounted for 11 per cent and infectious diseases 7.7 per cent.

Some infectious diseases were associated by doctors specifically with

---

52   H-J. Voth and T. Leunig, 'Did Smallpox Reduce Height? Stature and the Standard of Living in London, 1770–1873', *Economic History Review*, 49 (1996), 541–60 (p. 558). Some northern medical men also observed that infectious diseases had become more prevalent during the second half of the eighteenth century: J. V. Pickstone, 'Ferriar's Fever to Kay's Cholera: Disease and Social Structure in Cottonopolis', *History of Science*, 22 (1984), 401–19 (p. 410); J. Roberton, 'Remarks on the axiom of political economists, that a general improvement in the duration of life indicates a corresponding improvement in public health', *Manchester Guardian*, 18 June 1831, p. 3; J. Roberton, *General Remarks on the Health of English Manufacturers; and on the Need for Convelescent Retreats as subservient to the medical charities of our large towns* (London: J. Ridgway, 1831). See also the review of Roberton's book, *Medico-Chirurgical Review*, 20, 31 (1832), 77–83.

53   Hardy, 'Rickets and the Rest'. Studies such as Riley's analysis of the morbidity of workers are not possible for children because of a lack of structured source materials: J. C. Riley, *Sick, Not Dead: the Health of British Workingmen during the Mortality Decline* (Baltimore: Johns Hopkins University Press, 1997).

54   H. Freudenberger, F. J. Mather and C. Nardinelli, 'A New Look at the Early Factory Labor Force', *Journal of Economic History*, 44 (1984), 1085–90 (p. 1088, tab. 3).

Table 2: The morbidity of cotton workers, 1818–19

Classification	Number	% of total	% of total sick
Healthy	1008	55.3	0.0
Nonspecific Systemic	359	19.7	44.0
Pulmonary	226	12.4	27.7
Musculoskeletal	90	4.9	11.0
Miscellaneous	78	4.3	9.6
Infectious Disease	63	3.5	7.7
Total	1824		

Source: Calculated from H. Freudenberger, F. J. Mather and C. Nardinelli, 'A New Look at the Early Factory Labor Force', *Journal of Economic History*, 44 (1984), 1085–90 (p. 1088, tab. 3).
Note: Freudenberger *et al.* defined the classification as follows:
Nonspecific Systemic: delicate, feeble constitution, underweight, debility, fever, enlarged glands.
Pulmonary: cough, asthma, difficulty in breathing, hydrothorax, pleurisy.
Musculoskeletal: amputation, deformity, limpness, swelling, stiffness, pain, rheumatism.
Miscellaneous: cardiovascular complaints, genito-urinary (including menstruation), headache, rickets, mental disorder, dyspepsia, hernia, indigestion, stomach pain, sore breast (suckling), unknown.
Infectious Disease: consumption, measles, smallpox, scrofula, typhus, abscess, sore throat.

manufacturing work. Scrofula was reported as a disease peculiar to factories and was said to result from a general debility associated with indoor work and a lack of exercise and fresh air.[55] Mill work was said to lead to a loss of vitality which could bring 'particles' of scrofula 'into Action, and generate it where it is combined with Moisture ... and subject to Changes or Vicissitudes of Temperature.'[56] An 'exciting cause' was often necessary such as excessive heat, or cold, or a poor diet. Scrofula amongst working children was linked with warm temperatures in mills whilst the transition of workers from a warm humid atmosphere to cold external air was often said to initiate the disease. Doctors pointed to the particular circumstance of mill workers walking home in cold winter

55   PP 1816 (397), pp. 328–9. Scrofula was implicated in bone distortions and a lack of fresh air was thought to render children more susceptible to rickets (Farrer, p. 72).
56   PP 1819 (24), pp. 290–91.

air with perspiration remaining on the skin.[57] As early as 1796, Ferriar had advised workers in Manchester to wear flannel next to their skin to counteract the adverse effects of perspiration and cold.[58] Climatic and topographical factors were also widely cited as a cause of scrofula. Water-powered mills were invariably situated in river valleys where humidity and 'unwholesome mists' were thought to contribute further to the development of the disease.[59] Heredity was also though to play an important role. Engels observed in 1845, 'Scrofula is almost universal among the working class, and scrofulous parents have scrofulous children, especially when the original influences continue in full force to operate upon the inherited tendency of the children.'[60] However, most of the theoretical links between manufacturing and scrofula had been drawn by doctors largely unacquainted with industrial work. Little quantifiable evidence was ever offered to demonstrate any higher incidence of the disease amongst factory children and, in a letter to the Sadler Committee, the experienced Manchester doctor, Edward Carbutt, expressed himself highly critical of

the gross exaggerations of medical witnesses, particularly those of London, on the subject of the diseases of cotton factories. These gentlemen, hardly any of whom have ever had any opportunity of seeing persons employed in cotton factories, do almost universally attribute to factory labour the production of scrofulous diseases. Now the fact is, that scrofula is almost unknown in cotton factories, although the climate of this town and neighbourhood is particularly cold and

57   E. Lomax, 'Hereditary or Acquired Disease? Early Nineteenth Century Debates on the Cause of Infantile Scrofula and Tuberculosis', *Journal of the History of Medicine and Allied Science*, 32 (1977), 356–74 (pp. 363–4, 366); see Hamlin, 'Predisposing Causes'. The predisposition theory continued into the early nineteenth century. See also the discussion about temperature, scrofula and consumption in Kinder Wood's evidence in PP 1816 (397), pp. 198–203.
58   PP 1818 (90), pp. 173–4, 237. The finest spinning required the highest temperatures to stop the thread sticking to rollers and to prevent breakage. This meant that a temperature of 68–74°F had to be maintained; lower temperatures were required in woollen mills: PP 1818 (90), p. 185; J. Ferriar, letter 'To the Gentlemen meeting at the Bridgewater-arms', reproduced in J. E. M. Walker, 'John Ferriar of Manchester. M.D.: His Life and Work' (MSc thesis, University of Manchester, 1973), Appendix V, p. 4.1; PP 1831–2 (706), p. 516.
59   C. E. Tonna, *Helen Fleetwood* (London: R. B. Seeley & W. Burnside, 1841), p. 263, cited in *Factory Lives: Four Nineteenth-Century Working-Class Autobiographies*, ed. J. R. Simmons, intro. J. Carlisle (Toronto: Broadview Editions, 2007), pp. 483–91 (p. 483).
60   Lomax, p. 357; Engels, p. 132.

humid ... of four hundred and one persons employed, eight persons only were affected with scrofula, with no case of distortion of the spine or limbs ... This remarkable absence of scrofula I presume, with perfect deference to the medical gentleman who is one of your number, to attribute to the dryness and warmth of the cotton factories, to the lightness of the work, and to the superior food and clothing which the superior wages of the work-people enable them to obtain.[61]

Medical witnesses at the earlier Kenyon Committee of 1818 had found no excess of scrofula amongst Manchester mill workers and one medical examiner at the time noted an 'almost a total absence of Scrofula, of which I expected to have found a great deal.'[62] As part of their examinations, the Manchester medical investigators palpated the lymph glands of cotton spinners and found no greater incidence of scrofulous swellings or deformities compared with the urban population at large:

> We made each Person walk across a long Room, to ascertain whether there was any thing like Deformity; we were very particular in examining their Appearance, particularly inquiring whether they eat well and slept well, whether they had any Ailment, and not trusting to their Report; we were very exact in feeling whether we could find any glandular Swellings which could indicate Scrofula, particularly among the younger Part of them ... The Result of this Investigation was, that the Hands whom we examined ... were as healthy as could be expected in any Class of Society who were obliged to work at a manufacturing Employment.[63]

The committee found that workers suffering from 'scrofulous affections', rickets, weak limbs and distorted spine (including those displaying evidence of having suffered in the past) amounted to less than 2 per cent of the labour force.[64] Moreover, a later survey of around four thousand patients admitted to the Leeds Dispensary between 1831 and 1833 indicated that cases of scrofula were rare amongst both manufacturing

---

61   Letter from Dr. E. Carbutt, cited in A. Ure, *Philosophy of Manufactures: or, an exposition of the scientific, moral, and commercial economy of the Factory System of Great Britain* (London: Charles Knight, 1835), pp. 376–7.
62   PP 1818 (90), pp. 38, 56, 107.
63   PP 1818 (90), p. 141 and *passim*.
64   PP 1818 (90), p. 109. The substantial tabular results of medical surveys contained in the Kenyon Committees has hardly featured in standard accounts of factory welfare. On this see Freudenberger *et al.*, 'Early Factory Labor Force'.

and non-manufacturing urban patients. By the mid-century Phillips claimed that the disease was more fatal amongst rural than urban populations and the incidence of deaths from scrofula in the factory districts of Lancashire, Yorkshire and Cheshire was claimed to be less than half that in south-eastern, south midland and south-western English agrarian counties.[65] Phillips also pointed out that scrofula mortality amongst factory workers was about equal to that of masons, shoemakers and tailors in industrial towns, observing that it would 'seem improper to refer to manufactures an evil, which is not peculiar to them.'[66]

Sexual health and adolescence

Reports of industrial diseases and deformities were supplemented by claims of premature sexual development amongst adolescent mill and factory workers. Some early advocates of factory reform were concerned about the presence together of young female and male children in the workplace at around the ages of puberty.[67] Many thought that mills were sites of prostitution and some early legislation such as Peel's Act of 1802 included explicit stipulations that male and female apprentices should have separate sleeping arrangements.[68] By the time of the major factory debate in the early 1830s, sexual precociousness was said to be widespread amongst adolescent operatives. A witness to the Sadler Committee claimed that in mills, the 'means preventive of impregnation are more

---

65   PP 1833 (519), C3, pp. 19–20, tab. 1; B. Phillips, *Scrofula; its Nature, its Causes, its Prevalence, and the Principles of Treatment* (Philadelphia: Lea & Blanchard, 1846), pp. 184–5.

66   With regard to an occupational predisposition to scrofula, however, Phillips observed 'evidence which has hitherto been collected on the subject, consists for the most part of general statements, of the condition of the Factory population, and estimates of the general mortality of particular districts' (Phillips, *Scrofula*, pp. 203–5).

67   Horrell and Humphries point out that contemporaries 'generally did not distinguish prepubescent boys and girls. Sex only became significant at puberty, whereupon it led to condemnation of the employment of adolescent girls outside the confines of the family': S. Horrell and J. Humphries, '"The Exploitation of Little Children": Child Labor and the Family Economy in the Industrial Revolution', *Explorations in Economic History*, 32 (1995), 485–516 (p. 487); see also Pelling, 'Child Health', pp. 150, 154.

68   T. Bernard, 'Extract from an Account of Mr Dale's Cotton Mills at New Lanerk, in Scotland', *Reports of the Society for Bettering the Condition and Increasing the Comforts of the Poor*, 2 (1800), 250–7 (p. 254); 42 Geo. III, c. 73, s. vii.

likely to be generally known and practised by young persons'. Moreover, the low illegitimacy rate in factory towns was attributed to the alleged freer use of abortifacients.[69] In 1832, a case was reported of a twelve-year-old Lancashire mill girl who had given birth to a stillborn child.[70] Much of the blame for supposed factory depravity was placed on the decline in customary forms of supervision. In traditional rural society, masters had generally employed no more than one or two apprentices or servants and this was thought to ensure an adequate regulation of interpersonal relationships within a broader pattern of juvenile socialisation to work. Young workers in factories, by contrast, spent long periods of the working day or night away from home in the company of strangers. This was said to prevent young girls in particular from acquiring essential feminine domestic skills whilst at the same time exposing them to sexualised adult language and behaviour. Bisset Hawkins, in his report for the 1833 Factory Commission noted:

> With respect to debauchery, an easy preparation is afforded for it by the mixture of a large number of both sexes in the same room; an overlooker, who has generally passed his youth in a similar room, is the only restraint upon bad example, coarse tricks, and corrupting language; add to this, that usually the closet is in each of these crowded rooms, and that the entrance and exit of every one are conspicuous ... An estimate of sexual morality is scarcely possible to be reduced into figures; but if I may trust my own observations, and the general opinion of those with whom I have conversed, and the spirit of our evidence, then a most discouraging view of the influence of the factory life upon the morality of female youth obtrudes itself.[71]

---

69   PP 1831-2 (706), p. 545; A. McLaren, 'The Early Birth Control Movement: an Example of Medical Self-Help', in *Health Care and Popular Medicine in Nineteenth-Century England*, ed. J. Woodward and D. Richards (London: Croom Helm, 1977), pp. 89–104 (p. 93).

70   Mottram, p. 125.

71   Medical reports by Dr Hawkins (on Lancashire, Cheshire and Derbyshire), PP 1833 (519), D3, p. 4. In pottery workshops, Samuel Scriven reported: 'In eight cases out of ten of the whole, the places of convenience for the sexes are indecently and disgustingly exposed and filthy' (PP 1843 [432], C3). Such fears were fuelled by the Glasgow mule-spinner who reported that a number of his female child piecers had gone on to become prostitutes: cited in P. Bolin-Hort, *Work, Family and the State: Child Labour and the Organisation of Production in the British Cotton Industry, 1780–1920* (Lund: Lund University Press, 1989), p. 61.

Witnesses to the Sadler Committee claimed that the heat of the factory floor and the physical process of factory spinning induced premature sexual development amongst girls. This, in turn, would have harmful effects upon conception and parturition. Long periods of standing were thought to result in a narrowing of the pelvis and greater difficulties in childbirth.[72] Such ideas were supported by prevailing anthropological beliefs that females in warmer countries achieved puberty earlier than those in colder climes (the earlier ripening of fruit in warmer regions was frequently cited in support of such ideas).[73] Heat was thought also to be implicated in the premature development of the passions. 'Heat, I have observed', wrote Falconer in 1781, 'increases the faculty or power, as well as the accuracy, of sensation and feeling. This sensibility of the body is by sympathy communicated to the mind'.[74] Factory reformers such as Peter Gaskell seized upon such 'scientific' theories of premature development to support their campaign against child labour. Gaskell described how the

'crowding together [of] numbers of the young of both sexes in factories, is a prolific source of moral delinquency. The stimulus of a heated atmosphere, the contact of opposite sexes, the example of lasciviousness upon the animal passions − all have conspired to produce a very early development of sexual appetencies ... the female population engaged in manufactures, approximates very closely to that found in tropical climates; puberty, or at least sexual propensities, being attained almost coeval with girlhood.'[75]

72   Thompson reported this supposed pelvic narrowing in a somewhat matter-of-fact way: E. P. Thompson, *The Making of the English Working Class* (1963; London: Penguin, 1980), pp. 327–8. It was also thought that the exposure of pregnant women to immoral speech and behaviour might influence the physical development of the foetus (Figlio, pp. 190–1). See also C. E. Rosenberg, 'The Bitter Fruit: Heredity, Disease, and Social Thought', in *No Other Gods: On Science and American Social Thought* (Baltimore: Johns Hopkins University Press, 1997), pp. 25–53 (pp. 27–8); C. Hamlin, *Public Health and Social Justice in the Age of Chadwick: Britain, 1800–1854* (Cambridge: Cambridge University Press, 1998), pp. 98, 40.
73   Mottram, p. 116; see J. Roberton, 'An Inquiry into the Natural History of the Menstrual Function', *Edinburgh Medical and Surgical Journal*, 38 (1 October 1832), 227–54 (p. 228).
74   W. Falconer, *Remarks on the Influence of Climate, Situation, Nature of Country, Population, Nature of Food and Way of Life* (London: n.p., 1781), Book I, p. 6. Such views had earlier been articulated by Montesquieu (Roberton, 'Menstrual Function', pp. 249–50).
75   Gaskell cited examples of Tahitian girls commencing sexual intercourse when they

Little evidence of differential sexual maturity between factory girls and those in other occupations was ever produced, however, and by the early 1830s the thesis that factory girls matured earlier than others was challenged by the obstetrician John Roberton (surgeon to the Manchester Lying-in Hospital), whose 'Inquiry into the Natural History of the Menstrual Function' of 1832 largely dispelled fears about the influence of heat and climate upon premature menarche.[76] The more generalised claims that premarital sex was more prevalent amongst manufacturing populations were also largely inaccurate. Overcrowding in manufacturing towns and factory workplaces may well have compromised 'the social intimacy and sexual distance' that characterised traditional family structures, however rates of illicit sex were probably no greater than in early-modern rural society where premarital sex was regarded as a 'normal ... part of the courtship process'. In rural society between one third and a half of all brides capable of child-bearing between the late sixteenth and the early nineteenth centuries were pregnant at the time of marriage.[77]

Adolescent industrial workers nonetheless remained at risk of many conditions associated with puberty and early adulthood.[78] A higher incidence of chlorosis or 'green sickness' (a portmanteau description of

were six or seven years old: P. Gaskell, *The manufacturing population of England: its moral, social, and physical conditions, and the changes which have arisen from the use of steam machinery; with an examination of infant labour* (London: Baldwin & Cradock, 1833), pp. 68–9. A belief in the sexual precociousness of less 'civilized' infants was common: Roberton, 'Menstrual Function', pp. 247–8; Falconer, *Influence of Climate*, Book I, pp. 38–9.

76   Roberton was among the earliest doctors to apply the principles of anthropology to obstetrics. As Crawford has noted for earlier periods, assessments of the ages at which girls first menstruated were 'influenced more by theoretical notions than by any quantifiable observations': P. Crawford, 'Attitudes to Menstruation in Seventeenth-Century England', *Past & Present*, 91 (May 1981), 47–73 (p. 66); Roberton, 'Menstrual Function'.

77   M. Anderson, 'The Social Implications of Demographic Change', in *Cambridge Social History of Britain, 1750–1950*, ed. F. M. L. Thompson (Cambridge: Cambridge University Press, 1990), vol. 2, pp. 1–70 (p. 36). A report from Wales for the Committee of the Council on Education, for example, deplored the rural practice of 'courtship on beds': PP 1847 [870], p. 57; A. S. Wohl, 'Sex and the Single Room: Incest among the Victorian Working Classes', in *The Victorian Family: Structure and Stresses*, ed. A. S. Wohl (London: Croom Helm, 1978), pp. 197–216 (pp. 198, 204); P. E. H. Hair, 'Bridal Pregnancy in Rural England in Earlier Centuries', *Population Studies*, 20.2 (1966), 233–43 (pp. 239–240).

78   T. M. McBride, *The Domestic Revolution: The Modernisation of Household Service in England and France, 1820–1920* (London: Croom Helm, 1976), p. 100.

a variety of ailments associated with menarche) was reported amongst workers in Leeds factories.[79] Domestic servants, too, were said particularly to suffer from higher rates of the condition. Stockman discovered that 60 per cent of his sample of chlorosis sufferers were female servants, with factory girls accounting for 21 per cent. Causes were said to range from nutritional imbalances to overwork and lack of exercise.[80] Since the condition was normally thought to affect pubescent girls, the youthful age and gender structure of the mill labour force almost certainly accounted for its reported higher incidence. It is likely that ailments related to menstruation were also amongst the most important causes of absenteeism amongst factory females in the early nineteenth century. Indeed, the largest number of days lost through sickness or injury at the Deanston Cotton Works in Kilmadock in 1818 was reported as due to the 'Indisposition of Girls about the Age of Puberty'.[81]

Migration imparted an important range of effects upon the health of children and adolescents of working age. Young rural-to-urban migrants were usually reported as physically robust and less susceptible to chronic illnesses but the physical act of migration from the 'pure air' of the country to urban districts was also thought to expose them to a some infectious diseases to which urban-born adolescents enjoyed greater resistance.[82] Percival reported that, during the third quarter of

---

79 PP 1833 (519), C3, pp. 19–20, tab. 1.

80 H. King, *The Disease of Virgins: Green Sickness, Chlorosis and the Problems of Puberty* (London: Routledge, 2004), p. 78; Figlio, pp. 182–3. However, the overall proportion of sufferers from this ailment was low compared with the major diseases and the slightly higher levels of hypochromic anaemia amongst manufacturers are not sufficiently great to explain the fairly frequent references by medical witnesses to paleness among mill workers.

81 A total of 257 days were lost *per annum* from such indispositions compared with, for example, 140 days for 'Cattarrh' and 139 for pulmonary phthisis (PP 1819 (24), App., p. 106). Marx pointed out that urban homeworkers and those in sweated trades were often of a higher risk of diseases of 'bad air' such as tuberculosis: Figlio, p. 182; K. Marx, *Capital: A Critical Analysis of Capitalist Production*, vol. 1, trans. S. Moore and E. Aveling (New York: International Publishers, 1947), vol. I, pp. 254–5; J. Rule, *The Experience of Labour in Eighteenth-Century Industry* (London: Croom Helm, 1981), p. 77.

82 J. Landers, 'Mortality and Metropolis: the Case of London, 1675–1825', *Population Studies*, 41, 1 (1987), 59–76 (p. 69); McBride, p. 100. Excesses of male or female mortality have also been suggested according to different labour market structures: E. A. Hammel, S. R. Johansson and C. A. Ginsberg, 'The Value of Children during Industrialization: Sex Ratios in Childhood in Nineteenth-Century America', *Journal of Family History*,

the eighteenth century, smallpox was much more common amongst young migrant workers in Manchester.[83] Moreover, recent research on smallpox mortality amongst young migrants suggests that the disease had become endemic outside cities by the final quarter of the century and that this led to a decline in the vulnerability of young rural migrants.[84] Unfortunately, the rate at which young migrant workers suffered from other infectious diseases has not been researched, though it seems likely that they reacted in different ways to different diseases. Around 1810, Ferriar reported a much greater prevalence of fevers amongst recently arrived young migrants in city lodging houses, noting that 'persons newly arrived from the country are most liable to suffer ... and as they are often taken ill within a few days after entering an infected house, there arises a double injury to the town, from the loss of their labour, and the expense of supporting them in their illness.'[85] Such was the spread of smallpox amongst adolescents and young adults that some indentures contained exclusion clauses in case apprentices contracted the disease and in some urban districts it was customary for masters to have a reduced responsibility for apprentices during epidemics.[86] Some illnesses also imparted disfiguring or disabling complications which might limit the ability of young people to obtain or carry out work.[87] The health of children and adolescents was therefore crucial to the formation of contracts with employers and masters would not normally accept a child with an obvious illness or disability.[88] The capacity of servants to infect a family by whom

8 (1983), 346–66; Scola, pp. 281–2; M. E. Pooley and C. G. Pooley, 'Health, Society and Environment in Nineteenth-Century Manchester', in *Urban Disease and Mortality*, ed. Woods and Woodward, pp. 148–75 (p. 149); McBride, p. 53. Aitchison points out, however, that farm servants in pastoral rural districts were probably equally likely to contract tuberculosis through daily contact with dairy animals: J. Aitchison, *Servants in Ayrshire, 1750–1914* (Ayr: Ayrshire Archaeological & Natural History Society, 2001), p. 85. I am extremely grateful to Romola Davenport for an informative correspondence on the subject of smallpox amongst young migrants.

83   R. B. Hope, 'Dr Thomas Percival, a Medical Pioneer and Social Reformer, 1740–1804' (MA thesis, University of Manchester, 1947), pp. 70–2.

84   Davenport *et al.*, p. 1301. Infant mortality also declined over the period 1740–1840 and this led to a natural increase in the supply of urban child and adolescent labour.

85   J. Ferriar, *To the Committee for the Regulation of the Police in the Towns of Manchester and Salford* (Manchester: n.p., 1792), p. 211.

86   Indentures sometimes stipulated a literal duty upon a master to care for apprentices 'in sickness and in health': Pelling, 'Child Health', pp. 155, 158–9, 163.

87   Walker, p. 3.2.

88   Pelling, 'Child Health', pp. 159–60.

they were employed was a major preoccupation and some employers therefore preferred servants displaying smallpox scarring or those who had been inoculated.[89] Meanwhile, widespread and repeated infections would weaken children and adolescents and render them less desirable workers. High sickness and absenteeism rates almost always slowed down progression in the factory workplace, reduced the acquisition of skills and led to fewer training opportunities for young workers.[90]

Although urban districts harboured greater health risks for children and adolescents, therefore, it is crucial to avoid any crude dichotomy between the health of urban and rural child labourers. The relative decline in employment opportunities for women and children in agriculture and the decline in cottage industries during the later eighteenth century often resulted in similarly harmful health effects. This was particularly the case amongst young unmarried rural females. In the mid-eighteenth century, the predominantly rural occupation of domestic spinning had probably grown to employ in excess of a million women and children but suffered a precipitate decline from the 1780s as competition with new spinning mills increased.[91] At the same time, relative levels of unemployment amongst females in agriculture increased significantly.[92] Indeed, excess mortality among rural girls has been linked closely with the long-term decline in demand for female labour in agricultural districts. Between 1851 and 1860, the death rate amongst females aged ten to fourteen in the eastern rural counties of England was 29 per cent greater than among those at the same ages in London, whilst amongst those aged fifteen to nineteen the rate was 41 per cent greater in rural districts. Much of the increased mortality amongst young females is thought to have resulted from higher rates of pulmonary tuberculosis, a condition frequently linked with poor nutrition.[93] More generally, the unfavourable living standards of young

89   Davenport *et al.*, p. 1301. A majority of London apprentices lived 'out-door' and therefore had frequent opportunities to convey disease to a master's home: Aitchison, p. 82; McBride, p. 100.

90   Freudenberger *et al.*, 'Early Factory Labor Force'.

91   C. Muldrew, '"Th'ancient Distaff" and "Whirling Spindle": measuring the contribution of spinning to household earnings and the national economy of England, 1550–1770', *Economic History Review*, 65 (2012), 498–526 (p. 498).

92   On this see K. D. M. Snell, 'Agricultural Seasonal Unemployment, the Standard of Living, and Women's Work in the South and East, 1690–1860', *Economic History Review*, 34 (1981), 407–37.

93   K. D. M. Snell, *Annals of the Labouring Poor: Social Change and Agrarian England, 1660–1900* (Cambridge: Cambridge University Press, 1985), pp. 15–66; K. McNay,

females in rural districts (particularly in the south and east of England) also compelled many adolescents to migrate in search of work in domestic service and the new manufacturing sectors.[94]

The health of child workers in early nineteenth-century industrial districts was therefore affected by a wide variety of economic and epidemiological factors that were often not related directly to the workplace. The effects of household poverty and high rates of orphanage in eighteenth and early nineteenth-century society exposed very poor children to higher rates of ill-health. Poor children were also much more likely to commence work at exceptionally young ages. Infectious diseases were ubiquitous amongst children and it is likely that many young people commenced their working lives carrying physical impairments conferred by disease in early childhood. This almost certainly led medical commentators to confuse broader epidemiological effects such as deformity and short stature with the influence of the workplace. By the 1820s and 1830s, contemporary doctors had developed a complex explanatory framework for the principal causes of ill-health amongst child workers. This frequently involved the effects of specific working practices such as awkward posture, long periods of standing, contact with raw materials and extended hours of work, together with a growing concern about the frequency of industrial injuries amongst factory children. The importance of these specific hazards is considered at greater length in the next chapter.

J. Humphries and S. Klasen, 'Excess Female Mortality in Nineteenth-Century England and Wales: A Regional Analysis', *Social Science History*, 29 (Winter 2005), 649–81. The mortality of young females in rural north Lancashire was significantly greater than those at the same ages in Liverpool: T. A. Welton, 'On the Effect of Migrations in Disturbing Local Rates of Mortality, as Exemplified in the Statistics of London and the Surrounding Country, for the years 1851–1860', *Journal of the Institute of Actuaries and Assurance Magazine*, 16 (1870–2), 153–86 (pp. 154, 156). However, Welton ascribed some of the greater rural incidence of young female mortality to a tendency of individuals suffering from longer-term health problems such as phthisis to return to their parental home or parish of settlement prior to death. This subject is ripe for further exploration; see also Wrigley *et al.*, p. 300, tab. 6.24.

94   K. D. M. Snell, 'The Apprenticeship System in British History: The Fragmentation of a Cultural Institution', *History of Education*, 25 (1996), 303–21. At the 1851 census, nearly 15 per cent of female domestic servants in the northern town of Rochdale are recorded has having been born in the impoverished rural counties of southern England: E. Higgs, *Domestic Servants and Households in Rochdale, 1851–1871* (New York: Garland, 1986), pp. 340–1, tab. 40.

2

Child Health in the Industrial Workplace

It is crucial that the occupational health of early industrial children is set within an analysis of the complex epidemiology of early factory towns. However, specific occupational ailments amongst working children were often explained in terms of particular aspects of work practices and environments. Accounts of the effects of work upon the body were based upon long-established medical knowledge. Most eighteenth and early nineteenth-century doctors expressing opinions about the health of working children tended to draw largely upon theoretical approaches by established authorities such as Ramazzini who, in the late seventeenth century, had ascribed industrial ailments to two major sets of causes:

> The first and most potent is the harmful character of the materials that they handle, for these emit noxious vapors and very fine particles inimical to human beings and induce particular diseases; the second I ascribe to certain violent and irregular motions and unnatural postures of the body, by reason of which the natural structure of the vital machine is so impaired that serious diseases gradually develop therefrom.[1]

Charles Thackrah's studies of occupational health, for example, were heavily influenced by Ramazzini's theories about materials and ergonomics and for much of the early nineteenth century the debate about the health of mill and factory children revolved around the relative importance of these major factors. Doctors at the early factory inquiries highlighted, in particular, the effects of the heated environment of mills and pointed to the large amount of suspended cotton dust which was already implicated in the production of pulmonary complaints amongst

---

1   B. Ramazzini, *Treatise of the Diseases of Tradesmen* (English edn, London: Andrew Bell, 1705), cited in M. Gochfeld, 'Chronologic History of Occupational Medicine', *Journal of Occupational and Environmental Medicine*, 47, 2 (February 2005), 96–114 (p. 103).

adult workers. They also emphasised factors such as the sustained pressure on children's bones created by standing for long periods or the unusual physical positions adopted by child mill workers as causes of widespread deformities amongst children.

Deformities

The most common occupational complaints to emerge from the factory inquiries of the early nineteenth century were leg, foot or spinal deformities and stunted growth. In the eighteenth century, 'craft palsies' (occupational deformities) had been readily attributed to the stresses and strains of repetitive workplace tasks.[2] Jonas Hanway had reported the case of a climbing boy thought to have become deformed by working 'before he was five years of age, his bones not having acquired a fit degree of strength.' He noted that climbing boys were 'generally bandy-leg'd, beginning to climb before the bone has acquired a solidity, the daily pressure necessarily gives the leg a twist.'[3] Charles Wing, moreover, reported a severe postural effect upon an articled clerk who had a chronic habit of stooping over his desk: 'he became visibly round-shouldered, and before the articles expired he had a backward protuberance, decided difficulty in breathing, and palpitation of the heart ... The spinal complaint was obviously produced, in this case, by stooping down, and bending constantly to the desk'. Wing, however, drew a distinction between 'simple deformity' (i.e. those not caused by disease, but rather originating in infancy) and other 'constitutional defects, occasioned by bad nursing, by residing in heated apartments, by a scanty supply of unwholesome food [and] by excessive labour in manufacturing employments'.[4] Variation in the class and wealth of parents was also associated with different deformities. The children

2   J. Rule, *The Experience of Labour in Eighteenth-Century Industry* (London: Croom Helm, 1981), pp. 81–2.
3   Cited in J. P. Andrews, *An appeal to the humane, on behalf of the most deplorable class of society, the climbing boys, employed by the chimney-sweepers* (London: John Stockdale, 1788), pp. 17–19. Will Thorne, the trade union leader and autobiographer, blamed a developing 'hump back' on his work as a child in the brickyards of the 1860s: J. Humphries, *Childhood and Child Labour in the British Industrial Revolution* (Cambridge: Cambridge University Press, 2010), p. 245.
4   C. Wing, 'Pathology of Curvature of the Spine', *The Lancet*, 1, 24 December 1836, 463–4 (p. 463); C. Wing, 'Dr Harrison's Treatment of Spinal Deformity', *The Lancet*, 1, 22 October 1836, 166–8 (p. 166).

of wealthy parents were 'phthisical, nervous, dyspeptic, and laterally curved in their spines', whilst those of the poor suffered from 'rickets, mesenteric disease, scrofula, anteriorly bent spines, and twisted limbs.'[5] Ergonomics lay at the root of most contemporary diagnoses of skeletal distortion amongst children. In his 1802 treatise on child development, Struve cautioned that 'Every species of labour ... should be carefully adapted to their juvenile strength; for, while the body is in a growing state, hard work, such as lifting, carrying, or drawing heavy burthens in carts, is frequently the cause of ruptures, crooked limbs, and other deformities; of which there are but too many instances among the youth of the country.'[6] Struve considered, in particular, the causes of asymmetrical physical development amongst children:

> All partial exercise of the body, by which only one arm or leg is exerted, has a tendency to give the body a crooked form. Hence, playing at nine pins, drawing hand carts, carrying burthens on one arm, or shoulder, all are pernicious. The principal injury however arises from continuing such employment for several hours together; because, if it be practised with moderation, and but occasionally resorted to, its tendency is beneficial, rather than hurtful. Young people therefore ought to be taught to make use of both arms; for we generally neglect the improvement of the left hand; and it would be very desirable to contrive games in which both arms may be alternately exercised ... Long standing is likewise detrimental to the straight growth of children: and as their legs are too feeble, by preponderating to one side, the same injurious effect is produced.[7]

The postural origins of workers' deformities proved highly influential upon scholars of occupational health such as Thackrah, who identified ergonomic effects in a variety of trades.[8] Between 1816 and 1832, such

5   J. Black, 'Remarks on the Influence of Physical Habits and Employment', *London Medical Gazette*, 2, 12 (1833), 143–8 (p. 144).
6   C. A. Struve, *A Familiar View of the Domestic Education of Children during the early period of their lives: being a compendium addressed to all mothers, who are seriously concerned for the welfare of their offspring* (London: Murray & Highley, 1802), p. 367. The ancient belief that unsatisfactory or disturbing sights and shocks could lead pregnant women to give birth to deformed children still had currency in the nineteenth century.
7   Struve, p. 420.
8   This included coopers, ropemakers, miners, well-sinkers, tailors, frizers, shoemakers, printers, glue and size boilers, school children and lawyers: C. T. Thackrah, *The Effects*

ideas were applied increasingly to the deformities found amongst factory children. The factory committees chaired by Peel, Kenyon and Sadler all received reports from factory operatives and medical men that claimed a causative link between the physical demands of mill work and the distortion of children's limbs.[9] Francis Sharp, a house surgeon from the Leeds Infirmary, observed a

> peculiar twisting of the ends of the lower part of the thigh bone. This affection I had never seen before I came to Leeds and I have remarked that it principally affected children from eight to fourteen years of age. At first I considered it might be rickets; but from the numbers which presented themselves, particularly at an age beyond the time when rickets attack children, and finding they were of recent date, and had commenced since they began work at the factory, I soon began to change my opinion. I now may have seen of such cases ... nearly 100, and I can most decidedly state they were the result of too much labour. So far as I know they all belonged to factories, and acquired this knock-kneed appearance from the very long hours the children are worked in the mills. The greatest number have attributed their disease to this cause themselves ... I have seen a person whose legs became distorted and stature stinted from factory labour, and how, by changing his employ for mason's work, became a fine, full formed, stout person in the upper part of his body, but continued a bandy-legged knock-kneed man all his life.[10]

The surgeon, Samuel Smith, argued that long periods of standing led to knock-knees and skeletal distortions that had sometimes caused factory workers to lose twelve inches in height.[11] Smith told William Dodd (the

---

of Arts, Trades, and Professions ... on Health and Longevity (London: Longman, Orme, Brown & Green, 1831; 1832), pp. 13, 17–18, 21–2, 24, 27, 35, 93, 96.

9   The unnatural posture sometimes adopted by young piecers was referred to by the anti-factory lobby as 'frame gait': G. J. Holyoake, *History of Cooperation*, vol. 2 (London: T. Fisher Unwin, 1908), p. 426.

> From six o'clock to noon, we've neither – breakfast time nor play,
> I'm certain this is slavery, whatever they may say.
> From dinner time to seven at night in *frame-gait* I must stand,
> No time for *drinking* is allow'd – Is this a Christian Land?
>
> (Extract from Anon., 'The Piecener's Complaint',
> *Short Time Tracts*, no. 4 (November 1835), 2).

10   PP 1833 (519), C3, pp. 12, 14.
11   PP 1831–2 (706), p. 501.

'factory cripple') about a seventeen-year-old male who had become deformed after working for only three months in a factory.[12] The bones of children and adolescents, it was thought, were soft and incapable of bearing their own body weight for long periods. The *London Medical Gazette* echoed the proposition, arguing that it was 'inevitable that their muscular and osseous systems can never be properly developed.'[13] One doctor suggested that the Almighty would have provided children with stronger bones had He intended them to work in factories.[14] Some of the metropolitan medical witnesses to Peel's Committee of 1816 even considered that sedentary work in a mill might be injurious to skeletal development – a point roundly refuted by those with experience of mill work who stressed that workers were more or less continually in motion.[15] Congenital and idiopathic causes of factory deformity were largely dismissed by supporters of factory reform whilst conditions such as rickets were stated to have had no effect upon children of working age.

Workers' own explanations of deformities tended to be obtuse. In 1819, it was suggested that 'When the Children have been working all Day they generally grow very tired, and ... give way to stooping with their Legs, and that causes them to become crippled.'[16] Another operative claimed that leg deformities mostly resulted from 'holding one Leg up to ease the other, and then holding the other up to ease that, and that made it grow

---

12   Dodd reported that on his visit to Leeds in 1841 he received a kindly reception 'particularly by Mr Samuel Smith', who was of the opinion that standing for long periods led to both 'knock knee' and 'bow-leggedness' due to the collapse of the ligaments of the knee joint: W. Dodd, *The Factory System Illustrated in a Series of Letters to the Right Hon. Lord Ashley* (London: John Murray, 1842), pp. 7–10.

13   Anon., 'The Ten Hours' Labour Bill', *London Medical Gazette*, 26 January 1833, pp. 562–6 (p. 563). Hamlin notes that 'The chief diagnoses applied to factory children were scrofula (terminating in consumption) and rickets': C. Hamlin, *Public Health and Social Justice in the Age of Chadwick: Britain, 1800–1854* (Cambridge: Cambridge University Press, 1998), p. 39.

14   R. Gray, 'The Languages of Factory Reform in Britain, c.1830–1860', in *The Historical Meanings of Work*, ed. P. Joyce (Cambridge: Cambridge University Press, 1987), pp. 143–79 (p. 148).

15   As late as the 1850s, leading public health doctors such as John Simon continued to emphasise a lack of physical exercise amongst industrial workers as a cause of ill-health: A. S. Wohl, *Endangered Lives: Public Health in Victorian Britain* (1983; London: Methuen, 1984), p. 258. Ramazzini, too, had placed his emphasis upon the dangers of unusual postures amongst sedentary occupations such as shoemaking and tailoring (cited in Gochfeld, p. 103).

16   PP 1819 (24), p. 20.

out.'[17] When workers were asked if deformities were common amongst their comrades, they frequently answered in the affirmative though were usually unable to offer causative links with particular forms of labour.

> You say Children frequently become deformed; give the Committee the Names? – I cannot say the Names; but standing so long, it makes them grow crooked.

> State the instances in which they have become so deformed? – I cannot speak to the Names at present; but there are various Children in the Mill where I am that are growing quite deformed.

> What are the Names of those Children? – One, Fairhurst.

> Are there any other besides Fairhurst to your Knowledge? – There are several young Children, but I cannot speak to the Names unless I was to go into the Mill.

> How many more? – May be Three or Four.

> What Age? – That I really do not know; in-kneed People are so frequent in Cotton Factories I do not know.

> Do you know whether these deformed Children were sickly when they first came in? – That I cannot speak to.[18]

Another answered as follows:

> Do the Spinners or Children often become deformed? – Yes.

> Do you know any who have become so? – Yes.

> How many in your own Mills? – In my own Mill I do not think there is one, but I have heard of them.[19]

Claims of widespread deformity amongst factory children were countered by many medical men practising in manufacturing districts. The Preston

---

17 PP 1819 (24), p. 152.
18 PP 1819 (24), pp. 103–4.
19 PP 1819 (24), p. 135. Another operative claimed that each of his three children were lame and crooked through factory work (PP 1819 (24), p. 65).

certifying surgeon, James Harrison, described the notion of factory deformities as 'wholly unfounded. Persons who entertain such notions must be entirely unacquainted with the nature of the employment they condemn; for that employment requires very varied motions of the body, and by no means fixes the body in an unnatural position.'[20] Harrison studied the orthopaedic health of doffers in throstle spinning and noted, 'in consequence of kneeling when first they begin work, [they] often suffer a little from *synovitis*, or a slight inflammation of the knee-joint, excited by friction and pressure; but I have not met with a single instance of any permanent injury being sustained from this cause.'[21] Chadwick, too, argued that claims of factory deformity rested upon mistaken theoretical assumptions. He maintained that only a comprehensive study of factory and non-factory populations could demonstrate the case one way or another, adding that the burden of proving factory deformities largely lay with those who had reported them.[22] Medical witnesses at the subsequent 1833 Factory Commission were also highly sceptical about claims of deformity. Robert Baker noted:

> The bow legs and in-knees ... I have seen occasionally; but, in my opinion, had the individuals had proper support and nourishment these effects would not generally have occurred, and I have been very careful in my inquiries. I do not mean to say, however, that very long labour might not produce this effect. My reasons for forming the above opinion are grounded on having observed the same results in persons in other occupations, and in a given number of the population, much more frequently than amongst a given number of factory children. Notwithstanding most careful examination, I have not been able to find a case of the morbid state of the bones of the foot alluded to by Mr Smith, and feel convinced, that if such a state exists, it must be exceedingly rare.[23]

Baker had worked as a mill surgeon for at least five years prior to giving evidence and had been in regular contact with mill children throughout

---

20 J. Harrison, 'Extracts from the Report of the Inspectors of Factories, Illustrating the State of Health in the Different Factories', *Edinburgh Medical and Surgical Journal*, 44 (1835), 425–32 (pp. 426–7).

21 Harrison, 'Extracts from the Report of the Inspectors', p. 426.

22 Hamlin, *Public Health and Social Justice*, pp. 99–100. Black expressed similar reservations ('Physical Habits and Employment', p. 144).

23 PP 1833 (519), C3, p. 14.

that time. Further investigations, such as Sir David Barry's examination of 111 Scottish mill girls failed to find any evidence of distortion of the arches of the feet.[24] Adam Hunter of the Leeds Infirmary noted that, although he objected fundamentally to the employment of young children in factories, he could not identify any specific conditions such as leg ulcers, injuries to the arch of the foot, distortion of the spine and pelvis, loosening of the ligaments or twisting of the knee joint that were said to be produced by working in factories.[25] Hunter thought that distortion of the spine caused by factory work was 'a favourite subject with some practitioners ... and as to the arch of the foot, in many families the splay-foot, for as I understand the question it means nothing more, is congenital ... All these I have seen in people who never wrought in a factory. I cannot doubt that such cases have occurred in factories, but I neither think them so frequent nor so appalling as has been represented.'[26] James Black, meanwhile, suggested that some deformities amongst cotton operatives might be caused by the widespread custom amongst textiles workers of wearing wooden-soled clogs, particularly where tight lacing was adopted. Clog wearing resulted in poor muscular development and an awkward gait in which the foot merely needed to be lifted up and set down. Clogs were thought to damage 'the elastic symmetry of the leg' and had a tendency to 'mishape the ancle [sic], elongate the heel, and flatten the sole of the foot, by neutralising nearly all exercise of the plantar muscles and the posterior ones of the leg and ancle.'[27] Chest and spinal distortions were also said to result from practices such as swaddling and

24 PP 1833 (519), p. 3. He had not 'been able to detect any deformities by individual personal examination ... This mode of proceeding has produced two or three spinal curvatures, as many cases of swelled ancles [sic] and feet, and one shortened thigh from disease of the hip-joint, with some cases of flax-dust dyspnœa; but the deformities, upon being investigated, were all found to have occurred previously to mill-service' (PP 1833 (519), A3, p. 32).

25 PP 1833 (519), C3, p. 18.

26 PP 1833 (519), C3, p. 18. Hunter was a committee member and lecturer to the Leeds Mechanics' Institute: A. D. Garner and E. W. Jenkins, 'The English Mechanics Institutes: The Case of Leeds, 1824–42', History of Education, 13:2 (1984), 139–52 (p. 142).

27 J. Black, 'A Medico-Topographical, Geological, and Statistical Sketch of Bolton and its Neighbourhood', Transactions of the Provincial Medical and Surgical Association, 5 (1837), 125–224 (pp. 169–70). The effects of clog wearing were 'readily observed in the youth of both sexes belonging to factories, or employed in weaving, and in the otherwise stout and healthy lads that are brought up as colliers, carters, and as farm servants' (Black, 'Physical Habits and Employment', p. 144).

bandaging or from the restricting influence of boys' waistcoats and girls' stays.[28] William Farrer in his *Particular Account of the Rickets* (1773), believed that 'the most evident cause is the violence done to the parts of the tender bodes of infants, by pressure, or swathing, which may wreath the fibres of the bones while they remain in a cartilaginous state, and so prevent the equable growth and increase thereof. Add to this external injuries as falls, blows, &c. whereby luxations, distortions, fractures, &c. may be occasioned.'[29]

Much of the testimony of operatives about factory deformity was influenced by leading figures in the short time campaign. Joseph Hebergam, a disabled seventeen-year-old fatherless worsted spinner from Huddersfield, who had commenced work at the age of seven, declared that throstle spinning led to repetitive injuries caused by children stopping the 'flies' with their knees.[30] Hebergam's evidence was highly questionable however. He told the Sadler Committee that he was unable to walk due to a leg condition caused by early mill work, as a result of which he required to be carried to and from work by his brother and sister – though at another part of his testimony he recounted an incident in which, at the age of fourteen, he had been able to run away from an adult overlooker.[31] Hebergam met with leading opponents of the factory system in the two weeks prior to giving his evidence and his account provides an insight into the relationship between Sadler's witnesses and activists in the short time movement:

---

28 V. A. Fildes, 'The English Disease: Infantile Rickets and Scurvy in Pre-Industrial England', in *Child Care Through the Centuries: An Historical Survey from Papers Given at the Tenth British Congress on the History of Medicine*, ed. J. Cule and T. Turner (Cardiff: British Society for the Social History of Medicine, 1986), pp. 121–34 (p. 126); A. Combe, *Principles of Physiology* (New York: Harper & Brothers, 1834), p. 159, cited in W. H. Hutt, 'The Factory System of the Early Nineteenth Century', in *Capitalism and the Historians*, ed. F. A. Hayek (Chicago: University of Chicago Press, 1954), pp. 160–88 (p. 177); D. Hunter, *The Diseases of Occupations* (1955; London: Hodder & Stoughton, 1978), p. 46. The view was supported by W. Farrer in his *A Particular Account of the Rickets in Children; and Remarks on its Analogy to the King's Evil* (London: J. Johnson, 1773), pp. 4, 7. The stays of young girls were 'preventing the growth and formative contour of the ribs and muscles of the chest and spine, so essential to the requisite strength of the vertebral column and the proper freedom of the thoracic and digestive organs' (Black, 'Physical Habits and Employment', p. 144).

29 Farrer, p. 7.

30 PP 1831–2 (706), p. 158.

31 PP 1831–2 (706), p. 164.

Dr Walker ordered me to wear irons from ankle to the thigh; my mother was not able to get them, and he said he would write a note, and she might go to some gentleman in the town and give them that note, and see if they would not give her something towards them; and so she did, and I have got the bare irons made; and I was coming into the yard where I live; and there was a man who worked at the same place that I did, asked me to look at them; I told him I could not get money to line them with, and he said, 'I will tell you where there is a gentleman who will give you the money;' he told me of Mr. Oastler, and he said, 'I will go and see if he is at home, that you may not "lose your trouble." Mr. Oastler was at home ... Mr. Wood of Bradford gave me a sovereign, and Mr. Oastler gave me 3s. 6d., and so I had them made. He asked me questions what my lameness came on with, and I told him, and he happened to mention it at the County Meeting at York; my master saw it in the newspaper ... and he sent the foreman on to our house where I lived ... and he said to my mother, 'I suppose it is owing to our place that your Joseph got the use of his limbs taken away?' and my mother said he was informed wrong, that he had it before he went to that factory.[32]

According to Hebergam, Oastler had referred him to a sympathetic doctor at Leeds Infirmary who told him that 'it was come on with the factory system. He said, he thought he could have done me good if he had had me a few years ago; there would have been means of bringing me straight; he said it was all from the factory system, working so long, and standing so many hours.'[33]

Factory deformities were central to the campaign literature of the short time committees and numerous accounts were published of individuals who claimed to have been crippled by factory work. In 1832, John Doherty, the spinners' trade union leader in Manchester, published the *Memoir of Robert Blincoe*. Blincoe had been bound apprentice more than thirty years earlier at around the age of six or seven and claimed to have been deformed as a result of working in factories at an early age (though, curiously, Blincoe would later testify in evidence to the Factory Commission that the inward deformity of his legs had not begun until the age of fifteen).[34] The image of Blincoe on the title page of the *Memoir* (Figure 2) certainly

---

32   PP 1831–2 (706), pp. 163–4.
33   PP 1831–2 (706), pp. 162, 163.
34   A. E. Musson, 'Robert Blincoe and the Early Factory System', in *Trade Union and Social History*, ed. A. E. Musson (London: Frank Cass, 1974), pp. 195–206 (p. 195–6).

A

MEMOIR

OF

ROBERT BLINCOE,

An Orphan Boy;

SENT FROM THE WORKHOUSE OF ST. PANCRAS, LONDON,
AT SEVEN YEARS OF AGE,

TO ENDURE THE

Horrors of a Cotton-Mill,

THROUGH HIS INFANCY AND YOUTH,

WITH A MINUTE DETAIL OF HIS SUFFERINGS,

BEING

THE FIRST MEMOIR OF THE KIND PUBLISHED.

BY JOHN BROWN.

MANCHESTER:

PRINTED FOR AND PUBLISHED BY J. DOHERTY, 37, WITHY-GROVE.

1832.

Figure 2: Title page of J. Brown (ed.), *A Memoir of Robert Blincoe, an orphan boy* (Manchester: J. Doherty, 1832)

suggests a noticeable shortness of stature and deformity of the knees. Another important figure in the contemporary literature on factory deformities was William Dodd – the self-styled 'factory cripple' – who claimed to have 'both knees in' as a result of working in a spinning mill between the ages of six and fourteen. Dodd argued that many child piecers had their right knees bent inward as a result of the awkward postures and movements required in their work and he described the activities which gave rise to such deformities:

> The position in which the piecer stands to his work is with his right foot forward, and his right side facing the frame: the motion he makes in going along in front of the frame, for the purposes of piecing, is neither forwards nor backwards, but in a sidling direction, constantly keeping his right side towards the frame. In this position he continues during the day, with his hands, feet, and eyes constantly in motion. It will be easily seen, that the chief weight of the body rests upon his right knee, which is always the first joint to give way. The number of cripples with the right knee in, greatly exceeded those with the left knee in.[35]

Dodd toured the factory districts collecting evidence against the factory system which he dispatched in a series of letters to his patron, Lord Ashley, in return for which he was paid 45s per week and coach hire. According to Ashley, his informant was a 'wretched object. He had lost his hand, and ... almost his shape. He hardly looked like a human being ... My poor cripple Dodd is a jewel, his talent and skill are unequalled; he sends me invaluable evidence'. Dodd was also put on public display in London as an example of the effects of working in factories,[36] though the

---

The authenticity of the *Memoir* has been cast into doubt by Chapman who labelled the author of the memoir a 'gullible sensationalist, whose statements must be treated with the utmost caution': S. D. Chapman, *The Early Factory Masters: the Transition to the Factory System in the Midlands Textile Industry* (Newton Abbot: David & Charles, 1967), pp. 208–9; PP 1833 (519), D3, p. 17.

35   It can be inferred from Dodd's text that he ceased to be a piecer at fourteen: W. Dodd, *A Narrative of the Experiences and Sufferings of William Dodd, a Factory Cripple, Written by Himself* (2nd edn, London: L. & G. Seeley, 1841), pp. 273, 273–80. Dodd also thought that deformity of the bones of the lower bodies of factory workers resulted from standing for very long periods (*Factory System Illustrated*, pp. 7–13).

36   W. H. Chaloner, 'New Introduction', in W. Dodd, *The Factory System Illustrated* (London: Frank Cass, 1968), pp. v–xiii. John Bright pointed out in the House of Commons that Ashley 'had shown [Dodd] to his visitors as a cripple, as a specimen of what the

spectacle was derided by Cooke Taylor who chided Ashley for allowing himself to be misled by both Dodd and the operatives' union:

> A cripple was procured from the north of England, deformed from his infancy, and whose defects were in no way derived from the mill or the factory. He was exhibited as a kind of show in the hall of a benevolent nobleman, who was duped by the arts of the trades' unionists; and this spectacle was repeated night after night to impress upon the fashionable world of London the belief, that this unhappy wretch was a fair specimen of the injurious results produced by factory-labour.[37]

Dodd moved to London later in life where, in 1840, he developed pain in his right wrist 'arising from the general weakness in my joints, brought on in the factories' and he was admitted to St Thomas's Hospital where he remained for six months until his hand was finally amputated 'a little below the elbow in order to clear the affected part of the bone'.[38] Dodd reported on the bone pathology:

> On dissection, the bones of the fore-arm presented a very curious appearance – something similar to an empty honeycomb, the marrow also having totally disappeared; thus accounting at once for the weakness and pain I had occasionally felt in this arm for years, and

factories were doing for the population employed in them' (Chaloner, 'New Introduction', pp. vi–vii). The Hammonds later thought Bright's intervention 'needlessly offensive': J. L. Hammond and B. Hammond, *Lord Shaftesbury* (London: Constable & Company, 1923), p. 95.

37   W. Cooke Taylor, *Factories and the Factory System; from Parliamentary Documents and Personal Examination* (London: Jeremiah How, 1844), pp. 71–2. The exhibition of diseased or disabled people in support of charitable causes was not uncommon. Charitable institutions in the early nineteenth century exhibited deaf children during fund-raising events. There is also some evidence that the factory lobby of the 1830s had earlier 'exhibited diseased and crippled objects in London': A. Borsay, 'Deaf Children and Charitable Education in Britain, 1790–1944', in *Medicine, Charity and Mutual Aid: The Consumption of Health and Welfare, c.1550–1950*, ed. A. Borsay and P. Shapely (Aldershot: Ashgate, 2007), pp. 71–90 (pp. 74–77); Anon., *Exposition of the Factory Question* (Manchester: T. Sowler, 1832), pp. 4–5; M. W. Thomas, *The Early Factory Legislation: A Study in Legislative and Administrative Evolution* (Leigh-on-Sea: Thames Bank Publishing, 1948), p. 50. Bronstein reports a similar case of the exhibition of an injured railway worker: J. L. Bronstein, *Caught in the Machinery: Workplace Accidents and Injured Workers in Nineteenth-Century Britain* (Stanford: Stanford University Press, 2008), pp. 1–2.

38   Dodd, *Experiences and Sufferings*, p. 315.

which, without doubt, may be clearly traced to the same cause as the rest of my sufferings – *viz.* the factory system.[39]

The complexity of working-class nutritional deficiencies and the industrial disease environment render it impossible to determine the extent to which Dodd's later bone condition was connected with his early work in woollen mills. The osteoporotic appearance of his bone may have resulted from poor nutrition or infection, or may equally have been a complication of a Colles' fracture of the wrist (a common site of osteoporotic fracture in men).[40] Whatever the cause or extent of Dodd's disability, however, his connection with St Thomas's brought him into contact with leading London doctors and it is likely that during his stay there he was first introduced to Lord Ashley and the metropolitan anti-factory lobby. Indeed, it was only following his discharge from St Thomas's that Dodd embarked upon his tours of the factory districts and his series of writings highly critical of mill owners. Despite his taking on the epithet 'factory cripple', the extent of Dodd's disability must remain in doubt. He subsequently reported in his autobiography that following the onset of his leg deformity he was able to walk two miles each Sunday and climb the steep half-mile incline from Kendal town to the top of Castle Hill.[41] Indeed, when doubts were raised about Dodd's integrity he was immediately shunned by Ashley. He later wrote to the leading factory owners Henry and Edmund Ashworth, 'I have been held up to public view by these philanthropists(?) as an object of charity, and as an instance of the cruelty of the manufacturers, and you will be surprised when I say that after all this fuss, I have been extremely ill-used by them'. Dodd also claimed that Ashley's contacts in the Ten Hours Movement had instructed him to visit factories and to bribe operatives to obtain information against owners.[42]

Although the early nineteenth-century factory reform lobby placed great stress upon factory-induced deformities, it is likely that many of the

39   Dodd, *Experiences and Sufferings*, pp. 315–6.

40   E. Seaman, *Osteoporosis in Men* (Nyon, Switzerland: International Osteoporosis Foundation, 2004), p. 7. Dodd claimed to have suffered from wrist weakness and pain 'for years' but also stated that painful symptoms began only a matter of months prior to his admission to hospital. In the Preface to *Factory System Illustrated*, he repeated his claim that the amputation had been brought about by 'disease of the bone, brought on entirely by unremitting and exhausting labour' (p. iv).

41   Dodd, *Experiences and Sufferings*, pp. 289–90.

42   Letter to Messrs. H. and E. Ashworth, 26 September 1842, cited in Chaloner, 'New Introduction', pp. v, ix–x.

physically disabled witnesses to early factory inquiries were suffering from conditions largely unconnected with the workplace.[43] Most malformations of the legs and spine amongst industrial children were likely to have been due to physiological conditions such as severe *genu valgum* (knock-knees) or Blount disease (which causes the legs to bow outwards just below the knee).[44] Some disabled operatives at Kenyon's 1819 Committee also observed that their deformities had commenced from around the age they had commenced work and it is possible that some spinal curvatures resulted from scoliosis, a condition which generally affects children between ten and sixteen.[45] Other discrete conditions such as congenital talipes (club foot), kyphosis, spastic diplegia (Little's disease), infantile hemiplegia and poliomyelitis were little known or understood at the time and may well have contributed to the variety of deformities observed in factory children.[46] Rickets was another widespread complaint amongst nineteenth-century working children which tended largely to be associated with smoky northern industrial towns and enclosed living spaces which reduced children's exposure to ultraviolet light. As early as the 1780s, Percival had identified some 'cases of premature decrepitude' which he attributed to 'immoderate labour' and for which he routinely prescribed cod liver oil as a remedy.[47] Some factory deformities may also have resulted

43   Dodd, *Factory System Illustrated*, pp. 7–13.
44   A. Hardy, 'Rickets and the Rest: Child-care, Diet and the Infectious Children's Diseases, 1850–1914', *Social History of Medicine*, 5 (1992), 389–412 (p. 391); L. M. Osborn, T. G. DeWitt, L. R. First and J. A. Zenel (eds), *Pediatrics* (Philadelphia: Elsevier Mosby, 2005), pp. 368–9.
45   PP 1819 (24), p. 171. Scoliosis is mostly idiopathic, rather than the result of unusual postures. In 2008 adolescent idiopathic scoliosis affected 1–3 per cent of individuals in the age group 10–16 (though only a small number of these cases were severe enough to require treatment): S. L. Weinstein, L. A. Dolan, J. C. Cheng, A. Danielsson and J. A. Morcuende, 'Adolescent Idiopathic Scoliosis', *The Lancet*, 371, 3 May 2008, 1527–37 (p. 1527).
46   Hunter listed several such conditions as likely causes of supposed factory deformities (p. 121).
47   Floyer, in 1706, observed that 'No distemper is more frequent in infants than the rickets' (cited in Fildes, p. 121); W. F. Loomis, 'Rickets', *Scientific American*, 223(6) (1970), 76–91; T. Percival, 'Observations on the Medicinal Uses of the Oleum Jecoris Aselli, or Cod Liver Oil, in the Chronic Rhumatism, and Other Painful Disorders', in *Essays Medical, Philosophical, and Experimental* (Warrington: J. Johnson, 1789), pp. 354–62 (p. 355); Hardy, 'Rickets and the rest'. A British Medical Association survey of 1889 reported the largest concentrations of rickets existed in densely populated urban and industrial districts: I. Owen, 'Geographical Distribution of Rickets, Acute and Subacute Rheumatism, Chorea, Cancer, and Urinary Calculus in the British Islands', *British*

from scrofulous bone disease, though it should be noted that scrofula was no more common amongst factory workers than among the general population. A contemporary medical study of scrofula as it affected the bones made no mention of occupational causes but noted that where the disease affected the spine, it tended to cause spinal curvature and could affect the hip or the long bones of the arms or legs.[48] Physical injury to the lower limbs may also have caused changes in the knee angle or the shape of the foot, though leg trauma was mentioned only occasionally in state reports as a cause of leg deformity. Indeed, although most contemporary complaints about factory deformity tended to be focused on the lower limbs and spine, the overwhelming majority of factory-related injuries affected the upper limbs, hands and fingers.[49] Moreover, labour intensity was unlikely to have been a primary factor in factory deformities since the work of young textiles workers amounted to little more than cleaning, fetching and carrying. By contrast, there was a striking absence of comparable bone deformities amongst children working in heavier labouring or agricultural occupations. The effects of hard labour at early ages can therefore largely be ruled out as a contributory factor in physical distortions amongst mill children and it is not easy to comprehend how the comparatively light work available in textiles factories might have caused the kinds of profound deformities described by medical men in early parliamentary reports. Indeed, complaints of factory deformity largely disappeared after the resolution of the Ten Hours campaign in 1847 (though the internal environment of mills and factories did not change dramatically at the time). By the 1860s and 70s the only conditions said to affect the legs and feet of operatives were varicose veins and occasional oedema.[50]

If there was a greater incidence of physically weak or disabled children in the textiles labour force, this might be explained by a reshaping of

Medical Journal, 1 (1889), 113–16 (p. 114); see also Loomis, p. 79. A lack of ultraviolet light coupled with the stresses of early working has been shown to have caused rickets among relatively well-fed and well-paid nineteenth-century child coalminers: P. Kirby, 'Causes of Short Stature among Coalmining Children, 1823–1850', *Economic History Review*, 48 (1995), 687–99.

48   PP 1819 (24), p. 326; J. G. A. Lugol, *Researches and Observations of the Causes of Scrofulous Disease* (London: Churchill, 1844), pp. 291–306.

49   W. R. Lee, 'Robert Baker: the First Doctor in the Factory Department, Part 1. 1803–1858', *British Journal of Industrial Medicine*, 21 (1964), 85–93 (p. 89, tab. 1).

50   J. A. Smiley, 'Background to Byssinosis in Ulster', *British Journal of Industrial Medicine*, 18, 1 (1961), 1–9 (pp. 4–5).

labour demand based upon the lower labour intensity of mill work.[51] There is considerable evidence that slender or disabled children were positively selected to work in factories. In 1809, it was observed that 'crippled and feeble-minded' children worked as cleaners and helpers in mills on the ground that they were considered unemployable in heavier and more demanding domestic industry or agricultural work.[52] The Kenyon Committee of 1818 noted that textiles employers would often take on disabled children where their parents were too poor or infirm to care for them. Moreover, according to a pamphleteer of 1832, such children found in factories 'an asylum in a dry, warm atmosphere, which suits their constitutions, and their general health is improved.'[53] Although the slight build of mill children was often commented upon, it was also observed that they were for the most part 'better suited to the work, than if they were more tonic in fibre and robust. A pliancy, not a strength of muscle, is required; an endurance of continued attention to small objects, and not great or repeated displays of physical strength.'[54] Disabilities, therefore, may often have been decisive in the types of jobs open to children. Operatives' organisations certainly regarded low-paid disabled children as a threat to their own security of employment in much the same way that they deprecated the employment of women or parish apprentices. A treatise supportive of the Ten Hours Movement in 1833 lamented the lack of attention amongst legislators to 'removing cripples'.[55] Some disabled workers continued with remunerative work in mills for many years. When William Dodd attempted to gain employment outside the woollen mill where he worked, he was summarily dismissed on account of his disabilities and subsequently 'settled for life in the factories, as it was then pretty evident I should not be able to do anything else.'[56] Physically less demanding work in textiles mills may have provided

51   PP 1819 (24), p. 29.
52   F. B. Smith, *The People's Health, 1830–1910* (London: Weidenfeld & Nicholson, 1979), p. 171. The Hammonds famously reported an instance of a Lancashire mill-owner who agreed 'to take one idiot with every twenty sound children supplied' from urban workhouses: J. L. Hammond and B. Hammond, *The Town Labourer, 1760–1832: The New Civilisation* (1917; London: Longmans, Green & Company, 1966), p. 147.
53   PP 1818 (90), pp. 16–17; Anon., *Exposition of the Factory Question*, p. 5.
54   Black, 'Statistical Sketch of Bolton', p. 181.
55   Anon., *The Commissioners' Vade Mecum whilst engaged in collecting evidence for the Factory Masters* (Leeds: n.p., 1833), p. 13.
56   Dodd, *Experiences and Sufferings*, pp. 281, 284.

new opportunities for disabled children to earn an income and almost certainly served as a form of limited social inclusion for many disabled child workers.[57]

Materials

Cotton mills also brought together large numbers of operatives in confined work spaces where the processing of raw cotton wool produced large amounts of suspended dust. Inhalation of dust particles over long periods led to high rates of pulmonary disease amongst cotton workers. Indeed, medical witnesses at the Kenyon Committee of 1819 observed that spinners mostly left their occupations aged between thirty and forty due to 'asthma' and other chronic pulmonary disease whilst operatives themselves frequently complained of 'Stoppage of the Breast' and persistent coughs which they blamed on dust.[58] Dust in the scutching room of a Preston mill was described by one mill visitor as so thick that he could 'scarcely see the women who worked at the engine.'[59] Thackrah noted the gradual development of respiratory disease amongst workers in the preparatory stages of flax processing. These progressed from a cough with bronchitis-like symptoms to more marked difficulty in breathing which increased in severity over a number of years. According to Thackrah, men aged forty or fifty who had worked in dusty mill occupations were 'almost universally diseased'.[60] Ramazzini, too, had observed in the late seventeenth century that hemp-combers and hacklers breathed 'a foul mischievous Powder, that entering the Lungs by the Mouth and Throat, causes continual Coughs, and gradually makes way for an Asthma'.[61] An operative witness at the Sadler Committee provided a

57   See also A. Borsay, *Disability and Social Policy in Britain since 1750: a history of exclusion* (Basingstoke: Palgrave Macmillan, 2005), p. 177; A. Levene, *Childcare, Health and Mortality at the London Foundling Hospital, 1741–1800: 'Left to the Mercy of the World'* (Manchester: Manchester University Press, 2007), pp. 165–6; Thomas, *Early Factory Legislation*, p. 49.

58   PP 1819 (24), pp. 21, 83, 100 (many examples).

59   PP 1816 (397), pp. 121, 294; PP 1818 (90), pp. 177, 260.

60   PP 1831–2 (706), pp. 513–14. Most medical witnesses in the Factory Commission supplementary report of 1834 noted that carding and other preparatory stages were the most unhealthy (PP 1834 (167), pp. 150–1).

61   Ramazzini, p. 175. Kay categorised such complaints as phthisis: J. P. Kay, 'Observations and Experience concerning Molecular Consumption and on Spinners' Phthisis', *North of*

contemporary description of progressive lung disease (probably a classic case of byssinosis) in a mill worker:

> We had a book-keeper, who thought that when the men were ill they made pretence, but by-and-by he himself was taken ill, and he began to be as bad as he well could be.
>   Was he exposed to the dust? – He had been for years, and he stood it well; and he therefore thought that people were not so bad as they pretended to be, but in the end it affected him; he had stood it for several years; and after that he began to be a book-keeper, but it had affected him so, that if he was in the room for ten minutes he could scarcely breath; he had become very asthmatical.[62]

Operatives commonly accepted the development of lung disease as a normal consequence of the job. Many believed that cotton dust was little more than an inconvenience and that regular expectoration was sufficient to purge it from the lungs.[63] Mechanical ventilation of mills was advocated to improve the respiratory health of workers, particularly those in preparatory processes. Well-conducted mills such as Marshalls of Leeds employed fans and air blowers which changed the air every twenty minutes, with the carding and hackling machinery afforded special attention. Thackrah reported the use of similar ventilators in preparatory processes in Manchester mills in 1831.[64] Such machines must have been effective in reducing levels of suspended dust but tended to be installed only in the larger mills and, in general, little was done to preserve the respiratory health of cotton workers.[65] Pulmonary diseases formed the

England Medical and Surgical Journal, 1 (August 1830–May 1831), 348–63 (pp. 358–60).

62   PP 1831–2 (706), p. 286.

63   At least one medical witness at the 1818 Committee suggested that dust was not a problem and that 'daily Expectoration throws off the Cotton; there is no Accumulation takes place in the lungs' (PP 1818 (90), pp. 50, 60).

64   W. G. Rimmer, *Marshalls of Leeds: Flax Spinners, 1788–1886* (Cambridge: Cambridge University Press, 1960), p. 216. Thackrah describes a ventilating fan rotating at 1,200 revolutions per minute (p. 144). Thackrah advocated the creation of downward currents of air in flax preparation which would escape through channels in the floor of the mill (Smiley, p. 3). Mechanical ventilation had been advocated by Hales as early as 1743: S. Hales, *A Description of Ventilators: Whereby Great Quantities of Fresh Air May With Ease be Conveyed into Mines, Gaols, Hospitals, Work-Houses and Ships, in Exchange for their Noxious Air* (London: W. Innys, 1743).

65   The Kenyon Committee, however, noted that ventilation was adequate in most of the larger Manchester mills (PP 1818 (90), p. 42).

major group of ailments that distinguished textiles factory workers from other trades and it is likely that a substantial part of the greater incidence of chest complaints amongst manufacturing workers reflected extensive byssinosis (though, curiously, few workers who gave evidence to state inquiries reported the classic 'start of the week' or Monday morning symptoms associated with the disease).[66] Records of 4,000 applicants for medical aid at the Leeds Dispensary between 1831 and 1833 showed that factory workers (many of whom would have worked in the woollen and flax industries) had a 68 per cent greater incidence of major pulmonary disease compared with those not in factories (with pulmonary phthisis and bronchitis at twice the level of non-manufacturers).[67]

Long-term exposure to dangerous materials and chemicals often did not become apparent until later in adult life and chronic respiratory conditions did not immediately affect child workers.[68] Indeed, Charles Thackrah suggested that children appeared to 'bear dusty occupations with much less annoyance than adults'.[69] Much more important for the health of factory children was the inhalation and digestion of biological contaminants and pathogens present in raw cotton.[70] A Manchester surgeon at the Kenyon Committee of 1819 observed how cotton dust and

66   S. Bowden and G. Tweedale, 'Mondays without Dread: The Trade Union Response to Byssinosis in the Lancashire Cotton Industry in the Twentieth Century', *Social History of Medicine*, 16, 1 (2003), 79–95. The lack of identification of specific symptoms in historic sources probably results simply from the occupational effects of the disease being subsumed by the higher general incidence of pulmonary complaints such as bronchitis, tuberculosis and emphysema.

67   PP 1833 (519), C3, pp. 19–20, tab. 1; see also H. Freudenberger, F. J. Mather and C. Nardinelli, 'A New Look at the Early Factory Labor Force', *Journal of Economic History*, 44 (1984), 1085–90 (p. 1088).

68   The mean age of presentation with 'sweeps' cancer' in the late eighteenth century, for example, was thirty-eight years though most sufferers had worked with soot only in childhood or adolescence: H. A. Waldron, 'A Brief History of Scrotal Cancer', *British Journal of Industrial Medicine*, 40 (1983), 390–401 (pp. 391–4); R. D. Passey, 'Experimental Soot Cancer', *British Medical Journal*, 2 (1922), 1112–13; Andrews, *Appeal to the humane*, pp. 19–20; PP 1817 (400), p. 24.

69   PP 1831–2 (706), pp. 512–13. Kinder Wood, the Oldham surgeon and the only medical witness with any practical experience of mill work at the Peel Committee of 1816, observed that dust-induced asthma in cotton workers developed only after long exposure and mostly affected those in preparatory processes (PP 1816 (397), pp. 194–5, 204).

70   D. A. Zuberer and C. M. Kenerley, 'Seasonal Dynamics of Bacterial Colonization of Cotton Fiber and Effects of Moisture on Growth of Bacteria within the Cotton Boll', *Applied and Environmental Microbiology*, 59, 4 (1993), 974–80; PP 1819 (24), p. 87.

waste 'passes into the Stomach of the Children, and they are seized with Sickness, and they have in some Instances thrown up accumulated Dust and Filth.'[71] The spectrum of health challenges associated with imported raw cotton has been extended considerably in a series of recent occupational health studies which have shown the presence of significant levels of biological contamination, including Gram-negative bacteria, fungal spores and endotoxin. These are capable of causing severe allergic and inflammatory conditions as well as carcinogenic effects.[72] In early mills, preparatory processes such as mixing, blowing, scutching and carding would have created optimum conditions for particulates and pathogens to become suspended in the internal atmosphere of the workplace. Spinners' reluctance to open mill windows for fear that draughts would blow threads about and spoil the yarn meant that workers were exposed to a dense cocktail of contaminants (Figure 3).

Recent studies show that levels of biological contamination of raw cotton wool and the prevalence of cotton-related diseases also vary enormously according to the global region of production. Major cotton-related diseases affect 14 per cent of cotton workers in Turkey, 30 per cent in India, and nearly half of those in Ethiopia, whilst in the United States the incidence of cotton-related disease is almost negligible. Accumulations of harmful bacterial and fungal contamination in raw cotton are also related to the relative heat and humidity in which the crop is grown and the length of time the cotton boll is left in the field after opening.[73] Cotton samples from tropical countries such as Zimbabwe

71   PP 1819 (24), p. 279.
72   S. R. Lane and R. D. E. Sewell, 'Correlative Measurement of Four Biological Contaminants on Cotton lint, and their Implications for Occupational Health', *International Journal of Occupational and Environmental Health*, 12 (2006), 120–5 (pp. 124–5); E. Piecková and Z. Jesenská, 'Filamentous Microfungi in Raw Flax and Cotton for the Textile Industry and their Ciliostatic Activity on Tracheal Organ Cultures in Vitro', *Mycopathologia*, 134 (1996), 91–6; R. Rylander, P. Haglind and M. Lundholm, 'Endotoxin in Cotton Dust and Respiratory Function Decrement among Cotton Workers in an Experimental Cardroom', *American Review of Respiratory Disease*, 131, 2 (1985), 209–13; M. Hitchcock, '*In Vitro* Histamine Release from Human Lung as a Model for the Acute Response to Cotton Dust', *Annals of the New York Academy of Sciences*, 221 (1974), 124–31; P. D. Blanc, *How Everyday Products Make People Sick: Toxins at Home and in the Workplace* (Berkeley: University of California Press, 2009), p. 175; P. D. Blanc, 'Inhalation Fever', in *Environmental and Occupational Medicine*, ed. W. N. Rom and S. B. Markowitz (Philadelphia: Lippincott, Williams & Wilkins, 2007), pp. 402–17.
73   Lane and Sewell, pp. 120–2; R. Altin, S. Ozkurt, F. Fisekci, A. H. Cimrin, M. Zencir

Figure 3: 'Children opening up compressed raw cotton in preparation for spinning', in G. Dodd, *The Textile Manufacturers of Great Britain* (London: Charles Knight & Co., 1844), p. 104. Wellcome Library, London, number M0013539. Slide number 4829 (available under Creative Commons).

and Ivory Coast typically contain counts of Gram-negative bacteria up to four times greater than those from more temperate climes such as the southern United States. Similarly, fungal cell counts in cotton imports from Benin are around fifteen times greater compared with American sources.[74] Nineteenth-century authorities also blamed contamination of imported cotton on the climatic conditions under which crops were grown and the length of time cotton was left in the field prior to harvesting. In his major work on the cotton industry of 1835, Edward Baines noted

and C. Sevinc, 'Prevalence of Byssinosis and Respiratory Symptoms among Cotton Mill Workers', *Respiration*, 69 (2002), pp. 52–6.
74   Lane and Sewell, p. 121–2.

that any dampness on the cotton boll 'would make it afterwards become mouldy' and he highlighted in particular the 'slovenly' manner of Indian cotton cultivation and harvesting which rendered the raw product 'so much inferior to that of the United States.'[75] The differential health effects of contaminated and clean raw cotton were adverted to by J. P. Kay, who noted in 1830 that respiratory infections were 'more frequent, *cœteris paribus*, in mills where coarse and therefore dirty cotton is spun, than where a finer and cleaner material is used.'[76] There is no reason to suppose that the wide variations in biological contamination in raw cotton shown in comparatively recent studies of raw cotton samples did not also affect historic raw material imports. Indeed, changes in the global supply of raw cotton closely paralleled crucial changes in the reporting of ailments amongst factory workers. In the 1780s, workers were said to suffer predominantly from febrile conditions whereas by the 1830s, the major complaints were digestive and 'constitutional' disorders.[77] Changes in supply of raw cotton, therefore, may have been the crucial factor in levels of exposure to pathogens and cotton-related diseases amongst both adults and children. Quantitative evidence underpins such speculations. First, the overall supply of cotton wool to British mills increased rapidly from the mid-1780s to the 1810s with gross imports rising from around 16–18 million lbs to about 70–90 million lbs. By the mid-1830s gross imports had reached 366 million lbs.[78] Secondly, the global sources of imported cotton changed fundamentally over the same period. During the closing decades of the eighteenth century, imports from the tropical British West Indies formed the mainstay of supplies to British mills but by the middle of the 1810s the share had fallen to 19 per cent and, by the 1830s, West Indian cotton imports had become insignificant. Montgomery's 1833 treatise on

75   E. Baines, *History of the cotton manufacture in Great Britain: with a notice of its early history in the East and in all the quarters of the globe: a description of the great mechanical inventions which have caused its unexampled extension in Britain: and a view of the present state of the manufacture and the condition of the classes engaged in its several departments* (London: H. Fisher, R. Fisher & P. Jackson, 1835), pp. 288–9.

76   Kay, 'Molecular Consumption', p. 359.

77   C. S. Paterson, 'From Fever to Digestive Disease: Approaches to the Problem of Factory Ill-Health in Britain, 1784–1833' (Ph.D. thesis, University of British Columbia, 1995), pp. 175–6.

78   R. Davis, *The Industrial Revolution and British Overseas Trade* (Leicester: Leicester University Press), 1979, p. 41, tab. 26; M. M. Edwards, *The Growth of the British Cotton Trade, 1780–1815* (Manchester: Manchester University Press, 1967), App. C1–C3, pp. 250–1.

cotton processing, for example, listed all the major cotton wool sources for making up warp and weft but contained no reference whatsoever to West Indian cotton.[79] Meanwhile, by the mid-1820s, imports from north America (which had hardly been evident in the 1780s) rose to 65 per cent of total cotton imports and by the mid-1830s more than three-quarters of British cotton imports came from temperate America.[80] The substantial growth in imports of American raw cotton in the wake of the American War of Independence was also boosted by the availability to landowners in the southern states of cheap cultivable land as well as the diffusion of Whitney's cotton gin from the 1790s, which greatly improved the process of cleaning the crop by separating the seed from the cotton boll.[81] The rapid move to a different source of cotton wool, together with more efficient processing of raw cotton prior to export, almost certainly resulted in cleaner imports and reduced levels of bacterial and fungal contamination.

The shift in global origins of imported raw cotton was clearly evident from changes in the reporting of cotton workers' health. Between the 1780s and the 1830s medical opinion about factory workers' ailments shifted away from an emphasis upon largely unexplained 'mill fevers' towards a much greater stress upon general constitutional weakness, 'debility' and digestive ailments.[82] Therefore, the decline in reports of mysterious fevers such as those reported by Percival's Committee of 1784 ('a low, putrid fever, of a contagious nature') is likely to have paralleled fundamental changes in the profile of pathogens and other contaminants in imported raw cotton.[83] Crucially, as Hamlin pointed out, as early as 1817–19, outbreaks of fevers may have been common in manufacturing districts but factories were not by that time regarded as hotbeds of contagion.[84] By the 1830s, complaints that factories gave rise to fever had abated almost entirely. In 1834, the Preston factory surgeon James

79   Though evidence from 1818 suggests that imports from 'Demerara, Berbice, Surinam, Cayenne, West India Islands and Spanish Colonies' amounted to only 7.9 per cent: PP 1818 (90), p. 117; J. Montgomery, *The Theory and Practice of Cotton Spinning; or the Carding and Spinning Master's Assistant* (2nd edn, Glasgow: J. Niven, 1833), p. 45.

80   Davis, *British Overseas Trade*, p. 41, tab. 26.

81   G. Timmins, *Made in Lancashire: a History of Regional Industrialisation* (Manchester: Manchester University Press, 1998), pp. 140–1.

82   Paterson, pp. 10, 175–6.

83   Paterson, pp. 12, 25–6; A. Meiklejohn, 'Outbreak of Fever in Cotton Mills at Radcliffe, 1784', *British Journal of Industrial Medicine*, 16, 1 (1959), 68–70 (p. 68).

84   Hamlin, *Public Health and Social Justice*, p. 39.

Harrison conducted a survey of the health of 1,656 factory children. His long experience had led him to expect that carding processes would prove the least healthy; however, he found children in carding to be have a similar disease profile to weavers: 'a circumstance for which I was wholly unprepared, and for which I am at present unable to account. There is by far the most fluke in the carding-rooms, and the children generally look paler than those employed in weaving and spinning-rooms, but still the sickness in these rooms is small.' The increasing tendency towards large-scale mixing of raw cotton in the bigger enterprises prior to processing may also have further diluted the effects of cotton pathogens from specific global origins.[85] It is also possible that many of the mysterious factory ailments of the final quarter of the eighteenth century had been attributable to imported tropical infections. When inexplicable fever broke out in a pickers' room in Ashton-under-Lyne, workers were convinced that raw cotton bales had harboured the infection.[86] Moreover, the fever symptoms that afflicted Radcliffe, Manchester and Ashton-under-Lyne in the 1780s and 1790s were entirely different from the kinds of constitutional and chronic progressive, digestive and pulmonary conditions thought to affect cotton workers from the 1830s and 1840s.[87]

A belief that diseases could be imported in ships' cargoes was, in fact, a long-standing concern.[88] A Select Committee of 1819 warned of the potential for cotton to transmit disease through the infection of bales 'by those who are employed in packing it having contagion about their clothes … or from the interior part of the package having passed through

85   Harrison, 'Extracts from the Report of the Inspectors', p. 427; Montgomery, pp. 44–6.
86   Paterson, p. 57.
87   The open fibres of cotton and other finished textiles were implicated in the transmission of infections between places and individuals whilst ventilation was said to dissipate the influence. J. Ferriar, 'Origin of Contagious and New Diseases', in *Medical Histories and Reflections* (London: W. Bulmer & Co., 1810), vol. 1, 261–92 (p. 287); W. Clerke, *Thoughts upon the Means of Preserving the Health of the Poor, by Prevention and Suppression of Epidemic Fevers, Addressed to the Inhabitants of Manchester* (London: J. Johnson, 1790), p. 9.
88   Letter from John Ferriar, *Manchester Mercury*, 2 February 1796, cited in J. Innes, 'Origins of the Factory Acts: the Health and Morals of Apprentices Act, 1802', in *Law, Crime and English Society, 1660–1830*, ed. N. Landau (Cambridge: Cambridge University Press, 2002), pp. 230–55 (p. 237); M. Harrison, *Disease and the Modern World: 1500 to the Present Day* (Cambridge: Polity Press, 2004), pp. 97–9; D. Ingram, *An Historical Account of the Several Plagues that have Appeared in the World since the Year 1346* (London: R. Baldwin, 1755).

dwellings where contagion might have subsisted.'[89] It was thought that textiles had a particular propensity to harbour infections. John Howard thought in 1791 that effluvia were 'capable of being carried from one place to another, upon any substance where what is called scent can lodge, as upon wool, cotton, &c.'[90] The cholera *Vibrio* has been shown to survive for days or weeks in moist linen and imported rags which contemporaries thought to be a major source of the disease.[91] One of the major functions of the principal lazarettos was to purge infections from quarantined cotton bales by exposure to air.[92] However, it was difficult in practice to ventilate compressed cargoes such as mohair, cotton or goats' wool during the Atlantic crossing because they were normally sealed against the ingress of water:

> during the voyage, the hatches are firmly caulked down, and every crevice completely closed with pitch. In the like manner, the ship, between decks, is stowed full of these goods. The upper deck hatches are covered with equal care by tarpawling [sic], and battened down, for as to keep out water. Whatever portion of pestilential poison may be thus enclosed, could not infect the crew.[93]

Such conditions would have provided the optimum environment for the survival of pathogens in cotton. It is likely therefore that many of the unexplained mill fevers said to affect late eighteenth-century cotton workers and their children resulted from a range of contaminants in West Indian raw cotton and, possibly, the importation of tropical pathogens.

89   PP 1819 (449), p. 19. Barnes suggested that ships carrying contaminated cotton bales, rags and cloth had, by the nineteenth century, 'carried smallpox all over the world': E. Barnes, *Diseases and Human Evolution* (Albuquerque: University of New Mexico, 2005), p. 230.

90   Howard argued that 'If the poison of the plague were lodged in a bale of cotton, the air which passes through every infectious portion of it, would acquire a pestilential quality. This air would soon be blown away. But fresh air would, in like manner, acquire a pestilential quality.' An infected parcel of clothes had been blamed for an outbreak of plague in Derbyshire in 1665. J. Howard, *An Account of the Principal Lazarettos in Europe* (London: J. Johnson, 1791), vol. 2, s. 1, p. 24; s. 2, p. 24n. The plague was rumoured to have been imported to Britain in a bale of Turkish cotton (PP 1819 (449), p. 91).

91   A. Hardy, 'Cholera, Quarantine and the English Preventive System', *Medical History*, 37 (July 1993), 250–69 (pp. 252, 261).

92   Howard, vol. 2, s. 1, pp. 5, 20–1, 25.

93   Imports of wax and tallow candles were also subject to quarantine on the grounds that they contained cotton (Howard, vol. 2, s. 1, pp. 23–4, 21).

The global potential for imported raw cotton to harm the health of workers was further demonstrated during the later 'cotton famine' of the 1860s when east Indian (Surat) cotton wool was imported in large quantities as a substitute for the disrupted American supply. East Indian cotton was unpopular amongst both operatives and manufacturers for its low quality, high levels of waste and tendency to produce large volumes of dust during processing.[94] Surat cotton was blamed by workers and surgeons for an outbreak of throat and lung disorders. The Lancashire factory surgeon Jesse Leach observed a powerful irritation of the throat and nasal passages. The lungs of young preparatory workers produced a 'slaty-coloured expectoration which, when placed under the microscope, [was] seen to consist of fine short fibres of cotton in air-bubbles and mucus'.[95] The condition of the Surat bales was reported by another surgeon:

> on opening the bales of cotton there is an intolerable smell, which causes sickness. The fibre being so short, a great amount of size, both animal and vegetable, is used before the cotton is spun into weft. The cotton is also very dirty and dusty … The weft is very soft, and breaks frequently, and is also filled with 'chips' (pieces of leaves, &c.) Bronchitis is more prevalent, owing to the dust. Inflammatory sore throat is common from the same cause.[96]

The short fibres and organic contaminants in Surat cotton were also said to give rise to inflammatory skin conditions amongst preparatory workers. 'The arms and hands of mixers are … affected with a cutaneous rash, much resembling nettle rash. This may partly arise from fine sand and short fibres of cotton destroying the epidermis, and irritating by their presence the true skin.'[97] The profound effects of pathogens in

94   G. S. White, *Memoir of Samuel Slater, the Father of American Manufactures, connected with a History of the Rise and Progress of the Cotton Manufacture in England and America* (Philadelphia: n.p., 1836), p. 362. Spinners of coarser yarn thought that even the waste from American cotton was superior to the Surat cotton supply (PP 1864 [3309], p. 31).
95   J. Leach, 'Surat Cotton, as It Bodily Affects Operatives in Cotton Mills', *The Lancet*, 2, 5 December 1863, 648–9 (p. 648).
96   PP 1864 [3309], p. 62.
97   Leach, p. 648; PP 1864 [3309], p. 63; V. Murlidhar, V. J. Murlidhar and V. Kanhere, 'Byssinosis in a Bombay Textile Mill', *National Medical Journal of India*, 8 (1995), 204–7; Lane and Sewell, p. 120; Altin *et al.*, 'Prevalence of Byssinosis'.

textiles imports was further demonstrated with fatal consequences in the mid-1880s with outbreaks of cutaneous and inhalation anthrax amongst woolsorters in the Bradford worsted industry. The disease had been carried into west Yorkshire in infected mohair and alpaca imports from as far afield as Asia Minor and Peru.[98] Such was the fatality of anthrax that in some districts woolsorters drew lots to see who would sort certain batches of mohair.[99]

Clearly, the role of imported raw materials in causing ill-health provides opportunities for further research. Whilst it is tempting to regard reports of fever in the cotton districts of the 1780s and 90s as part of a global endemicisation of disease, such influences require to be considered within the context of factors such as rising industrial wages and improvements in hygiene which may also have played an important part in the decline of fevers amongst manufacturing workers.[100] It has been suggested that febrile diseases were highly sensitive to standards of personal and domestic hygiene and therefore a decline in reports of mill fevers may also have reflected improvements in the overall cleanliness of mills and workers' homes between the 1780s and 1830s (though there is little evidence that the domestic or sanitary arrangements of mill workers improved significantly over that period).[101]

Other pulmonary and dermatological complaints amongst textiles children were attributed to the widespread use of contaminated animal and vegetable lubricants. A mill visitor in 1818 remarked on the overall disagreeable smell of hot organic lubricating oil. William Dodd noted during his tours of the factory districts that the 'fat of horses, dogs, pigs,

---

98   Similar outbreaks occurred in Leicester in 1880 and 1886–7 and in London in 1886–7 and 1893 (Wohl, *Endangered Lives*, p. 265). Mandatory disinfection of the most dangerous woollen imports was not introduced until the early twentieth century.

99   F. M. Laforce, 'Woolsorters' Disease in England', *Bulletin of the New York Academy of Medicine*, 54 (1978), 956–63 (p. 957). See also P. S. Brachman, 'Inhalation Anthrax', *Annals of the New York Academy of Sciences*, 353 (1980), 83–93; J. Stark, 'Bacteriology in the Service of Sanitation: The Factory Environment and the Regulation of Industrial Anthrax in Late-Victorian Britain', *Social History of Medicine*, 25 (2012), 343–61.

100   S. J. Kunitz, 'Speculations on the European Mortality Decline', *Economic History Review*, 36 (1983), 349–64. It has been suggested more recently that the importation of harmful pesticides in cotton bales may have resulted in a higher incidence of Paget's disease in some Lancashire mill towns: J. H. Lever, 'Paget's Disease of Bone in Lancashire and Arsenic Pesticide in Cotton Mill Wastewater: a Speculative Hypothesis', *Bone*, 31 (2002), 434–6.

101   Pickstone, 'Dearth, Dirt and Fever', p. 130.

and many other animals, which ... are killed with some incurable disease upon them, is sold to the manufacturers, and kept for the purpose of greasing the heavy machinery. It may be imagined what sort of effluvia will arise from the application of this fat to shafts almost on fire ... as one piece melted away, another was laid on till it got cooled, and all the time the smoke was arising almost sufficient to suffocate me.'[102] A major recommendation of Percival's Committee following the outbreak of 'mill fever' in 1784 was that rancid lubricating oil should be changed more frequently or substituted.[103] The use of animal fats as lubricants had declined significantly by the 1840s and 50s, by which time many mills and factories had adopted palm oil or mineral oils as their primary lubricants. The further transition to the use of mineral oil from the mid-nineteenth century would lead to a rise in scrotal cancers amongst mule spinners.[104] Meanwhile, other chemicals used in the processing of textiles caused irritation to children's lungs and eyes. The use of calcium hydroxide, for example, as a depilatory agent on animal hides was reported by Dodd who observed how lime dust saturated the atmosphere of carpet and rug factories:

> skin-wool and cow's-hair are used in the manufacture of coarse rugs, carpets, &c. This is obtained from the skins of the animals after they are killed, by means of a strong solution of lime-water. This lime thus gets intermixed with the wool and hair ... it is then put through the teaser ... the workpeople, the machine, and all around, are covered with the lime; and consequently, every inspiration of air in such an atmosphere, must carry with it and lodge upon the lungs a portion of these pernicious ingredients: the result is, difficulty of breathing, asthma.[105]

102 PP 1818 (90), p. 242; Dodd, *Experiences and Sufferings*, p. 283.

103 Meiklejohn, 'Outbreak of Fever', p. 69. A contemporary writer had noted that 'The rancid oil which is employed in the machinery is a copious source of putrid effluvia. We apprehend that a purer oil would be much less unwholesome, and that the additional expense of it would be fully compensated by its superior power in diminishing friction': Anon., *A Short Essay written for the Service of the Proprietors of Cotton-Mills and the Persons employed in Them* (Manchester: C. Wheeler, 1784), pp. 9–10.

104 British imports of palm oil from West Africa increased from 200 tons in 1808 to 4,700 tons in 1827 and 13,945 tons in 1834 (PP 1842 (551), App. 3, p. 33). Waldron, pp. 396–9; T. Wyke, 'Mule Spinners' Cancer', in *The Barefoot Aristocrats: A History of the Amalgamated Association of Operative Cotton Spinners*, ed. A. Fowler and T. Wyke (Littleborough: George Kelsall, 1987), pp. 184–96.

105 Dodd, *Experiences and Sufferings*, pp. 283–4.

Textiles processes involving hot water and steam could also prove hazardous to children. In flax mills the use of very hot water to divide the flax meant that children's arms were sometimes scalded. In the wet-spinning of flax, children also suffered continual wetting from spray which flew out from the frames and concerns were expressed about the effects of child workers walking home soaked to the skin. The Factory Act of 1844 prohibited wet-spinning by children and young persons (i.e. at ages eight to twelve and thirteen to eighteen) except where adequate means were provided to prevent them from becoming wet.[106]

Injuries

Industrial injuries probably had the most damaging effect upon the lives of child workers but until the 1830s and 40s were amongst the least reported aspects of their industrial health.[107] Despite the growing debates over the health of factory children from the 1780s, it was not until the Factory Act of 1844 that legislation was introduced to regulate the safety of factory machinery. Moreover, it was only from that point that any meaningful records of the numbers of industrial injuries began to be kept by the factory inspectors.[108] Records of child injuries and deaths in earlier periods rarely distinguished between work and non-work related causes, though Coroner's records often indicate wide spatial divergences in the type and location of fatal injuries. These suggest a great variety of

106   PP 1831–2 (706), pp. 293–4, p. 170; 7 Vict., c. 15, s. xix. The Act also included provisions for the protection of child workers against the escape of steam into rooms: A. M. Anderson, 'Historical Sketch of the Development of Legislation for Injurious and Dangerous Industries in England', in *The Dangerous Trades: the Historical, Social and Legal Aspects of Industrial Occupations as Affecting Health*, ed. T. Oliver (London: John Murray, 1902), pp. 24–43 (p. 32).

107   The incidence of workplace injuries amongst modern child workers remains little understood, though see some statistics in J. McKechnie, 'A Peculiarly British Phenomenon? Child Labour in the USA' in *A Thing of the Past? Child Labour in Britain in the Nineteenth and Twentieth Centuries*, ed. M. Lavalette (Liverpool: Liverpool University Press, 1999), pp. 193–215 (pp. 211–14).

108   Sambrook suggests that the recording of causes of death was, even by the mid-nineteenth century, 'medically imprecise': P. A. Sambrook, 'Childhood and Sudden Death in Staffordshire, 1851 and 1860', in *Staffordshire Histories: Essays in Honour of Michael Greenslade*, ed. P. Morgan and A. D. M. Phillips (Stafford: Staffordshire Record Society, 1999), pp. 216–52 (p. 221).

children's economic activity according to age and gender. Evidence from the late medieval and early-modern periods shows that from around the age of two, the causes and locations of injuries to boys and girls followed an increasingly divergent pattern similar to those affecting adults of the same sex. Male children were more likely to die in accidents at a greater distance from the home whilst females died in larger numbers closer to home, predominantly from scaldings or injuries involving domestic equipment.[109] Fatal accidents can also be used to some extent as a proxy to locate children within the workplace. Indeed, the location of industrial injuries was often highly age-specific. A majority of fatal injuries to children in coalmines, for example, occurred whilst child workers were *in transit* within the workplace (i.e. in transportation or ancillary roles) whereas deaths at the coalface from falling coal or stone tended overwhelmingly to affect adult face workers.[110] In domestic industries, meanwhile, living spaces were so closely integrated with production that it is frequently difficult to discern any direct relationship between play and work activities. Often, these activities overlapped and young children playing near machinery were at risk of injury or death. The three-year-old son of a machine-maker in Newchurch, east Lancashire:

> was playing by himself in a room in which some machinery was at work, when his clothes became entangled and he was drawn between a shaft and the floor. The accident was not discovered until blood was observed dripping through the ceiling into the room below whereupon his body was discovered lying on the floor near the shaft, and his head, totally dissevered therefrom, about a yard from the body.[111]

Similarly, fatal accidents to children in and around the workplace included falling down disused or unfenced mine shafts, falling from the decks of canal boats, or merely becoming injured whilst trespassing on work premises.[112] Transportation was also responsible for large numbers of

109   B. A. Hanawalt, 'Childrearing among the Lower Classes of Late Medieval England', *Journal of Interdisciplinary History*, 8 (1977), 1–22 (pp. 16, 19).

110   F. A. Bailey, 'Coroner's Inquests held in the Manor of Prescot, 1746–89', *Transactions of the Historic Society of Lancashire and Cheshire*, 86 (1934), 21–39; Sambrook, p. 227; Anon., 'Fatal Accident', *Blackburn Standard*, 11 December 1839, p. 2.

111   Anon., 'Awful Death', *Blackburn Standard*, 22 July 1840, p. 2.

112   Anon., 'Death by Falling Down a Coal Pit', *The Manchester Times and Gazette*, 12 April 1834, p. 2; Anon., 'Coroner's Inquest – Child Drowned', *The Manchester Times and Gazette*, 31 July 1841, p. 3; Sambrook, p. 241. Child workplace deaths in the late

child deaths and injuries. In late eighteenth and early nineteenth-century Leicestershire, incidents involving transportation and horses accounted for around 10 per cent of accidental violent deaths whilst three-quarters of accidental deaths relating to transportation in Prescot during the second half of the eighteenth century involved young children.[113] Of the seventy cases of fatal injury by carts, coaches, drays and wagons, heard at the Old Bailey between 1679 and 1770, more than half the victims were children (with incidents involving carts accounting for two-thirds of child accidental deaths).[114]

Urban and industrial growth resulted in increasing numbers of accidents to children attributable to the industrial workplace. In the 1850s and 60s, work-related injuries were the most common cause of death amongst children aged eleven to fifteen in the Potteries and the Black Country. Police reports show that the incidence of work-related deaths amongst children in industrial districts was more than a third greater compared with those in nearby rural areas (Table 3).[115] The relatively higher accidental death rate among young females in Manchester in the mid-century has also been attributed to their greater presence in relatively more dangerous

twentieth-century workplace overwhelmingly affected children who were not working but nonetheless were present (often trespassing) on industrial premises: *Hansard* (Commons), 13 November 2000, vol. 356, cc. 478–9W; Health and Safety Executive, *Reporting of Injuries, Diseases and Dangerous Occurrences Regulations* 1995 (RIDDOR) statistics, http://www.hse.gov.uk/statistics/demographic.htm, Excel files: ridagegen1 (Injuries to men employees by age of injured person and severity of injury') and ridagegen2 (Injuries to women employees by age of injured person and severity of injury').

113   P. J. Fisher, 'The Politics of Sudden Death: The Office and Role of the Coroner in England and Wales, 1726–1888' (Ph.D. thesis, University of Leicester, 2007), p. 122, n. 13; Bailey, 'Coroner's Inquests'.

114   E. Cockayne, *Hubbub: Filth, Noise and Stench in England, 1600–1770* (New Haven: Yale University Press, 2007), p. 170. Many incidents involved the intoxication of a driver or a horse turning 'vicious' and running amok. Substantial deodands might be levied against horses and vehicles but criminal prosecution of drivers and riders was rare: Fisher, p. 123, n. 18, p. 123–4, n. 13; J. S. Cockburn, 'Patterns of Violence in English Society: Homicide in Kent, 1560–1985', *Past & Present*, 130 (1991), 70–106 (p. 92). See also C. Spence, 'Accidentally Killed by a Cart: Workplace Hazard, and Risk in Late Seventeenth Century London', *European Review of History*, 3 (1996), 9–26.

115   Sambrook, p. 226. Rural children were not immune from machinery accidents. Verdon reports a female servant assisting at a threshing machine, whose 'clothes unfortunately became entangled in the wheel, and she was not rescued before one of her legs had been lacerated in the most dreadful manner': N. Verdon, *Rural Women Workers in Nineteenth-Century England: gender, work and wages* (Woodbridge: Boydell Press, 2002), pp. 89–90.

Table 3: Work-related deaths of children under fifteen as a proportion of all sudden child deaths: Staffordshire, 1851–2 and 1860–1

	Black Country	Potteries	Rural	Total
Work-related deaths	13.8	12.4	9.0	12.8

Note: Calculated from P. A. Sambrook, 'Childhood and Sudden Death in Staffordshire, 1851 and 1860', in *Staffordshire Histories: Essays in Honour of Michael Greenslade*, ed. P. Morgan and A. D. M. Phillips (Stafford: Staffordshire Record Society, 1999), pp. 216–52.

manufacturing occupations.[116] Non-fatal injuries, meanwhile, were more widespread amongst industrially employed children but frequently went unrecorded in official reports. Some of the early factory inquiries provided a partial insight into the scale of the problem. A doctor at the Kenyon Committee in 1819 examined bodily injuries amongst cotton mill children and found that nearly half had suffered 'considerable' and 3 per cent 'very considerable' injuries in the course of their work. A survey of Manchester Sunday schools, meanwhile, found that about a third of factory-employed boys and a fifth of girls were 'materially hurt', with injuries ranging from slight lacerations to missing fingers.[117] The extent and type of mill injuries to children would later be underlined by Robert Baker's study of 1840, which showed that injuries were almost always confined to the upper limbs of mill workers. Of those admitted as in-patients to the Leeds General Infirmary during that year, 97 per cent of injuries fell into this group.[118] Such injuries would often render a child incapable of future productive work but rarely attracted any form of compensation or support from employers. Employers also did not normally take a systematic approach to the treatment of workplace injuries to children. In 1833, around half of mills in the East Midlands paid no subscriptions to local hospitals or charities and, of those that did, less than one in five actually paid for medical treatment for accidents. Huzzard noted that in one factory, injuries would be allocated care according to their severity, with those of a minor nature referred to 'an old woman in the neighbourhood' who

---

116 T. A. Welton, 'On the Effect of Migrations in Disturbing Local Rates of Mortality, as Exemplified in the Statistics of London and the Surrounding Country, for the years 1851–1860', *Journal of the Institute of Actuaries and Assurance Magazine*, 16 (1870–2), 153–86 (pp. 164–5).

117 PP 1819 (24), p. 357.

118 Lee, 'Robert Baker', p. 89, tab. 1; see also PP 1819 (24), p. 250.

had knowledge of customary treatments. More serious injuries might be treated in the first instance by the owner's family surgeon with major cases referred to the local charity hospital.[119]

The frequently gruesome or spectacular nature of factory injuries provided sensational reading for a growing early nineteenth-century newspaper audience. Such reports attracted even greater sympathy because the factory workforce was made up predominantly of women and children. The sheer physical violence produced upon the body by mill and factory machinery was also of a different magnitude to those occurring in small workshops or domestic manufacture. Early steam-powered technologies involved complex transmission and power take-off via extensive systems of shafts and belts. Moreover, new textiles machinery was frequently crammed into older buildings not originally designed for their use, thus reducing the workspace between machines. Low ceilings and cramped working areas tended to place transmission shafts and gearing within reach of child operatives and injuries frequently occurred as a result of clothing becoming caught on unguarded horizontal or vertical shafts.[120] As a consequence, young factory workers were 'obliged to wear their clothes rather short and close to the body, to preserve them from being caught by the machinery.' Girls and women wore their hair set close to their heads secured by combs or by caps and wore pinafores or tight and short gowns.[121] The inappropriateness of many factory buildings to house new machinery was pointed out by several factory inspectors and engineers and, by the 1840s, the increasingly ubiquitous self-acting mule was singled out more and more frequently as an important cause of fatal accidents to children:

> This to some will appear ridiculous and absurd; but go into some mills, and you will find but *one* passage, and that *only* ten or twelve inches wide at the most; there you will see a boy or a girl with a box or skip upon the head, carrying it along this narrow passage, and in order to avoid coming in contact with the wall or some part of the machinery, the child is compelled to lean its body with the weight upon the head first to one side and then to the other ... Now in such a situation, if

119   S. Huzzard, 'The Role of the Certifying Factory Surgeon in the State Regulation of Child Labour and Industrial Health' (MA thesis, University of Manchester, 1976), pp. 8–9.
120   PP 1841 [311], p. 5.
121   Black, 'Statistical Sketch of Bolton', p. 169. In 1816 Kinder Wood noted the higher incidence of such accidents in smaller mills (PP 1816 (397), p. 195).

the child's clothes should become entangled, or a slip of the foot cause it to fall, then it must necessarily be exposed to considerable danger, especially if *self-acting mules* are in operation ... In this department children (generally boys) are employed who are called 'scavengers;' they are exposed to imminent danger from having to go underneath to 'wipe down' *while the machinery is in operation*, in doing which, should they not get out of the way when the carriage is 'running in,' they may be caught between the carriage and the roller beam, and either sustain considerable injury, or death may be the consequence.[122]

The maintenance and cleaning of such machinery would normally entail either the slowing down or the complete cessation of production, which was unpopular amongst both employers and operatives. As one overlooker complained, they 'should have to stop all the mill for one drum, and this might occur twenty times in the mill during the day.'[123] Alternative methods were sometimes adopted to save time and child workers were taught how to remove belts from pulleys using sticks whilst the machinery was in motion.[124] Factory superintendents in the 1830s and 40s remarked upon the numbers of children suffering injuries involving transmission machinery and belts which frequently involved the rapid and violent amputation of a finger, hand or arm.[125] Rudimentary power transmission in many mills also meant that it might take several minutes to stop machinery in the wake of an injury or entanglement.[126] A female operative described the sustained level of violence attending the death of an eleven-year-old boy in a Manchester mill:

the boy worked ... as a winder, and about half-past eight, when the machinery was about to be stopped for the breakfast hour, she observed him standing close to the winding frame, holding a strap in his hand which was connected with a shaft that ran within six or eight inches of the roof of the building. She called to him and told him he was in danger, but he only smiled at her. She went to her own frame and soon afterwards hearing a crash behind her she turned round and saw

---

122   Letter from Mr B. Fothergill of Messrs. Sharp and Roberts, Engineers, Manchester, 16th May 1840, Report from L. Horner, PP 1841 [311], p. 14.
123   Appendix to Horner's report, PP 1841 [311], p. 19.
124   PP 1819 (24), p. 20; PP 1841 [311], pp. 3–4.
125   PP 1841 [311], p. 4.
126   Anon., *Caledonian Mercury*, 21 March 1836, p. 3; Anon., 'Fatal Accident', *The Manchester Times and Gazette*, 11 June 1836, p. 2.

deceased going round an iron shaft at the top of the room, which turned at the rate of about 120 revolutions in a minute. She screamed and almost fainted, and whilst in this state she saw one of the deceased's legs flung past her by the shaft. She got down the stairs to the next floor as well as she could, and met with a man named William Grant ... when [the witness] told him of the accident he ordered the engine to be stopped, and went upstairs. At that time both deceased's legs were off, and pieces of flesh flew about him in every direction, and the roof of the building was broken by the body being forced against it.[127]

There is some evidence that by the 1830s, in the most technically advanced mills, the threat of injury from machinery was decreasing. In the newer, purpose-built, steam-powered mills, transmission shafts were often conveyed beneath floors whilst vertical shafts were increasingly boxed in.[128] Montgomery observed in 1833 that:

The make up and plan of the shafts and other gearing fitted up in mills that have been lately built, forms a most striking contrast for neatness and simplicity to that which is to be seen in old establishments erected about thirty or forty years ago. Not only does the former excel the latter for neatness and simplicity, but it is also more safe and durable – not so liable to accident, and exhausts less of the moving power.[129]

The larger and more highly capitalised mills were frequently praised by the factory inspectors for their provision of safety guards. Marshalls of Leeds had fenced in its dangerous carding machinery prior to the Factory Act of 1833 and, by 1841, the superintendent for Preston noted that the large Horrockses mill there had operated for fifteen to twenty years without any injuries from unguarded machinery.[130] The boxing in of transmission machinery was not always successful, however, since access to shafts and gearing was required for maintenance and lubrication. There was little supervision of access doors and the vertical boxing in of shafts

127   Anon., 'Another Fatal Accident', *The Manchester Times and Gazette*, 18 June 1836, p. 3. An operative suggested to the Kenyon Committee in 1819 that he had seen 'as many as Two or Three killed in one Day by the Straps' (PP 1819 (24), pp. 20–1).
128   Report from J. Heathcote, Superintendent of Factories, PP 1841 [311], p. 22. See also J. Tann, *The Development of the Factory* (London: Cornmarket, 1970).
129   Montgomery, pp. 39–40.
130   Rimmer, p. 216. Report from J. Heathcote, Superintendent of Factories, PP 1841 [311], p. 22.

across several floors could sometimes create strong currents of air that might draw in loose clothing.[131]

Apportioning the blame for industrial injuries in mills was no easy task for either legislators or the early factory inspectorate. The notion that child workers might be held tacitly responsibility for workplace injuries had been largely dismissed by the Factory Commissioners of 1833 but the matter of who was responsible for industrial accidents remained unclear until the later 1840s. Parents would frequently blame their own injured children for stupidity or negligence, whilst inspectors and managers often argued that penalties for injuries to children could only be effective were they to fall upon the operative spinners who permitted their piecers and scavengers to clean machinery whilst in motion. The argument advanced was that cleaning took only a moment to perform and that overlookers and managers could not be expected to exercise continuous scrutiny of child workers throughout the working day.[132] The factory inspectors also highlighted the 'natural heedlessness' of very young children who would 'run about and play, and ... run against the machinery.'[133] In the wake of the Factory Act of 1833 there was a growing tendency among superintendents and surgeons to report workplace injuries together with a greater willingness by the provincial press to carry stories about spectacular fatalities and serious industrial injuries such that, by the early 1840s, this had become the single most important issue for the factory inspectorate. A series of special reports was produced by the inspectors on the practicality of legislation to make fencing compulsory and several high-profile court cases placed responsibility for injuries increasingly upon employers.[134] A case for damages was brought in 1840 at the Liverpool Assizes by Elizabeth Stocks, aged 16 years, who had been employed in a cotton mill and who had been caught in unguarded machinery 'whereby she was mutilated, much injured and suffered excruciating pain, lost her wages in consequence of her inability to attend her work, and was put

---

131   Anon., 'Accidents by Machinery', *The Manchester Times and Gazette*, 7 February 1835, p. 2.
132   Bronstein, pp. 100–2; PP 1841 [311], pp. 10, 63. Cases relying on the culpability of children persisted. In the early twentieth century, a ten-year-old who had her arms torn off by machinery in a US cotton mill had her court case dismissed on the ground that she had assumed all the risks of her work: J. Mitchell, 'Burden of Industrial Accidents', *Annals of the American Academy of Political and Social Science*, 38 (1911), 76–82 (pp. 81–2).
133   PP 1841 [311], p. 4.
134   See Bisset Hawkins' reports in PP 1834 (167), pp. 271–4; PP 1841 [311].

to considerable expense in her cure.' The girl was supported by 'her next friend and guardian', Lord Ashley. The plaintiff initially pleaded guilty, though 'after some private discussion between the counsel' the plea was withdrawn and the sum of £100 damages was agreed.[135] Ashley's select committee the following year suggested a prohibition on the cleaning of machinery whilst in motion and this, together with the compulsory fencing of flywheels, gearing and shafts, became incorporated into the subsequent Factory Act of 1844.[136] This marked the first occasion upon which factory legislation had laid down minimum standards of industrial safety. The 1844 Act also included formal reporting provisions and the introduction of fines against employers for non-compliance.[137] It was not until the late 1840s, however, that the reporting requirements ushered in by the Act disclosed for the first time the full extent of the problem of industrial injury. In the first six months of the new provisions, reports of accidents in Lancashire and Yorkshire alone totalled 996, of which 5 per cent involved amputation and 6 per cent the loss of at least one finger, whilst in 1849 the factory inspectors reported 2,021 accidents over a six-month period, more than half of which involved machinery, which resulted in 109 amputations and 22 deaths.[138] By 1854, the first decennial return of accidents reported 38,000 incidents including 477 deaths.[139] Given the proliferation of machine production and the progressive transition to steam power in the half century prior to the 1844 Act, it is likely that the proportions of machinery deaths and injuries in textiles were much more substantial at earlier dates. This renders it even more difficult to explain why decades of debate over the employment of children in factories between the 1780s and the 1830s had failed to highlight industrial injuries as the most significant threat to the welfare of industrial child workers.

135   Anon., 'Accident by Machinery – Liability of Mill-Owners', *The Manchester Times and Gazette*, 22 August 1840, p. 3; see also Anon., *Preston Chronicle*, 22 August 1840, p. 2.
136   Report from the Select Committee on the Act for the Regulation of Mills and Factories (says 18 February 1841) in PP 1841 [311], p. 189; 7 Vict., c. 15, ss. xx–xxiii.
137   7 Vict., c. 15. The legislation provided a model for the Mines Inspection Act of 1850 (13 & 14 Vict., c. 100): P. W. J. Bartrip and S. B. Burman, *The Wounded Soldiers of Industry: Industrial Compensation Policy, 1833–1897* (Oxford: Oxford University Press, 1983), pp. 54–63, 83–92.
138   Huzzard, pp. 39–41.
139   Bronstein, pp. 15–16. Such statistics may also underestimate injuries because the onus was upon employers to report incidents (Huzzard, pp. 39–40).

3

Certifying Surgeons, Children's Ages
and Physical Growth

The arrival of the first factory inspectorate in 1834 was accompanied
by new requirements to assess the ages and physical conditions of
factory children. The main provisions of the 1833 Factory Act excluded
children below nine from factory work and limited those aged nine to
twelve to forty-eight hours per week.[1] When the inspectors took up their
positions, however, they soon discovered that the age clauses of the Act
were largely inoperable because there existed no reliable documentary
means of verifying the ages of child applicants for factory work. Evidence
from parish registers was often unreliable because the gap between birth
and baptism could vary widely.[2] Civil registration, moreover, did not
commence in England and Wales until 1838 which meant that the earliest
date from which a nine-year-old applicant could provide any reliable
documentary proof of a date of birth for the purposes of the factory
acts was 1846. In Scotland, meanwhile, legislation requiring formal registration was not enacted until 1854 and the age limitations of the Act
could not practically be enforced until the mid-1860s.[3] The earliest civil
registers also frequently contained fewer personal details than parish
registers. Spaces were reserved for the insertion of a child's baptismal
name but these were often left blank. Registers also suffered from fictitious
entries by registrars themselves as they were being paid by the entry.
Moreover, parents were not legally bound to provide information about

---

1   The Act also limited those under eighteen years to not more than twelve hours work
per day (3 & 4 Will. IV, c. 103).
2   The general difficulty in assessing ages of working children had previously been raised
at the Kenyon Committee of 1818 (PP 1818 (61), p. 1, c. 2). In some districts, children were
not baptised. By contrast, it sometimes happened that four or five children of the same
parents would be baptised or christened at the same time: Anon., 'Information Under
the Factory Act', *Preston Chronicle*, 30 April 1842, p. 4.
3   6 & 7 Will. IV, c. 86; 17 & 18 Vict., c. 80.

a birth unless requested by a registrar and it was not until the Births and Deaths Registration Act of 1874 that the burden of registration of birth was placed (under penalty) upon parents or guardians rather than the registrar.[4] The age stipulations of the 1833 Act would ultimately prove the most problematical function of the new inspectorate and would within a short time require the recruitment of a large number of medical practitioners in an attempt to provide accurate assessments of the ages of child applicants.

Early factory legislation had placed upon parents the primary responsibility for confirming the ages of their working children. In fact, the Factory Act of 1819 permitted employers to blame parents for any errors or the fraudulent reporting of ages and a factory bill of 1825, similarly, sought to institute a register of names and ages along with confirmatory signatures of parents or guardians which would 'exempt such proprietor or occupier of such mill, manufactory or building, from any prosecution'.[5] The Act of 1833, however, marked an important departure by shifting much of the responsibility for avoiding taking on underage children onto employers. The Factory Commission, anticipating the possible difficulties of implementing any new age regulations, had recommended the appointment of certifying surgeons to confirm that child applicants were of 'the ordinary strength and appearance' of the ages prescribed in the legislation.[6] However, the framers of the legislation largely failed to appreciate how onerous the verification of children's ages would ultimately prove and almost as soon as the Act was passed, the size of the administrative burden became apparent. Robert Rickards, the first Lancashire and Yorkshire Inspector, noted 'the impossibility of an inspector and one

---

4   37 & 38 Vict., c. 88; M. Nissel, *People Count: A History of the General Register Office* (London: HMSO, 1987), pp. 22–6.

5   59 Geo. III, c. 66; 60 Geo. III, c. 5; PP 1825 (382), p. 2, l. 5, p. 3, ll. 31–5. Hobhouse's Act of 1831 (1 & 2 Will. IV, c. 39) also contained a similar clause: U. R. Q. Henriques, *Before the Welfare State: Social Administration in Early Industrial Britain* (London: Longman, 1979), p. 73.

6   PP 1833 (450), p. 67; S. Huzzard, 'The Role of the Certifying Factory Surgeon in the State Regulation of Child Labour and Industrial Health' (MA thesis, University of Manchester, 1976), pp. 15–16. The certificates were to be 'arranged in alphabetical order in a book to be kept by the certifying surgeon, whilst the counterpart, duly signed by the said surgeon, and countersigned by the Inspector or justice of the peace, will, on delivery to the mill-owner, be also registered in a book to be kept in the mills for this purpose, and open at all times to authorised inspection' (PP 1834 (596), p. 30).

superintendent in a division like this, attending to the state and condition of all its factories and mills, and of the children employed therein ... The thing was absolutely impossible.'[7] Rickards attempted to deal with the weight of applications by dividing the Manchester district into five separate areas and appointing a certifying surgeon in each. Having submitted a list of appointable surgeons from which the Medical Board of the Manchester Royal Infirmary chose five, Rickards declared himself to be satisfied 'that these nominations will be very acceptable to masters and men generally.'[8] His system was soon swamped, however, and within a year, Rickards' inspectorate (which contained around three-quarters of the British textiles industry) had appointed 151 surgeons who had granted 35,845 certificates. A similar rapid expansion in applications occurred in Leonard Horner's Scottish and Irish inspectorate which during its first year of operation employed 111 surgeons and issued 28,392 certificates.[9] The Commission had originally intended that age certificates would be granted in the presence of magistrates along the lines required in the binding of parish apprentices but by the end of the 1830s it had become common practice for certificate books 'containing perhaps a hundred certificates' to be sent up to the petty session, where it was said that 'the magistrate, as fast as he can sign, puts his name, without asking any questions whatever.'[10] The system was also marked by enormous variation between districts. Some justices would only countersign certificates where they were issued by a person with whom they were personally acquainted whilst others were under the impression that they were countersigning merely to confirm the signature of a surgeon.[11] Variations in practice and evasions of the regulations were therefore widespread throughout factory districts in the wake of the 1833 Act. Horner estimated that in

7   Report by R. Rickards, Factory Inspector, PP 1835 (342), p. 6.
8   Report by Robert Rickards, PP 1834 (596), p. 28. There was a precedent for this as the 1802 Act had permitted justices to divide those areas containing more than six factories or mills into two or more districts and to appoint two visitors for each district (42 Geo. III, c. 73, s. 9).
9   Huzzard, p. 23; PP 1835 (156), pp. 2–4. By 1838 Leeds alone had thirteen certifying surgeons (PP 1839 [159], p. 12). Understanding the relationship between the factory surgeons appointed in the wake of the 1833 Act and the inspectors is made more difficult by the fact that the formal inspectors' minutes only began in January 1837 (The National Archives, HO87, Home Office Factory and Mines Entry Books).
10   PP 1833 (450), p. 67; PP 1840 (203), p. 39.
11   PP 1840 (203), p. 40.

his own district one in three working children certified as aged twelve had obtained certificates by deceiving the surgeons.[12]

The Factory Commission had also failed to make clear how the competency of prospective certifying factory surgeons might be assessed and the Act itself had been imprecise in defining the status of medical men who might act, allowing only for the signing of certificates by 'some Surgeon or Physician of the Place or Neighbourhood'.[13] Most certifying surgeons were appointed on a strictly part-time basis and operated in a competitive market for health care. As such, they for the most part fitted Inkster's description of general practitioners as 'marginal men', combining certification duties with other contractual work such as caring for the sick poor or writing up assessments of the health of applicants for life assurance schemes or provident clubs.[14] Their practices were therefore deeply embedded in, and dependent upon, local economies and local manufacturing populations and they were often unwilling to upset their potential customers.[15] There was little formality in the granting of age certificates and most were issued in the residences of surgeons with no witnesses as to the identity or appearance of a certified child.[16] The

12   C. Wing, *The Evils of the Factory System Demonstrated by Parliamentary Evidence* (1837; London: Frank Cass, 1967), p. 417.

13   PP 1833 (450), pp. 68–71, quoted in M. W. Thomas, *The Early Factory Legislation: A Study in Legislative and Administrative Evolution* (Leigh-on-Sea: Thames Bank Publishing, 1948), pp. 58–9; 3 & 4 Will. IV, c. 103, s. xii.

14   I. Inkster, 'Marginal Men: Aspects of the Social Role of the Medical Community in Sheffield, 1790–1850', in *Health Care and Popular Medicine*, ed. J. H. Woodward and D. Richards (London: Croom Helm, 1977), pp. 128–63; 'Agonistes', 'Defence of the Payment for Medical Replies by the Life-Assurance Companies instead of the Party Petitioning to Assure', *The Lancet*, 38, 30 April 1842, 164–5; W. Sanders, *Rules and Tables for Provident and Independent Institutions* (Birmingham: T. Knott, 1834), pp. 9–10, 14–15, 20, 24–5, 27, 29, 37–47. Surgeon-apothecaries could earn a quarter to a third of their income from parish duties: S. Williams, 'Practitioners' Income and Provision for the Poor: Parish Doctors in the Late Eighteenth and Early Nineteenth Centuries', *Social History of Medicine*, 18 (2005), 159–86 (p. 175).

15   H. Marland, *Medicine and Society in Wakefield and Huddersfield, 1780–1870* (Cambridge: Cambridge University Press, 1987), pp. 75, 77, 275, 280; A. Digby, *Making a Medical Living: Doctors and Patients in the English Market for Medicine, 1720–1911* (Cambridge: Cambridge University Press, 2002), p. 109. As Digby pointed out, for most practitioners '[t]he concept of territoriality was implicitly understood as the basis for an economically viable practice' (p. 108).

16   As Robert Baker later recalled, 'I used to give such certificates in large numbers at my own house every Saturday night' (PP 1868–9 [4093-I], p. 196).

numbers of certificates issued annually by individual surgeons were also highly variable. Huzzard suggests that the numbers issued *per annum* by surgeons ranged from 21 to 7,164 with an average per surgeon of about 1,200.[17] Collusion between surgeons, factory owners and parents was also common, particularly where owners were permitted to carry the expense of their own surgeons. The 1833 Commission had foreseen that any measure

> by which the enforcement of the law shall be made chiefly dependent on those who have an interest in breaking it may be expected to prove as inefficient as the provisions of the existing law. On the part of the parent, who, under the existing law, is called upon to give the certificate of the age of the child, (which certificate forms at present the main security against evasion on this point), we find a strong interest in the commission of fraud; ... on the part of the immediate agents or overlookers, probably the friends of the parent, a willingness to connive at it; and on the part of the masters not especial motive to exert vigilance.[18]

The fact that surgeons merely offered an opinion as to the age of children also meant that they enjoyed virtual immunity from any legal action arising from erroneous or fraudulent certification. Indeed, the exceedingly small percentage of convictions for falsification of age certificates (1.1 per cent of all convictions under the Factory Act in 1836) underlined the extreme difficulty of disproving a mere opinion.[19] As Horner pointed out:

> as regards the surgeon, there is no possibility of reaching him, unless you can prove (an exceedingly difficult thing to prove) direct and intentional fraud; because the surgeon certifies his opinion, and we all know how indefinite that is. The surgeon might have met me, and said, 'Sir, I differ from you entirely; my opinion is that that child is 13;' and there it ends; his opinion may be perfectly absurd, but he shelters himself under that.[20]

---

17   Huzzard, p. 21.
18   PP 1833 (450), pp. 68–71, quoted in Thomas, *Early Factory Legislation*, pp. 58–9.
19   Convictions during June–August 1836 (PP 1837 [73], p. 5, tab.).
20   PP 1840 (203), p. 35. In one visit, Horner cancelled the certificates of a hundred children on the grounds that their physical appearance did not match their stated ages (PP 1837 [73], p. 43).

Factory owners, moreover, were under no obligation to introduce their own opinions about the age of an employed child. Where a child appeared grossly below the permitted age they could claim immunity from prosecution by referring merely to the age as stated on the surgeon's certificate. A case from 1839 hinged around the question of whether an owner who knew a child to be under age might be prosecuted even though the child had already been granted a certificate by a surgeon. The owner swore that he had not known the child to be under age but the superintendent produced a letter written by the owner proving otherwise. The magistrates declared the owner's behaviour 'highly reprehensible', though it was clear that there was no case answerable in law.[21] When an inspector discovered children whose appearance he considered significantly below the certified age, the normal course of action was to instruct a mill-owner or parent to have the child re-examined by the same surgeon and where differences could not subsequently be reconciled, a surgeon could bring the matter before a court to determine on production of the child in question.[22] In 1839, an inspector discovered a boy working with just his baptismal certificate:

> upon looking at that baptismal certificate, I found that he had been baptized about a week before. He had been rejected by the surgeon; he went to the parish church, was baptized, an extract was given from the register, and, what appears to me an exceedingly improper thing, the clergyman had stated that the boy was born so-and-so ... I immediately brought the subject under the notice of the curate, a very respectable gentleman, and he said he was not the least aware of the object for which the certificate was wanted, and that he should take care never to do so in future.[23]

Opportunities for evasion of the law also occurred where families migrated from one district to another. Child workers would have their initial certification fees paid by a master (at a 'moderate charge by the surgeons') but those who moved subsequently to a new employer were compelled to produce new certificates at their own expense upon each occasion.[24] Horner had speculated shortly after his appointment that certificates,

21   Anon., 'Violation of the Factory Act', *The Charter*, 24 March 1839, p. 137.
22   PP 1840 (203), p. 27; PP 1837–8 (399), p. 5.
23   PP 1840 (203), p. 41.
24   PP 1834 (596), p. 28.

once granted, might be freely transferable between employers during the time a child was subject to the restrictions of the Act but, as Rickards pointed out, certificates might easily be passed to other children. It was only where a surgeon re-examined a child in a new district that a proper assessment of strength and physical appearance could be obtained.[25] The practice of repeat certification was supported by employers who suspected that certificates issued outside their own districts might be filled out by unappointed surgeons or that fraudulent transfers of certificates from older to younger children might leave them open to prosecution.[26] Rickards supported the transfer of costs to parents because he believed that the disincentive to migrate would have the effect of partially 'binding' children to employers, thus deterring excessive migration of workers.[27] In reality, the movement of child workers between districts was almost always dependent upon the migration decisions of parents and the children of migrant workers were almost universally forced into multiple certification.

Problems with faulty assessments of ages continued throughout the 1830s and this led to repeated attempts by the inspectors to restrict the power to issue certificates to their own appointees or, at least, to surgeons who were members of medical colleges.[28] The inspectors had no statutory power to appoint surgeons and, as Fox Maule pointed out in the Commons, they 'could not exclude persons from certifying who called themselves surgeons, though they were often little better than cow-doctors.' Indeed, Rickards was said to have discovered a 'drunken ale-house keeper' issuing certificates.[29] These difficulties were

---

25   PP 1834 (596), p. 9; PP 1835 (342), p. 7.

26   In the Commons, Brotherton thought the practice injurious to the interests of the workpeople of Manchester whilst Hindley 'had been told by a respectable manufacturer in Manchester, that even if a child was under ten years' old the surgeon would grant a certificate that the child was twelve years if the manufacturer said that the child would be useful to him' (*Hansard* (Commons), 19 June 1835, vol. 28, cc. 894–6).

27   This, he thought, would keep children 'more steadily to their work, and prevent capricious removals'. Employers who had paid for certificates, moreover, usually had them made up into a book and resisted attempts to remove individual certificates fearing later prosecution: PP 1834 (596), p. 28; PP 1840 (203), pp. 38–9.

28   About a third of certifying surgeons were not members of a medical college: Huzzard, pp. 25, 31; PP 1839 (434), s. 29, pp. 8–9; *Hansard* (Commons), 25 February 1839, vol. 45, c. 882.

29   Fox Maule, *Hansard* (Commons), 25 February 1839, vol. 45, c. 881. In the opinion of the Crown lawyers, a mill owner was at liberty to accept a certificate from anyone who practised surgery ('a tooth drawer, would be entitled to grant a certificate ... [w]hether licensed or not'): PP 1840 (203), pp. 40–1; Huzzard, p. 23.

compounded by resistance from local practitioners themselves who felt that the appointment of surgeons by inspectors would have the effect of excluding them from what remained largely a free market in certification work. In April 1842, Joshua Ikin, surgeon to the Leeds Hospital for Women and Children, wrote to *The Lancet*, alerting the profession to a clause to be inserted in an amending bill to the Factory Act which sought to limit the numbers of certifying surgeons to the appointees of the inspectors – a proposal which he thought 'most prejudicial to the interests and highly objectionable to the general body of practitioners in manufacturing towns and districts'.[30] Ikin claimed that the factory inspectors were appointing their own favourites whilst refusing the attempts of others to obtain positions, thus procuring 'for themselves a nice bit of patronage, to be exercised for the benefit of friends or acquaintances'. Since the inspectors were not normally medical men, it was argued that they were not competent to question the accuracy of a surgeon's medical report and that their superintendents, meanwhile, might be general practitioners themselves and might be interested in appointing or negotiating with their own friends.[31] Despite a vociferous debate in the medical journals, however, the argument was ultimately lost in 1844 when the new Factory Act bestowed upon the inspectors the absolute power of appointment over certifying factory surgeons.[32]

30   Ikin had been surgeon to a small mill until his certificates were declined by an inspector. Though, as he himself pointed out, the Factory Act did not actually permit an inspector to refuse a surgeon's certificates: J. I. Ikin, 'Certifying Surgeons under the Factory-Amendment Bill', letter to *The Lancet*, 38, 30 April 1842, 165–7 (pp. 165–6).
31   Ikin, 'Certifying Surgeons', p. 166. Ikin railed against the 'scheme of the interested and already too powerful inspectors, who would ... unreasonably endeavour to deprive medical men of their just rights and privileges': J. I. Ikin, 'Appointment of Certifying Surgeons under the New Factory Bill', *Provincial Medical and Surgical Journal*, 6, 15 April 1843, 56–7 (p. 56).
32   Moreover, 'no Surgeon, being the Occupier of a Factory, or having a beneficial Interest in any Factory, shall be a certifying Surgeon' (7 Vict., c. 15, s. ix). From 1844, certificates not granted by a formally appointed certifying surgeon had no legality unless countersigned by a magistrate (7 Vict., c. 15, s. x). The Mines Act of 1842 (5 & 6 Vict., c. 99) contained a strict prohibition on the employment of children below ten but provided no administrative machinery whatsoever for assessing the ages of child applicants. It was assumed that ages would merely be assessed by coalowners on the basis of evidence of birth or baptism rather than inspection by a surgeon.

Surgeons and anthropometric standards

The continuing misunderstandings and evasions of the statutory age regulations drove the inspectors to seek out supplementary means of assessing children's ages. Despairing of any short-term improvement in documentary evidence and in the absence of any further statutory guidance, the inspectors turned to measurements of children's heights and the timing of the eruption of teeth. Horner circulated a letter of instructions to his surgeons, alerting them to the results of two independent surveys of the heights of child applicants, which had been carried out by James Harrison of Preston and Robert Baker of Leeds (both certifying factory surgeons).[33] Harrison based his survey on measurements of 1,270 factory applicants and recommended the exclusion of children who fell below the minimum height recorded for each of the ages in his survey.[34] Baker, meanwhile, noted that one of the practical advantages of the use of heights was that a shorter child could never be substituted for a taller one and that this would afford 'a degree of equality of advantage to all the mill-owners ... a child not being 4 feet 3 ½ inches for one mill cannot be so for any other, and thus all the parties are made alike.'[35] Horner circulated supplementary instructions to the factory surgeons:

> Until some more precise and accurate data can be obtained, it will be advisable for you to take the observations of Mr Harrison and Mr Baker as a guide; and therefore, unless in cases of unusual development of muscular strength, no child that, without shoes, measures less than

33   Statistical Society of London, 'Report on the Eleventh Meeting of the British Association for the Advancement of Science', *Journal of the Statistical Society of London*, 4 (October 1841), 181–2 (p. 181); J. M. Tanner, *A History of the Study of Human Growth* (Cambridge: Cambridge University Press, 1981), p. 154.

34   The average stature of children aged eleven years, for example, was 50.75 inches whilst the minimum was 46.50 inches. Harrison argued that 'ordinary appearance, of course, must be regarded as the average size, but as there are necessarily many under the average, who are really of the specified ages, it is obvious that considerable latitude must be allowed': J. Harrison, 'Extracts from the Report of the Inspectors of Factories, Illustrating the State of Health in the Different Factories', *Edinburgh Medical and Surgical Journal*, 44 (1835), 425–32 (p. 425). The average height of an eleven-year-old male factory worker in 1833 had been recorded at 50.76 inches, almost identical to Harrison's average for factory applicants (PP 1833 (450), D1, p. 88).

35   Though he stressed that heights were 'a guide, to be taken along with other evidence of a more satisfactory nature' (extract from a letter by Robert Baker, 8 September 1836, PP 1837 (99), p. 3).

3 feet 10 inches, ought to be considered as having the appearance of nine years of age, and no child less than 4 feet 3½ inches, ought to be considered as having the appearance of 13 years of age; there must, besides, be no deficiency of bodily health and strength to justify a certificate of 9 and 13 years respectively being granted to children of the above-mentioned stature.[36]

The directive was widely misunderstood by many surgeons and Horner was compelled to circulate further instructions, pointing out that some surgeons were

not only certifying all children who measure 4 feet 3½ inches as having the ordinary strength and appearance of 13 years of age, but have even gone to the mills and recertified children as 13, whom, a few weeks before, they had certified as 12 years of age. If my letter had been attentively read, it would have been seen that the heights of 3 feet 10 inches for nine years, and 4 feet 3½ inches for 13 years of age, are, with rare exceptions, to be held as the minimum and not the average for those ages.[37]

Horner also lobbied for compulsory barefoot height measurements of all child applicants but his attempt was stifled by the Crown law officers who ruled that any alteration to the form of certificate as laid down in the legislation would be illegal.[38] This did not prevent the inspectors pressing for changes in the law whereby all applicants for factory work would have their height, colour of eyes and colour of hair recorded by 'inspecting surgeons'.[39]

The inspectors also seized upon the stages of child dentition as a proxy for age.[40] In 1837 the London dentist, Edwin Saunders, published *The Teeth, a Test of Age, Considered with Reference to the Factory Children*, in which he argued that the timing of the eruption of teeth in children offered a more reliable standard as the variations in height at particular

---

36   PP 1837 (99), p. 2.
37   Like Baker, Horner stressed that the consideration of a child's height was an 'initiatory step in the inquiry' (extract from a Letter to the appointed Surgeons, 7 November 1836, PP 1837 (99), p. 4).
38   PP 1837 [73], p. 4.
39   PP 1837–8 (292), Schedule 1, p. 13. The bill never passed into law.
40   PP 1837–8 (119), p. 42.

ages were almost always relatively greater than that of the eruption of teeth.[41] He noted:

> the teeth appear to possess an economy of their own, and to be, to a great extent, uninfluenced by those affections and states of constitution in which the other parts of the system, more or less, participate, and with which, according to the degree of vitality which they possess, they are found to sympathize. Even in those more violent commotions of the system resulting from the catalogue of infantile diseases ... the progress of the formation of the teeth does not appear to be retarded.[42]

At the request of the inspectors, Saunders produced tables presenting the stages of tooth eruption at ages nine and thirteen.[43] Indeed, the inspection of teeth became so commonplace that Horner observed in one of his reports, 'when the doctors and I go round the mills, and call any to us that appear too young for their work, they sometimes come running up with their mouths open, and turn up their little heads without being told'.[44] The method was not universally popular in practical application, however, and in a case brought under the Factory Act in Carlisle in 1842, the certifying surgeon encountered a girl who had the requisite number of teeth on one side of her mouth but not on the other.[45] The inspection of teeth continued to be championed by the second Children's Employment Commission of 1843, which reported that, apart from the study of teeth, 'any judgment founded upon personal appearance ... or upon intelligence

---

41   Though the claim to a wide variation in heights appears to have been drawn from Edwin Saunders' erroneous reporting of Horner's recommended minimum height restriction as the 'average height'. E. Saunders, *The Teeth, a Test of Age, Considered with Reference to the Factory Children* (London: H. Renshaw, 1837), pp. 24–5, 54. Robert Saunders (the factory inspector) also cited studies by another London dentist, James Pattison Clark (PP 1837–8 (119), p. 42).

42   Letter from Edwin Saunders in Wing, *Evils of the Factory System*, p. c.

43   These advised that children aged nine would have four central and four lateral incisors and four anterior molars, whilst those of thirteen would have, in addition, four cuspid and four anterior and posterior bicuspids: E. Saunders, 'The Teeth A Test of Age', *The Lancet*, 2 (30 June 1838), 492–96 (p. 493). Saunders pointed out that 'the development of the teeth in the girls was more regular and a little in advance of that of the boys' but that there was little discernible difference in timing: Saunders, *The Teeth, a Test of Age*, pp. 51, 74–5.

44   PP 1840 (203), pp. 38–9.

45   Anon., 'Information Under the Factory Act'. The surgeon declared it impossible to judge the age of a thirteen-year-old to within six months using such methods.

... [was] ... a mere *guessing* at the age'. Nevertheless the use of heights and dentition by factory surgeons declined as civil registration of births became more accurate and more regularly observed.[46]

The physical growth of child workers

Despite the shortcomings of the early attempts to inform the age regulations of the Factory Act, the efforts of surgeons and inspectors to construct anthropometric standards resulted in the collection of large amounts of data from which it is possible to test various assumptions about the health and nutritional status of working children.[47] A major and long-standing complaint amongst medical critics of the employment of factory children was that they suffered significantly shorter stature compared with those in different regions and in other occupations. The Peel Committee of 1816 had heard such complaints and Peel himself observed the often 'stinted growth' of the children who worked in his own factories.[48] Evidence from supporters of factory reform such as William Osburn (a Tory Poor Law overseer and Chairman of the Leeds Short Time Committee) suggested that 'working in factories retards the growth of children upwards of a year; probably a year and a half'.[49] Osburn claimed that there was a difference of at least an inch and a half between factory and non-factory children:

> The difference in appearance is so perceptible that many other persons, as well as myself, are able to go into a Sunday-school and select at once all the children that are employed in factories; and persons more conversant with the factory system, than I am, persons employed

46   PP 1843 [432], D1, cited in W. C. R. Hicks, 'The Education of the Half-Timer', *Economic History: A Supplement of the Economic Journal*, 3 (1939), 222–39 (p. 223).
47   Important collections of child height statistics include: J. Fielden, *The Curse of the Factory System* (1836), ed. J. T. Ward (New York: A. M. Kelley, 1969), p. 9; PP 1831–2 (706), Q. 9887, pp. 465–6; PP 1833 (450), D1, p. 88; PP 1842 (381), App. C, pp. 212–14, App. D, p. 215, App. E, p. 216; PP 1842 (382), pp. 5, 31, 38, 65, App. A, pp. 77–86, tabs 1–5; J. Black, 'Remarks on the Influence of Physical Habits and Employment', *London Medical Gazette*, 2, 12 (1833), 143–8 (p. 147, table); Harrison, 'Extracts from the Report of the Inspectors'; Anon., 'Mr Fielden, MP, and the Factory Inspector', *The Champion*, 16 October 1836.
48   Fielden, p. 9.
49   PP 1831–2 (706), Q. 9878, p. 465.

themselves in factories are able not only to do that, but also to point out the particular occupation in which each individual is engaged.[50]

In 1837, following on from Saunders' tables of age-related tooth eruption, Horner embarked upon a substantial project to provide more objective height standards for the certifying surgeons. He obtained measurements of more than 16,000 children aged between eight and fourteen, representing the largest recorded sample of the stature of children in northern English manufacturing districts for the early nineteenth century. Twenty per cent of the sample lived in 'large towns', 37 per cent in 'small towns' and 43 per cent in 'rural districts' (see Appendix, Tables A.1–A.3).[51] The surgeons involved in the survey were instructed to 'confine the observation to the children of the working classes; to measure those only whose real ages can be ascertained with tolerable certainty; to distinguish the males and females; to exclude those who are not in an ordinary state of health, and to distinguish the measurements by differences of half years'. The subjects of the survey were almost certainly child *applicants* for factory work rather than children already employed, and their heights were probably recorded following the manner of Harrison's earlier sample 'taken, of course, without shoes'. The data recorded by the surgeons in 1837 provide valuable insights to the dynamics of growth of both male and female children in different industrial environments (see Table 4).[52] The data show that urban males and females were relatively shorter from

50   PP 1831–2 (706), Q. 9887, pp. 465–6.
51   Sixty-five surgeons were involved in the survey and the average number of children measured per surgeon was 228. The following towns made returns from more than one surgeon: Manchester (3); Stockport (2); Leeds (2); Rochdale (2); Huddersfield (2); Morley (2) (PP 1837 (99), p. 5). The samples contained approximately equal proportions of boys and girls.
52   PP 1837 (99), pp. 1–11; PP 1837 [73], pp. 21, 44. The minute book and other factory inspectorate papers contain no reference to Horner's survey, implying that he had concealed his project from the Home Department prior to the findings appearing in his report of March 1837: The National Archives, LAB15/1; PP 1837 (99), p. 3. The absence of Home Department funding suggests that the surgeons merely supplied Horner with the heights of the child applicants examined in their own townships. The presence of large numbers of females is also important since the armed forces recruitment data, from which historians have drawn most of their inferences about historic heights, do not contain measurements of females. Nor do the measurements suffer from the truncation of distributions arising from the minimum height restrictions imposed on military recruits: see R. Floud, K. Wachter and A Gregory, *Height, Health and History: Nutritional Status in the United Kingdom, 1750–1980* (Cambridge: Cambridge University Press, 1990).

Table 4: Stature of children in different occupations and by place of residence, 1833–41 (inches)

	Age	Factory children 1833	Non-factory 1833	Marine Society 1833	Large towns 1837	Rural districts 1837	Small towns 1837	Collieries 1841	Dorsetshire Farms 1841
Males	8	-	-	-	46.37	46.25	46.26	45.81	47.88
	9	47.64	48.06	-	47.99	48.15	47.40	47.26	48.45
	10	49.29	50.15	-	49.36	49.59	48.98	48.34	51.86
	11	50.76	50.51	-	50.00	51.17	50.45	49.24	51.53
	12	52.88	52.50	-	51.13	52.43	52.10	51.31	54.73
	13	53.98	54.50	54.05	52.99	53.65	53.74	52.09	54.59
	14	56.09	56.13	56.79	55.11	55.73	56.11	54.02	58.17
	15	-	-	57.00	-	-	-	55.61	58.29
	16	-	-	59.36	-	-	-	57.27	62.33
Females	8	-	-	-	46.24	45.84	45.14	-	-
	9	47.50	47.94	-	47.72	47.58	47.72	-	-
	10	49.12	48.87	-	49.12	49.84	49.09	-	-
	11	51.06	51.55	-	50.41	50.91	50.52	-	-
	12	53.20	53.17	-	51.60	52.69	52.01	-	-
	13	55.14	54.57	-	53.32	54.23	54.03	-	-
	14	57.25	57.77	-	55.68	55.87	56.26	-	-

Sources: Factory and non-factory employed children, PP 1833 (450), D1, p. 88; Marine Society, Floud et al., *Height, Health and History*, tab. 4.4, p. 173; Certifying factory surgeons (barefoot heights), PP 1837 (99), pp. 1–11; collieries and Dorsetshire farms, PP 1842 [381], App. C., pp. 212–14, App. D, p. 215, App. E, p. 216; PP 1842 [382], p. 65, App. A, pp. 77–86, tabs 1–5.

Note: The factory and non-factory children measured by S. Stanway for the Factory Commission in 1833 all attended the same Sunday schools. Their measurements have been reduced by a half inch on the basis of Quetelet's understanding that they were recorded with shoes. Given that many children at the time would have worn clogs, this might be thought a conservative reduction. Samples with fewer than 100 subjects have been omitted.

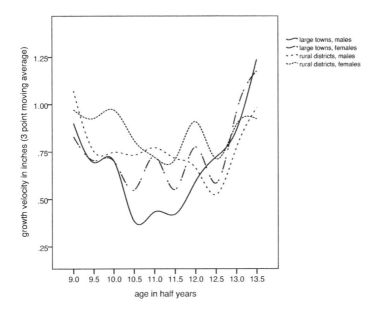

Figure 4: Half-year incremental growth velocities of urban and rural males and females: northern factory districts, 1837. Source: PP 1837 (99), pp. 1–11

around the age of eleven compared with those living in rural industrial districts and small towns. Despite adolescent 'catch up' growth thereafter, the urban–rural deficit was not removed for urban children by the age of fourteen.[53] The picture of slower urban growth is confirmed in estimates of the incremental rate of growth, which shows the velocity of growth of both male and female children to have been relatively slower from around the age of 10.5 (Figure 4).[54]

It is not clear why urban child applicants for factory work were affected by stunting at around these ages, though many child applicants would have been working in heavier or less healthy occupations prior to being

53 Since the variance of height distributions tends to increase with age, it is important not to attribute the increasing urban–rural divergence entirely to a declining nutritional status among the shortest group: A. M. Smith, S. Chinn and R. J. Rona, 'Social factors and Height Gain of Primary Schoolchildren in England and Scotland', *Annals of Human Biology*, 7 (1980), 115–24 (p. 116).
54 Cross-sectional data are used here as if they were longitudinal on account of their large number.

presented for factory work. It is likely that many of the applicants for factory work in the sample would have been members of distressed hand weaving families who accounted for around half of the total employees in textiles in the 1830s.[55] As early as 1817, applications for poor relief from weavers, winders and dyers to Manchester Poor Law overseers were said to be a hundred times greater than those from spinners and carders.[56] Hand weavers could also provide little in the way of employment for their own children since they normally required only a single 'winder' to assist. Those with several children of working age would be required to find work for them outside the home, frequently in spinning mills.[57] As Lyons pointed out, hand weaving was 'largely confined to adults from the mid-1830s onwards; the children of weavers were members of the wage labor force ... to a large degree in factories, beginning in the 1820s'.[58] Urban weavers suffered most severely from the decline in trade in the early part of the century due to their greater reliance on weaving as a sole source of income and it was in depressed urban districts that marginal child incomes became increasingly important to weaving households. A Scottish mill owner pointed out in 1818 that 'the little Children working with us often took more Money Home on the Saturday Night, for the Maintenance of the Family, than the Father could make on the Loom.'[59] For many poor families, the most acute point of life-cycle poverty also occurred when children reached the age of around nine or ten when poor relief payments for children would normally cease. It was around these ages that the children of weavers and others in distressed trades seem to have been pressed into spinning mills in greater numbers.[60] Hence, the

55   R. G. Kirby and A. E. Musson, *The Voice of the People: John Doherty, 1798–1854* (Manchester: Manchester University Press, 1975), p. 12.

56   PP 1818 (90), p. 247.

57   PP 1818 (90), p. 171.

58   J. Lyons, 'Family Response to Economic Decline: Handloom Weavers in Early Nineteenth-Century Lancashire', *Research in Economic History*, 12 (1989), 45–91 (p. 57). Hand weaving families in Lancashire in the 1830s typically received some form of poor relief: J. Brown, 'The Condition of England and the Standard of Living: Cotton Textiles in the Northwest, 1806–1850', *Journal of Economic History*, 50 (1990), 591–614 (p. 601).

59   PP 1818 (90), p. 72.

60   The tendency was deprecated by W. E. Hickson, a member of the Royal Commission on Unemployed Hand-Loom Weavers, who opined that weavers' children required 'protection even against the authors of their being': W. R. Greg, 'Protection of Children in Mines and Collieries', *Westminster Review*, 38 (July 1842), 86–139 (p. 138). In the early 1840s Chadwick referred to distressed domestic weavers as 'Lilliputians': E. Chadwick,

shortfall in the heights of urban child factory applicants probably reflects in large part the poor living standards of children who were *not* employed in factories and who were *not* subject to the factory acts. Because the data show the widespread deleterious effects of urban living, however, they also provide a valuable yardstick against which to compare heights of children in discrete industrial occupations and in different geographical environments at around the same time.

In 1833, the Factory Commission measured both factory and non-factory children who attended Sunday schools in Manchester and Stockport and discovered little difference in stature between the two groups (Table 4). The effect of factory occupation upon the health and growth of working children therefore appears to have been negligible. Indeed, some age cohorts of urban factory children in 1833 were taller than the broad body of northern English urban children in 1837. The similarity in heights amongst the 1833 (factory and non-factory) Sunday school subjects might be explained partly by the fact that the children would all have lived within walking distance of the schools and would have a common epidemiological environment. Their families were also likely to have had similar social class and religious backgrounds. The Children's Employment Commission observed that higher standards of cleanliness and dress were to be found amongst children in districts containing Sunday schools.[61] Boys recruited to the London Marine Society in 1833, similarly, enjoyed a considerable height advantage over northern urban children though they were not significantly taller than northern factory and non-factory boys attending the Sunday schools. Much of this might be explained by the fact that children who were able to gain admission to such associational groups by the 1830s were likely to have been drawn from somewhat better-off urban working-class families. It is also unlikely that the Marine Society would have accepted weak, sick or disabled children for sea-service training and, in such cases, those children not gaining admittance would not have been measured. It is also notable that southern agricultural workers, who were often reported to suffer from extremely low wages and poor diets compared with northern urban

Report on the Sanitary Condition of the Labouring Population of Great Britain (1842), ed. M. W. Flinn (Edinburgh: Edinburgh University Press, 1965), p. 252. In Manchester and many industrial towns the earnings of a working child would normally led to a reduction in outdoor relief: PP 1818 (90), pp. 246, 251; PP 1819 (24), pp. 369–70;
61   PP 1842 (380), p. 164.

children, were by far the tallest group of child workers.[62] Coalmining children in the early 1840s, by contrast, were consistently the shortest child occupation group (compare the heights of children working in collieries with those on Dorsetshire farms in Table 4).[63] The relative shortness of mining children does not appear to have resulted from a shortage of food, however, since miners and their children enjoyed an above-average food intake by working-class standards and their wages were often double those of agricultural and general labourers. Of eighty-six surgeons who gave evidence to the Children's Employment Commission in 1840–42, only one described miners' diets as poor and even in poorer marginal coal-districts it was reported that colliers were better fed than agricultural labourers.[64] Instead, postural factors, similar to those used to explain the deformities of mill children, were often cited in reports of short stature among mining children. Thackrah observed that coalminers working in pits containing thick coal seams were 'of good figure, and erect' whereas those required to adopt abnormal postures in thin seams had 'the spine permanently curved, and the legs frequently bowed'.[65] The Commission found that

---

62   J. Burnett, *Plenty and Want: A Social History of Diet in England from 1815 to the Present Day* (London: Scholar Press, 1979), p. 30–47; see also the arguments in S. Nicholas and and R. H. Steckel, *Tall but Poor: Nutrition, Health and Living Standards in Pre-Famine Ireland*, NBER Historical Paper 39 (Cambridge, MA: National Bureau of Economic Research, 1992).

63   P. Kirby, *Anthropometric Data Relating to working-class children, 1841* (database), UK Data Archive, University of Essex (1993), http://www.esds.ac.uk/findingData/snDescription.asp?sn=3108; P. Kirby, 'Causes of Short Stature among Coalmining Children, 1823–1850', *Economic History Review*, 48 (1995), 687–99. According to Tanner, 'there seems to be no evidence that the heights of children working in mines were actually measured' (p. 155).

64   B. R. Mitchell, *British Historical Statistics* (Cambridge: Cambridge University Press, 1988), p. 153; P. H. Lindert and J. G. Williamson, 'English Workers' Living Standards during the Industrial Revolution: a New Look', *Economic History Review*, 36 (1983), 1–25 (p. 4, tab. 2); J. G. Williamson, *Did British capitalism breed inequality?* (Winchester, MA: Allen & Unwin, 1985), p. 12, tab. 2.4; Mitchell, *British Historical Statistics*, p. 153; R. Church, *The history of the British Coal Industry, vol. 3: 1830–1913, Victorian Pre-eminence* (Oxford: Oxford University Press, 1986), p. 574; J. G. Williamson, 'Earnings Inequality in Nineteenth-Century Britain', *Journal of Economic History*, 40 (1980), 457–76; PP 1842 (381); PP 1842 (382), p. 34; F. Engels, *The Condition of the Working Class in England in 1844* (1845; Oxford: Oxford University Press, 1993), p. 250.

65   Kirby, 'Causes of Short Stature'; see also J. Humphries, 'Short Stature among Coalmining Children: A Comment', *Economic History Review*, 50 (1997), 531–7 and P. Kirby, 'Short Stature among Coalmining Children: A Rejoinder', *Economic History Review*, 50 (1997), 538–42. Thackrah equally condemned the confinement of children

'children who are employed at the pit mouth, or in farmers' service, are straighter on the legs and better looking than those working underground ... the children who do not work or have not from an early age worked in pits, are well and better formed than those, if even of the same family, who have worked at an earlier age than 12 years'.[66] Some observers claimed that the physical shape of miners was fundamentally different from that of other workers. It was thought that colliery communities were populated by a discrete shorter genotype which was sustained by the high degree of occupation succession between male members of coalmining families in isolated mining settlements.[67] Contemporary descriptions of the physical appearance of miners were frequently couched in terms of hereditary difference. John Leifchild was of the opinion that the short stature of colliers was 'hereditarily transmitted to the children' and that the evidence of this was to be found 'in some of the old collieries where the labour has been the uninterrupted occupation of generations.'[68] A contributor to the Penny Magazine observed in 1835 that 'the unions which they form [are] almost exclusively confined to families whose pursuit is similar to their own ... In these respects they are quite a distinct race from the neighbouring peasantry'.[69] Leifchild noted:

in the north, where the race has so long continued isolated, the pitman born and bred differs in his configuration from any other operative. His stature is rather diminutive, his figure disproportionate, his legs are more or less bowed, his chest protrudes, and his arms are oddly

in school rooms: 'To fix a child in a particular posture for hours, is vile tyranny, and a cruel restraint on nature', though he also argued 'that children ought not to work at all': C. T. Thackrah, The Effects of Arts, Trades, and Professions ... on Health and Longevity (London: Longman, Orme, Brown & Green, 1831; 1832), pp. 23–5, 178; PP 1831–2 (706), Q. 10502, p. 515.

66   PP 1842 (382), p. 256.

67   Kirby, 'Causes of short stature'; Humphries 'Comment'; Kirby 'Rejoinder'; R. H. Steckel, 'Heights and Human Welfare: Recent Developments and New Directions', Explorations in Economic History, 46 (2009), 1–23 (p. 4).

68   PP 1842 (381), p. 525; J. R. Leifchild, 'Life, Enterprise and Peril in Coal Mines', Quarterly Review, 110 (1861), 329–67 (pp. 341–2); J. R. Leifchild, 'Life and Labour in the Coal Fields', Cornhill Magazine, 5 (1862), 343–53 (p. 348). Rachitic causes of short stature are discussed below.

69   Anon., 'The Collieries, No. 1', Penny Magazine Monthly Supplement, 28 February–31 March 1835, 121–8 (p. 123). A Lancashire Sub-Commissioner observed in 1841 'that the colliers intermarry very much, and some portion of the deterioration in respect to their stature and physical condition is probably congenital' (PP 1842 (382), p. 188).

suspended ... In all these particulars we note the hereditary features of a class working in darkness and in constrained positions. Other men could not perform the work, and therefore the descendants of genuine pitmen do not look like other men.[70]

The distinctive body shape of child miners is evident from comparative measurements of their chest circumferences against those of children in other occupations. Mining children were by far the shortest occupation group, whilst farm boys were the tallest but miners had the largest mean chest measurements (Table 5). Here, it is possible that chest infections such as hypoxia, which can tend towards a deepening of the chest cavity, may have been responsible for some instances of 'barrel chest' amongst mining children. However there is little evidence to suggest widespread chest complaints specifically among child miners. Indeed, a 1905 report on deaths from lung diseases showed that young miners were less likely to die of lung diseases than the average of those employed in other industries whereas older miners in the age-group 55–65 had a 30 per cent greater chance of death from long-term lung disease compared with other occupations.[71] Chronic pulmonary diseases were therefore unlikely to have been responsible for the relatively larger chest circumferences of child miners). There was also a clear correlation between the thicknesses of coal seams being worked and the ages at which children were employed. The proportions of younger and smaller children were much greater in pits that worked narrow seams (Table 6).

A further factor to affect the growth of mining children was their complete deficiency of ultraviolet light during normal working hours, which is thought to have contributed to slow and abnormal bone growth.[72]

---

70   Leifchild, 'Life, Enterprise and Peril', pp. 358–9.

71   R. Wilson, 'On the Coal-Miners of Durham and Northumberland, their Habits and Diseases', *Transactions of the British Association for the Advancement of Science*, 33 (1863), 126; L. Ward, 'Effect of British Statutory Regulations Directed to the Improvement of Hygienic Conditions of Industrial Occupations', *Journal of the Royal Statistical Society*, 68 (1905), 435–525 (p. 511).

72   Kirby, 'Causes of Short Stature'. The effects of rickets in stunting growth was clearly demonstrated in a study of skeletons in 1832: A. Shaw, 'Upon Distortion of the Spine and Pelvis, from Rickets; with illustrations of a peculiar Conformation of the Skeleton produced by that disease, a paper read to the Medico-Chirurgical Society, 22 May 1832', *London Medical Gazette*, 10 (1832), 397–8. A study of the relationship between nutrition and human growth notes that 'variation in growth ... especially in height, is essentially an expression of the variation in rates of bone growth': L. A. Malcolm, 'Protein-Energy

Table 5: Mean chest circumferences, males working in collieries and on farms, 1841

Age	8	9	10	11	12	13
Collieries	23.72	24.75	25.22	26.40	26.48	27.42
Farms	22.96	25.85	25.19	26.15	26.17	26.72

Source: PP 1842 [381], App. C., pp. 212–14; App. D., p. 215; App. E, p. 216; PP 1842 [382], App. A, pp. 77–86, tabs. 1–5.

Table 6: Age-groups (per cent) of working miners by seam height: 5742 males in seventy-seven west Yorkshire pits, 1841

	Maximum height of seam (inches)								
Age-group	24	36	48	60	72	84	96	108	120
under-7	5.94	0.59	0.12	1.23	0.00	0.00	0.58	0.00	0.00
8–9	16.28	4.22	3.44	1.29	0.85	3.70	2.33	0.00	0.53
10–12	25.06	17.17	9.33	13.62	13.18	6.17	6.68	7.61	13.46
13–17	17.70	30.77	19.86	21.37	19.96	23.46	14.23	23.84	23.57
adults	35.02	47.24	67.25	63.49	66.01	66.67	76.19	68.55	62.44

Notes: Where two seam heights were entered for the same pit, the mean of both is used.
Source: Proportions derived from employers returns to the Children's Employment Commission (PP 1842 [381], App. B, pp. 210–11).

Most mining children were employed as hauliers and worked underground for around ten to twelve hours per day. The absence of pit-head lighting at many pits meant that coal needed to be landed at the pit head during daylight and this required child workers to be underground during daylight hours.[73] John Wilson, who began work in 1850 at the age of thirteen, recalled in his autobiography, 'In the winter time the boys hardly ever saw daylight except on Sunday', and Moses Horler recalled that in the mines of Somerset during the early 1840s children worked 'not

Malnutrition and Growth', in *Human growth*, ed. F. Falkner and J. M. Tanner (London: Plenum Press, 1979), vol. 3, pp. 361–72 (p. 367).
73   P. E. H. Hair, 'The Social History of British Coalminers' (D.Phil. thesis, University of Oxford, 1955), pp. 114–15. In the second quarter of the nineteenth century, the illumination of pit-heads was confined to a minority of technologically advanced north-east pits.

seeing daylight for a whole week in the winter time, as they had to go underground at 4 o'clock in the morning, not coming up again until after dark in the evening'.[74] Unsurprisingly, rickets was a common complaint amongst mining children.[75] Underground work deprived children of sufficient amounts of ultraviolet radiation necessary for the conversion of the pre-hormone 7-dehydrocholesterol into calciferol (an essential hormone which aids the calcification of bone). This deficiency would have resulted in the growth of soft bone, whilst the regular stresses and strains resulting from pushing or pulling coal trolleys would almost certainly have contributed further to retarded skeletal development.[76]

Sunlight deprivation also affected a wide range of children in urban manufacturing districts. The dense pall of smoke that hung over most industrial towns and cities at high northern latitudes led to poor light penetration and to widespread bone deformities.[77] Ferriar reported a tendency towards physical distortions among families occupying dark, enclosed, dwellings in Manchester during the early nineteenth century.[78] Early textiles mills and workshops, moreover, often crammed new machinery into sunless rooms and cellars and, as early as 1784, Percival's report on Radcliffe had remarked that the mill windows were too small to admit sufficient amounts of light. By the later 1880s, the British Medical Association had established that the greatest frequency of rickets was to

74   J. Wilson, *Memories of a Labour Leader* (London: T. Fisher Unwin, 1910), p. 69; M. Horler, *The Early Recollections of Moses Horler*, ed. M. F. and H. Coombs (Radstock: n.p., 1900), p. 14.

75   In 1842 Thomas Rayner, a surgeon of twenty-seven years' practice, noted: 'Collier children are liable to rickets ... The privation from light also tends to prevent the healthy action of the skin' (PP 1842 (381), p. 292).

76   W. F. Loomis, 'Rickets', *Scientific American*, 223(6) (1970), 76–91 (p. 77); A. Hardy, 'Rickets and the Rest: Child-care, Diet and the Infectious Children's Diseases, 1850–1914', *Social History of Medicine*, 5 (1992), 389–412. For children who left the pit during daylight, it is likely that a covering of coal-dust on the skin would have diminished further the penetration of ultraviolet radiation.

77   Ultraviolet light deprivation was also more intense during the darker winter months (Loomis, pp. 77, 88).

78   J. Ferriar, 'Prevention of Fevers in Great Towns', *Medical Histories and Reflections* (London: W. Bulmer & Co., 1810), vol. 2, 213–47 (p. 217). Fish can synthesise calciferol in the absence of ultraviolet radiation so fish products (particularly fish liver oil) are a very good substitute for the absence of ultraviolet radiation: T. Percival, 'Observations on the Medicinal Uses of the Oleum Jecoris Aselli, or Cod Liver Oil, in the Chronic Rhumatism, and Other Painful Disorders', in *Essays Medical, Philosophical, and Experimental* (Warrington: J. Johnson, 1789), pp. 354–62.

Table 7: Average stature and weight of adult males aged 23–50 years in different occupations, environments and classes, 1883

	inches	lbs	cases
Agricultural workers, Galloway	70.50	173.6	75
Fishermen, Flamborough	68.71	166.8	68
Athletes (running, jumping and walking)	68.34	143.7	89
Lead-miners, Wanlockhead	68.43	163.9	92
Coal-miners, Durham	66.38	152.4	51
Town population, Edinburgh and Glasgow	66.35	137.2	32
Lead-miners, Cardigan	66.30	155.2	328
Town population, Sheffield	65.80	142.5	100
Town population, Bristol	65.77	142.4	300

Source: British Association for the Advancement of Science, *Final report of the anthropometric committee*, p. 271, tab. 7.

be found in 'the manufacturing district belonging to the great coal-field of Lancashire and Yorkshire and its extensions southwards into Cheshire and Staffordshire and into Derbyshire and Notts ... The coalfield of the Black Country ... is even more closely set with industrial towns, and here the same thing is observable'.[79] A striking urban–rural difference in achieved heights was evident in a report of 1883 by the British Association which found the mean achieved height of male adult agricultural workers in Galloway to be 70.50 inches whilst the mean of Durham coal miners was 66.38 inches (the average for County Durham was 67.70). The average of male town dwellers in Bristol, meanwhile, was 65.77 inches (Table 7).[80]

Evidence of child heights recorded in the major state inquiries suggests strongly that (with the singular exception of coalmining children) urban environment, rather than industrial occupation, was the major factor in the relative short stature of children. This finding is underpinned by the fact that height differences between children in textiles mills and those in other urban occupations were largely insignificant. Although there is

79   I. Owen, 'Geographical Distribution of Rickets, Acute and Subacute Rheumatism, Chorea, Cancer, and Urinary Calculus in the British Islands', *British Medical Journal*, 1 (1889), 113–16 (p. 114).
80   British Association for the Advancement of Science, *Final report of the anthropometric committee* (London: J. Murray, 1884), p. 262, p. 271, tab. 7.

no quantitative evidence of child heights in factories prior to the 1830s, there is anecdotal evidence from doctors who lived and worked alongside factory workers that no height deficiency existed amongst mill children. In his evidence to the 1816 Peel Committee, for example, the Oldham surgeon, Kinder Wood, argued that the growth of textiles workers was:

> not at all stinted by this employment ... I have examined a great many of these for the army, who have been brought up in these works; they are generally tall, and of a slender configuration ... I know this differs from the common opinion [but] I have many reasons for thinking so ... I do not know how it may be found in other districts; I cannot speak as to them. I should wish to speak practically; the children in my own district rather gain height than otherwise ... My information is the result of general observations, and not of picked-up intelligence.[81]

The subsequent Kenyon inquiry of 1818 conducted a survey of Manchester Sunday schools and found 'not much Difference, in point of Health or Appearance, amongst those employed in Cotton Factories, when compared with those who worked at other Trades; but considerable Difference in favour of those Children who worked at no Employment at all.'[82]

There is much scope for further research to establish the relationship between occupation and children's physical growth. Data collected in the 1830s and 40s may provide the basis for more extensive quantitative analysis.[83] However, background epidemiological factors and occupational selection effects may pose major obstacles to the use of height records in drawing conclusions about the impact on health of child and adolescent occupations. It cannot be assumed that short stature and other aspects of poor physical growth will always result from poor working conditions. Indeed, in many child occupations, strong selection effects appear to have operated on the basis of height, strength and relative disability. As Hutt suggested, 'If there *was* a slightly larger proportion of deformity or puniness among the factory children, this might be accounted for by

---

81   PP 1816 (397), pp. 192, 197, 206. Charles Wing omitted Wood's observational evidence from his selected evidence on stature in *Evils of the Factory System*.
82   PP 1818 (90), p. 143; see also pp. 28–9.
83   See P. Kirby, *The Physical Stature of 16,402 Children in Northern English Factory Districts, 1837* (database), UK Data Archive, University of Essex (2010), http://www.esds. ac.uk/findingData/snDescription.asp?sn=6426.

bearing in mind the frequent statement that children who were insufficiently strong for other employments were sent to the cotton factories because of the lightness of the work there.'[84] By contrast, a large body size and a degree of physical strength were the chief criteria for agricultural work. When the 1843 Poor Law assistant commissioners asked what age children were first employed on farms, a puzzled Dorsetshire farmer replied that it depended 'upon their size a great deal' and that the rate of wages received depended largely 'on the size and strength of the boy rather than his age'.[85] If strength, stature and relative disabilities, rather than age, influenced the point of entry to the labour market and the occupation followed, such selection issues may render age-specific occupational height data unreliable as an indicator of general workplace health and welfare.

---

84   W. H. Hutt, 'The Factory System of the Early Nineteenth Century', in *Capitalism and the Historians*, ed. F. A. Hayek (Chicago: University of Chicago Press, 1954), pp. 160–88 (p. 178).

85   PP 1843 [510], pp. 29, 33, 176; see also pp. 200, 206, 341.

4

The Ill-Treatment of Working Children

The corporal punishment of working children occupies an important position in both the history of child labour and in wider discussions about the general welfare of children in the past. The majority of historical discussions of child punishment in early mills and factories have implied that physical abuse was common and many accounts have relied heavily upon contemporary anecdotal accounts of brutality gathered from government reports such as the Sadler Committee of 1831–32. The Hammonds, for example, argued that in cotton mills 'scarcely an hour passed in the long day without the sound of beating and cries of pain', whilst James Walvin has claimed that in textiles mills 'thousands of pathetic children were beaten awake, kept awake by beating and, at the end of the day, fell asleep too exhausted to eat'.[1] Such generalised statements have become a mainstay of social histories of eighteenth and nineteenth-century industrial life, although scholars have rarely questioned the evidence base upon which assumptions rest and few have investigated the methods or rationale of workplace violence. Indeed, the functions of workplace violence and the social origins of its victims have remained largely unexplored beyond the mainly selective evidence of early government inquiries. The consensus is that early factories and mines were intrinsically abusive places for children. This chapter moves towards a broader and more diffuse set of explanations of violence towards child workers. It suggests that the sheer diversity of forms of ill-treatment and the variety of social contexts in which such punishments were administered (coupled with a scarcity of trustworthy evidence) renders any generalised assumptions about the extent

---

1   J. L. Hammond and B. Hammond, *The Town Labourer, 1760–1832: The New Civilisation* (1917; London: Longmans, Green & Company, 1966), p. 160; J. Walvin, *A Child's World: A Social History of English Childhood, 1800–1914* (Harmondsworth: Penguin, 1982), pp. 64–5. An extensive narrative biography of the mill apprentice, Robert Blincoe, claimed to be 'a life that illuminates a violent age': J. Waller, *The Real Oliver Twist. Robert Blincoe: A Life that Illuminates a Violent Age* (Thriplow: Icon Books, 2006).

and severity of violence against industrial children extremely unreliable. A concentration upon supposed 'industrial' punishments has also largely overshadowed other important social, cultural and economic influences and it is therefore vital to explore the extent to which violence against children arose from specific workplace factors or was indicative of broader customs and practices. Cultural norms in the past, for example, may have served to legitimise violence because society itself accepted higher levels of aggression in everyday life. Moreover, the social background of children may have played a decisive role in predisposing them to violent behaviour. Groups such as parish apprentices, without parents or protectors in the workplace, often experienced greater levels of cruelty and violence, largely irrespective of the occupation they followed. The dependent position of such children also meant that they were not free to remove themselves from harsh and abusive situations. It has also been argued, controversially, that the beating of factory children may have been inflicted positively to increase their productivity and bring about a greater regularity of effort. Research on the relationship between workplace safety and corporal punishment has also shown how the increasing complexity of some industrial processes posed novel safety risks and led to regulated forms of corporal punishment, followed subsequently by legislative efforts to exclude young children from the production process.[2] It is crucial therefore that any analysis of violence against working children in the past is set within a broad range of economic, social and industrial situations in which such abuse occurred.

Corporal punishment and the working-class child

Eighteenth and early nineteenth-century children were exposed to greater levels of violence in everyday life compared with modern children. It was possible for a working-class child of the 1830s, for example, to witness

2   C. Nardinelli, 'Corporal Punishment and Children's Wages in Nineteenth-Century Britain', *Explorations in Economic History*, 19 (1982), 283–95; P. Kirby, 'The Historic Viability of Child Labour and the Mines Act of 1842', in *A Thing of the Past? Child Labour in Britain in the Nineteenth and Twentieth Centuries*, ed. M. Lavalette (Liverpool: Liverpool University Press, 1999), pp. 101–17 (pp. 106–8). See also the survey of household violence drawn from a sample of working-class autobiographies in J. Humphries, 'Childhood and Violence in Working-Class England, 1800–1870', in *Childhood and Violence in the Western Tradition*, ed. L. Brockliss and H. Montgomery (Oxford: Oxbow Press, 2010), pp. 135–40.

a public execution, a flogging, a drunken fight or the ill-treatment of animals for sport.³ The cultural lives of children also revolved around games and activities which often involved violence and which frequently mimicked adult attitudes and behaviours. One autobiographer recalled his 'boyish delight' at a day out with the local rat-catcher: 'In those days I loved to kill. In fact, everything that came my way had to die. This, I think, was the spirit of the times. All boys delighted in it. It was a hard cruel age.'⁴ Gang fighting and bullying were also commonplace, as the young Joseph Arch recalled:

> My clothing was the coarsest. I had to go to school in a smock-frock and old hobnailed boots, and my work-a-day garb was the same. The sons of the wheelwrights, the master tailor, and the tradesmen were just becoming genteel, and used to dress in shoddy cloth. These peacocky youngsters would cheek the lads in smock-frocks whenever they got the chance, and many a stand-up fight we used to have – regular pitched battles of smock-frock against cloth-coat, they were.⁵

Violence was also widely employed in political and industrial disputes. The Earl of Durham recalled the rough justice meted out to blackleg miners: 'One of the Union practices ... was to strip a recusant stark naked and flog him thro' a village before the eyes of women and children!'⁶ Employers, for their part, would readily call in the militia to deal with large-scale disputes and political demonstrations. The factory reformer Richard Oastler, meanwhile, proposed that factory legislation should allow for the flogging and pillorying of recalcitrant factory owners, whilst in 1833 effigies of the factory commissioners were burned by protesters.⁷ Casual violence was also ubiquitous in the domestic workplace: a weaver's son described his introduction to productive work: 'I had played at

3   Nardinelli, 'Corporal punishment', p. 286; M. A. Crowther, *The Workhouse System, 1834–1929: The History of an English Social Institution* (London: Methuen, 1983), p. 33.
4   A. Ireson, 'Reminiscences' (1929–30), in *Destiny Obscure: Autobiographies of Childhood, Education and Family from the 1820s to the 1920s*, ed. J. Burnett (London: Allen Lane, 1982), pp. 70–7 (p. 75).
5   J. Arch, *From Ploughtail to Parliament: An Autobiography* (1897–8; London: Ebury Press, 1986), p. 31.
6   L. Cooper, *Radical Jack* (London: Cresset Press, 1959), p. 107, quoted in B. Duffy, 'Coal, Class and Education in the North-East', *Past & Present*, 90 (1981), 142–51 (p. 147).
7   P. Kirby, *Child Labour in Britain, 1750–1870* (Basingstoke: Palgrave, 2003), p. 98; J. T. Ward, *The Factory Movement, 1830–1855* (London: Macmillan, 1962), p. 98.

turning a handle ... but now I must work. I was put to the bobbin-wheel. How I hated being chained to the stool and how I suffered the effects of having "bad bobbins" flung at my head!'⁸ The pages of the blue books are strewn with examples of ill-treatment in the small domestic industrial enterprises that characterised the first industrial revolution. In Birmingham metalware workshops, apprentices were said to be universally ill-used and treated 'with ferocious violence ... on bodies exhausted by overwork'.⁹ An acceptance of violence in the workplace seems to have been long-established. Medieval guild statutes enshrined the rights of masters to punish apprentices and indentures often contained explicit provisions for masters to administer physical punishment where it was thought appropriate.¹⁰ Physical discipline was also the customary method of keeping order in schools. The stick and whip were commonly found in Gothic art as symbols of the teaching profession, and eighteenth and nineteenth-century teachers have been described as 'at best, incompetents, at worst, vicious brutes'.¹¹ Indeed, Laslett observed that the most important material object in the world of early-modern children may have been the stick.¹² Few working-class children could therefore avoid some measure of violence either at home, school or work.¹³ Moreover,

8   D. Vincent, *Bread, Knowledge and Freedom: A Study of Nineteenth-Century Working-Class Autobiography* (London: Methuen, 1981), p. 76, cited in E. P. Hennock, 'Socialization and Working-Class Childhood in Nineteenth-Century England' (mimeo., University of Liverpool, 1989), p. 6.

9   PP 1843 [431], pp. 80–1 (and see the examples on pp. 80–5). See also E. Hopkins, *Childhood Transformed: Working-Class Children in Nineteenth-Century England* (Manchester: Manchester University Press, 1994), pp. 27–9.

10   S. Shahar, *Childhood in the Middle Ages* (London: Routledge, 1990), p. 173. Pelling has argued that physical injury was 'not necessarily pre-eminent in the minds of contemporaries among the wrongs done to early modern apprentices': M. Pelling, 'Child Health as a Social Value in Early Modern England', *Social History of Medicine*, 1 (1988), 135–64 (pp. 161–2).

11   Shahar, p. 175; A. Tropp, *The School Teachers: The Growth of the Teaching Profession in England and Wales from 1800 to the Present Day* (London: Heinemann, 1957), pp. 10–11. For a recent discussion of school punishments see J. Middleton, 'Thomas Hopley and Mid-Victorian Attitudes to Corporal Punishment', *History of Education*, 34 (November 2005), 599–615. Rooke observed that it 'was not until after the passage of the Education Act of 1870 that the administration of corporal punishment became an issue to capture the national imagination': P. J. Rooke, 'A Study of Rewards and Punishments in the Elementary Schools of England and Wales, 1800–1893' (MA thesis, University of London, 1962), p. 9.

12   P. Laslett, *The World we have Lost* (London: Methuen, 1965), p. 105.

13   J. M. Beattie, *Crime and the Courts in England, 1660–1800* (Oxford: Oxford

parents who had themselves suffered physical violence as children would be more likely to accept it as a normal part of the upbringing of their own offspring. The ill-treatment of children in the workplace was therefore embedded within a broader range of social conventions attached to both corrective and irrational violence.

Disabilities and unusual character traits also predisposed many children to ill-treatment. Shahar has pointed out that neglect and violence were more likely to be experienced by 'sickly or handicapped children who require special care, nervous children, and those who are particularly vulnerable emotionally, who make almost intolerable demands, and whose crying (which is a symptom of their condition) creates additional emotional pressure on the parent.'[14] The Jarrow waggonway wright, Anthony Errington, recalled in his autobiography that during his schooldays 'haveing a small stopage in my speach which made me Lisp, I oft got the Lether strap over me.'[15] Violence against child workers might also have longer-term social implications: a female servant recalled having her nose broken by her mistress which later 'dejected my fortunes in marriage'.[16] In rural society, high rates of family dependency, low earnings, and an ever-present concern with the supply of food all contributed to an often authoritarian work discipline.[17] In an increasingly high-dependency demographic regime, it would have been surprising had there not been a continual tension between the natural anarchy of childhood and efforts by older workers to impose discipline in production situations.[18] Arch suffered severe torments at the hands of his carter who

University Press, 1986), p. 75; G. Smith, 'Expanding the Compass of Domestic violence in the Hanoverian Metropolis', *Journal of Social History*, 41 (2007), 31–54 (pp. 31–44); D. D. Gray, 'The Regulation of Violence in the Metropolis: The Prosecution of Assault in the Summary Courts, c.1780–1820', *London Journal*, 32 (2007), 75–87.

14   Shahar, p. 111.

15   P. E. H. Hair (ed.), *Coals on Rails or the Reason of my Wrighting: the Autobiography of Anthony Errington, a Tyneside Colliery Waggon and Waggonway Wright, from his Birth in 1778 to Around 1825* (Liverpool: Liverpool University Press, 1988), p. 31.

16   T. F. Thiselton-Dyer, *Old English Social Life as told by the Parish Registers* (London: Elliot Stock, 1898), pp. 172–3, cited in Pelling, 'Child Health', p. 162.

17   Laslett, *World we Have Lost*, pp. 105–6. Similarly, in modern developing economies, children who, through physical illness or weakness, are unable to contribute to the family economy tend to be at greater risk of violence: M. Fekkes, F. I. M. Pijpers, M. Fredriks, T. Vogels and S. P. Verloove-Vanhorick, 'Do Bullied Children get Ill, or do Ill Children get Bullied? A Prospective Cohort Study on the Relationship between Bullying and Health-Related Symptoms', *Pediatrics*, 117 (May 2006), 1568–74.

18   High levels of mobility amongst young rural dwellers have been explained in part by

'liked to make us dance a quickstep to the tune of the stick and the whip
… He was a cruel flogger, and the very sight of him was enough to set
some of the lads shaking in their hobnailed boots.'[19] In the 1860s, agricultural gangmasters made use of 'kicking, knocking down, beating with
hoes, spuds, or a leather strap, "dyking," or pushing into the water, and
"gibbeting," *i.e.* lifting a child off the ground and holding it there by the
chin and back of the neck until it is black in the face'.[20] In the rural lace
industry, meanwhile, small girls were beaten to deter them from 'looking
off' the lace and, in the straw-plait schools of Victorian Buckinghamshire
and Bedfordshire, mistresses were equipped with 'formidable looking
sticks'.[21]

Working children were generally not easy targets for more severe
violence, however, and serious assaults represented only a small proportion
of cases towards them. Out of 555 assault charges in Westminster between
1850 and 1853 only two involved violence between master and servant.[22]
Warner and Griller, moreover, have suggested that recorded assaults
against minors in Portsmouth as a proportion of all assaults amounted
to less than 2 per cent (a remarkably low figure given that children formed
more than 35 per cent of the population).[23] Judicial records, however,
only permit the identification of trends in more serious crimes whilst
much day-to-day workplace violence appears to have gone unrecorded.[24]
Authorities were often reluctant to intervene in cases of violence unless
it resulted in a serious injury or a death. Common assault cases rarely

feelings of dissatisfaction with the treatment received from masters: A. Kussmaul, 'The
Ambiguous Mobility of Farm Servants', *Economic History Review*, 34 (1981), 222–35;
Kirby, *Child Labour in Britain*, p. 58.
19   Arch, pp. 31–2.
20   Anon., 'Agricultural Gangs', *Quarterly Review*, 123 (1867), 173–90 (pp. 179–80).
21   I. Pinchbeck and M. Hewitt, *Children in English Society, vol. 2, From the eighteenth
century to the Children Act 1948* (London: Routledge, 1973), p. 397; P. Horn, 'Child
Workers in the Pillow Lace and Straw Plait Trades of Victorian Buckinghamshire and
Bedfordshire', *Historical Journal*, 17 (1974), 779–96 (p. 790).
22   PP 1854 (523), p. 21. These statistics do not make it clear if the perpetrator was the
master or the servant.
23   J. Warner and R. Griller, '"My Pappa is out, and my Mamma is asleep." Minors, their
Routine Activities, and Interpersonal Violence in an Early Modern Town, 1653–1781',
Journal of Social History, 36 (Spring 2003), 561–84 (p. 576).
24   Although Amussen, through a study of court records, has provided a valuable insight
into the kinds of expectations and meanings of violence in the domestic context: S. D.
Amussen, 'Punishment, Discipline, and Power: The Social Meanings of Violence in Early
Modern England', *Journal of British Studies*, 34 (January 1995), 1–34.

proceeded beyond the summary level and even where cases were brought to court, they would often be quickly dismissed or the perpetrators bound over without further action.[25] The rarity of prosecutions against masters therefore probably concealed a more widespread acceptance of low-level abuse of child workers.[26] The study of early workplace ill-treatment of children is made even more difficult by the fact that a great deal of production took place in the mostly hidden domestic sphere where there was often a blurring of the boundaries between industrial and domestic violence.[27] Indeed, many child workers in domestic-industrial situations were the children or close relatives of masters and were therefore subject to customary levels of domestic violence. Such abuse in domestic situations was often tolerated or even condoned, although there seem to have been clear limits to which beating might be used, even within the privacy of the home.[28] As Tomes put it, 'In a community where physical violence occurred frequently, these crimes were deviant not in the nature but in the level of their violence.'[29]

Beatings were also much more common and more severe amongst apprentices against whom sanctions such as deprivation of wages or fines were likely to have been less effective.[30] As Adam Smith noted in 1776, 'A journeyman who works by the piece is likely to be industrious, because he derives a benefit from every exertion of his industry. An apprentice is likely to be idle, and almost always is so, because he has no immediate

25 P. King, 'Punishing Assault: The Transformation of Attitudes in the English Courts', *Journal of Interdisciplinary History*, 27 (Summer 1996), 43–74 (p. 46).
26 S. Cretney, 'Children, Cruelty and Corporal Punishment in Twentieth-Century England: the Legal Framework', in *Childhood and Violence*, ed. Brockliss and Montgomery, pp. 151–8 (p. 152); H. Leyser, 'Corporal Punishment and the Two Christianities', in *Childhood and Violence*, ed. Brockliss and Montgomery, pp. 113–22 (p. 121).
27 J. S. Cockburn, 'Patterns of Violence in English Society: Homicide in Kent, 1560–1985', *Past & Present*, 130 (1991), 70–106. As Cockburn pointed out, 'The true dimensions of domestic violence in earlier times are irretrievably lost behind a veil of domestic privacy, societal reticence and the common-law doctrine which sanctioned the "moderate" correction of wives, children and servants by heads of households' (pp. 93–5).
28 Amussen argues that 'Discipline used with restraint helped keep subordinate members of the community – wives, children, and servants – in order. Punishment without restraint created disorder' (p. 18).
29 N. Tomes, 'A "Torrent of Abuse": Crimes of Violence between Working-Class Men and Women in London, 1840–1875', *Journal of Social History*, 11 (Spring 1978), 328–45 (p. 329).
30 S. Pollard, 'Factory Discipline in the Industrial Revolution', *Economic History Review*, 16 (1963/4), 254–71 (p. 260).

interest to be otherwise.'[31] Significant variations existed in the intensity of beatings according to a child's employment contracts and status. This was the case even in individual sectors. In metal trades, for example, 79 per cent of apprentices were beaten in the workplace compared with only 48 per cent of free child labourers.[32] Apprentice initiation ceremonies often involved violence, humiliation and threats which were intended to impress upon the new apprentice his lowly position in the hierarchy of the workplace.[33] The failure amongst newly apprenticed shipwrights to pay 'footing' or 'maiden garnish' (the provision of alcoholic drink for the older 'mates') might result in a flogging. The young William Lovett recounted how, as a youth, he had to provide drink for his mates in cabinet-making workshops under pain of a beating. Meanwhile, newly recruited 'trappers' in the Durham coal district were sometimes nailed by their jackets to the ventilation doors.[34] For children apprenticed from institutional care, few efforts were made to judge the suitability of prospective masters and the high degree of social and spatial isolation amongst such children meant that their treatment was largely dependent upon the character and mental condition of the master to whom they were bound.[35] Isolated orphans and pauper children were unable to compare their own treatment with conditions elsewhere and their term of binding (usually over several years) meant that they had little chance of escape from abusive masters. Children locked away in remote rural apprentice-houses also had little opportunity to approach town magistrates.[36] The Children's Employment Commission reported an instance of the systematic battering of a fatherless apprentice which was brought to court following a long period of hidden and escalating abuse:

31   A. Smith, *An Inquiry into the Nature and Causes of the Wealth of Nations*, ed. R. H. Campbell, A. S. Skinner and W. B. Todd (Oxford: Clarendon Press, 1976), pp. 136–7, cited in Nardinelli, 'Corporal Punishment', p. 287. Pollard thought that workplace beatings 'clearly belonged to the older, personal relationships and were common with apprentices, against whom few other sanctions were possible' (p. 260).

32   Nardinelli, 'Corporal Punishment', p. 287.

33   L. Brockliss, 'Apprenticeship in Northwest Europe, 1300–1850', in *Childhood and Violence*, ed. Brockliss and Montgomery, pp. 171–80 (pp. 174–5).

34   I. J. Prothero, *Artisans and Politics in Early Nineteenth-Century London* (Folkestone: Dawson, 1979), p. 34.

35   M. Anderson, 'Sociological History and the Working-Class Family, Smelser Revisited', *Social History*, 1 (1976), 317–34 (p. 327); J. Lane, *Apprenticeship in England, 1600–1914* (London: University College Press, 1996), p. 219.

36   Ward, *Factory Movement*, p. 19.

His posteriors and loins were beaten to a jelly; his head, which was almost cleared of hair on the scalp, had the marks of many old wounds upon it which had healed up; one of the bones in one arm was broken below the elbow, and, from the appearance, seemed to have been so for some time ... The boy, on being brought before the magistrates, was unable either to sit or stand, and was placed on the floor of the office, laid on his side on a small cradle bed ... It appeared from the evidence that the boy's arm had been broken by a blow with an iron rail, and the fracture had never been set, and that he had been kept at work for several weeks with his arm in the condition above described. It further appeared in evidence, and was admitted by [the boy's master] that he had been in the habit of beating the boy with a flat piece of wood, in which a nail was driven and projected about half an inch. The blows had been inflicted with such violence that they had penetrated the skin, and caused the wounds described ... The boy had been starved for want of food, and his body presented all the marks of emaciation. This brutal master had kept him at work as a waggoner until he was no longer of use, and then sent him home in a cart to his mother, who was a poor widow, residing in Church-lane, Rochdale.[37]

Pauper children also faced greater workplace dangers compared with the 'free' children of established workers. The Midland Mining Commission of 1843 reported that apprentices were 'forced into places that make them run away from their masters ... they are forced to do jobs which other lads would not do without more money and extra pay'.[38] The most severe treatment was found amongst apprentices in subcontracting situations: for example, butties in the Derbyshire coal district sometimes kept gangs of children underground for thirty-six hours whilst working double shifts.[39] Competition for jobs was a major source of violent behaviour. Parish apprentices also tended to displace the children of established workers and this posed a major threat to marginal household incomes.[40]

---

37   PP 1842 (382), p. 182.
38   PP 1843 [431], p. xlii.
39   N. K. Buxton, *The Economic Development of the British Coal Industry from Industrial Revolution to the Present Day* (London: Batsford, 1978), pp. 125–6. Hair cited several similar cases: P. E. H. Hair, 'The Social History of British Coalminers' (D.Phil. thesis, University of Oxford, 1955), pp. 217–19.
40   Political economists, and factory reformers too, disliked the effects of the system on the freedom of labour. The Assistant Poor Law Commissioner, E. C. Tufnell, noted: 'If the parish premium displaces the labour of the child of an independent labourer, look

Bullying of pauper apprentices was extremely common. The overseer of the Oldham Union reported that he had had to summon three cases of severe bullying against apprentices:

> two of [the apprentices] were parish children, and one was the child of a widow, who was a pauper ... [The boys] ... had not brought dinners of their own down the pits, and being hungry, it was supposed they had stolen other boys' dinners which were missing; for this they were punished in the following manner: – one of the biggest of the boys and a young man got the boy's head between his legs, and each boy in the pit – and there were 18 to 20 of them – inflicted 12 strokes on the boy's rump and loins with a cat ... the flesh of the rump and loins was beaten to a jelly.[41]

The state took some limited steps towards alleviating the problems suffered by apprentices and successive attempts were made during the second half of the eighteenth century to afford them greater legal rights. From 1747, children who could prove ill-treatment could be released from their indentures and by 1792 provision had been made for the fining of violent masters.[42] The Health and Morals of Apprentices Act of 1802 marked a major effort to preserve the health of parish children. However, the practical application of such regulations was short-lived due to the decline in the numbers of parish apprentices in the labour force during the early nineteenth century. By the 1830s and 40s, the vast majority of child workers were employed on terms similar to those of free adults and were increasingly paid money wages, accompanied by a growing tendency for urban child workers to be based near to their place of work and to remain living in the parental home. The increased scrutiny and parental contact afforded by this transition almost certainly contributed to a decline in the proportions of working children at risk of serious abuse.[43]

Few first-hand accounts of pauper apprenticeship have survived and

---

at the result; the parish congratulates itself upon having got a pauper child into a good place, whilst an independent labourer is disappointed of his just hopes, and perhaps is instantly made a pauper' (PP 1837 [73], App. B, pp. 89–90).

41   PP 1842 (380), pp. 43–4; PP 1842 (382), p. 235.

42   20 Geo. II, c. 19; 32 Geo. III, c. 57.

43   R. Burr Litchfield, 'The Family and the Mill: Cotton Mill Work, Family Work Patterns, and Fertility in Mid-Victorian Stockport', in *The Victorian Family: Structure and Stresses*, ed. A. S. Wohl (London: Croom Helm, 1978), pp. 180–96 (p. 192).

"Love conquered Fear."

Figure 5: 'Love conquered Fear', in F. Trollope, *The Life and Adventures of Michael Armstrong the Factory Boy* (London: Henry Colburn, 1840), facing p. 82

Figure 6: 'Frontispiece', in J. C. Cobden, *The White Slaves of England,
Compiled from Official Documents* (2nd edn, New York: Saxton,
Barker & Co., 1860), p. 1

those that have are beset by serious problems of interpretation.[44] In 1779, an illegitimate orphan, Robert Blincoe, was one of around eighty pauper children bound from the St Pancras workhouse to mills in Nottingham and Derbyshire, and his *Memoir* highlights particular problems because of its subsequent anachronistic reporting during the factory reform campaign of the early 1830s.[45] Writing more than a quarter of a century after the events described, the author of the *Memoir* recounted insanitary conditions, regular and indiscriminate beatings, and intense hunger which, according to the *Memoir*, drove children to steal food from the trough of the mill-owner's pigs.[46] Blincoe's savage overlooker 'used to tie him up by the wrists to a cross beam and keep him suspended over the machinery till his agony was extreme [and] lift the apprentices up by their ears, shake them violently and then dash them down upon the floor with the utmost fury'.[47] Reports of abuse against vulnerable factory apprentices – many modelled on the Blincoe *Memoir* – appeared in popular periodical articles and novels which stressed the alleged cruelty of textiles mills.[48] Amongst these was Frances Trollope's highly romanticised account of Blincoe's life, *The Life and Adventures of Michael Armstrong, the Factory Boy* (1840) and contained evocative plates depicting hardships in the life of

44   Lane, *Apprenticeship*, p. 17.
45   W. Hutton, *History of Derby* (London: Nichols, Son & Bentley, 1791); J. Brown (ed), *A Memoir of Robert Blincoe, an orphan boy* (Manchester: J. Doherty, 1832). See also S. D. Chapman, *The Early Factory Masters: the Transition to the Factory System in the Midlands Textile Industry* (Newton Abbot: David & Charles, 1967); M. H. Mackenzie, 'Cressbrook and Litton Mills, 1779–1835', *Derbyshire Archaeological Journal*, 88 (1968), 1–15; S. D. Chapman, 'Cressbrook and Litton Mills: An Alternative View', *Derbyshire Archaeological Journal*, 89 (1969), 86–90; M. H. Mackenzie, 'Cressbrook and Litton Mills: A Reply', *Derbyshire Archaeological Journal*, 90 (1970), 56–9. See also M. H. Mackenzie, 'Cressbrook Mill, 1810–1835, *Derbyshire Archaeological Journal*, 90 (1970), 60–71.
46   Blincoe's amanuensis and publisher were avowed opponents of factory conditions and published his story with the intent to vilify factory owners; Blincoe's *Memoir* was first published in 1828 by Richard Carlile in the Radical paper *The Lion* but in 1832, at the height of agitation for factory reform, was republished by John Doherty, the Manchester printer and trade union leader. A. E. Musson, 'Robert Blincoe and the Early Factory System', in *Trade Union and Social History*, ed. A. E. Musson (London: Frank Cass, 1974), pp. 195–206 (p. 195–7).
47   L. C. A. Knowles, *Industrial and Commercial Revolutions in Great Britain During the Nineteenth Century* (London: Routledge, 1921), p. 92n.
48   I. Kovačević and S. B. Kanner, 'Blue Book into Novel: The Forgotten Industrial Fiction of Charlotte Elizabeth Tonna', *Nineteenth Century Fiction*, 25 (1970), 152–73; W. H. Chaloner, 'Mrs Trollope and the Early Factory System', *Victorian Studies*, 4, 2 (December 1960), 159–66.

the eponymous character.[49] However, even Trollope's emotive images were further embellished in subsequent polemical literature. One of her plates was re-engraved as the frontispiece of Cobden's *White Slaves of England* (1860) in which an invented figure of an overman had been added in the act of beating a child (compare figures 5 and 6).[50]

Industrial corporal punishments

It is not possible to show quantitatively whether punishments were more severe in the newer industries compared with smaller domestic enterprises. Pollard claimed that about 10 per cent of factory owners who provided returns to the 1833 Factory Commission admitted to using corporal punishment. However, this reported figure may be inaccurate since only the better employers provided returns. It would also have been foolish for factory owners to admit to beating children at a time when the issue formed an important point of attack by the factory reform lobby.[51] Nonetheless, mills and factories brought about high concentrations of workers, increasingly complex divisions of labour and a more rigid work discipline. Co-ordinated work efforts became essential to efficient and safe productivity.[52] Working hours in factories and large workshops were not limited to the hours of daylight or the cycle of the seasons

49 It was based around Blincoe's experiences together with information gathered by Trollope at meetings with Richard Oastler and John Doherty in Manchester in 1839. Chaloner, 'Mrs Trollope', pp. 159–60.

50 Cobden claimed that children 'may be *bought* at the workhouse at a cheap rate, and then they must trust to God alone for their future welfare. There is scarcely an instance in which the law ever interferes for their protection. The masters and overlookers are allowed to beat their younger operatives with impunity': J. C. Cobden, *The White Slaves of England, Compiled from Official Documents* (Cincinnati: Derby, 1853; 2nd edn, New York: Saxton, Barker & Co., 1860), p. 118.

51 Pollard, p. 263.

52 Literature on the subject of work discipline more generally includes: D. A. Reid, 'The Decline of Saint Monday, 1766–1876', *Past & Present*, 71 (May 1976), 76–101; D. A. Reid, 'Weddings, Weekdays, Work and Leisure in Urban England, 1791–1911: The Decline of Saint Monday Revisited', *Past & Present*, 153 (November 1996), 135–63; H-J. Voth, *Time and work in England, 1750–1830* (Oxford: Oxford University Press, 2000); E. P. Thompson, *The Making of the English Working Class* (1963; London: Penguin, 1980), pp. 337–8, 443–53; E. P. Thompson, 'Time, Work-Discipline and Industrial Capitalism', *Past & Present*, 38 (December 1967), 56–97; P. Kirby, 'Attendance and Work Effort in the Great Northern Coalfield, 1775–1864', *Economic History Review*, 65 (2012), 961–83.

and might be extended around the clock. Children and rural migrants often found it difficult to adapt to the regularity and time discipline imposed by large manufacturing processes.[53] The lower labour intensity of industrial work also permitted children to be engaged in work at earlier ages when they were most susceptible to violent conduct and least able to protect themselves. This often led to high levels of coercive violence. As one Scottish factory owner noted, when his works were first opened 'the children were all newcomers, and were very much beat at first before they could be taught their business'. Early factory employers such as Arkwright encountered difficulties in training his labour force 'to a precision and assiduity altogether unknown before, against which their listless and restive habits rose in continued rebellion'.[54] Moreover, most violence was inflicted upon children by their immediate supervisors on the factory floor – often their own relatives, operatives or overmen. Few examples can be found of factory owners or senior managers inflicting corporal punishment.[55] Many parents and employers also assumed that beating formed part of the training of child workers. The marginal value of child incomes meant that poor parents were often placed under great pressure to accept some measure of corporal punishment and would often beat children themselves if they were fined or dismissed from their employment. The underviewer at Hetton Colliery noted: 'The parents would prefer that the Children should be thrashed rather than fined, and sometimes propose this'.[56] A sub-commissioner of 1842 observed that a trapper dreaded being sacked because 'he knows that his discharge would be attended with the

---

53   'Alfred', the author of the *History of the Factory Movement*, described how 'little fingers and little feet were kept in ceaseless action, forced into unnatural activity by blows from the heavy hands and feet of the merciless over-looker, and the infliction of bodily pain by instruments of punishment invented by the sharpened ingenuity of insatiable selfishness': 'Alfred' [S. Kydd], *The History of the Factory Movement from the Year 1802 to the Enactment of the Ten Hours Bill In 1847* (London: Simpkin, Marshall & Co, 1857), pp. 21–2, cited in Pinchbeck and Hewitt, p. 403.
54   Pollard, pp. 255, 258.
55   By contrast, generalised reports of English cruelty to child workers appear to have been widespread throughout Europe. A Parisian professor noted in 1860: 'Many reports come from England of cruelty to children, but these are due to brutality by masters in industry, rather than ill-treatment by parents', cited in B. Knight, 'History of Child Abuse', in *Child Care Through the Centuries: An Historical Survey from Papers Given at the Tenth British Congress on the History of Medicine*, ed. J. Cule and T. Turner (Cardiff: British Society for the Social History of Medicine, 1986), pp. 109–19 (p. 112).
56   PP 1842 (380), p. 133.

loss of wages, and bring upon him the indignation of his father, more terrible to endure than the momentary vengeance of the deputy and the putters all taken together.'[57] More rarely, parents would exact retribution upon the perpetrators of excessive violence against their children. William Kershaw, who worked in a Gomersal mill in 1799, reported to his mother that he had been beaten at work with a billy-roller until he vomited blood:

> The next morning after I went to work, she followed me, and came to the slubber that had used me in that way, and gave him a sharp lecture; and when she had done she retired into the engine-feeder's house, and left me to my work; and as soon as she was gone, he beat me severely again for telling, when one of the young men that served the carder, went out and found my mother, and told her, and she came in again and inquired what instrument it was I was beaten with, but I durst not do it; some of the by-standers pointed out the instrument, the billy-roller, and she seized it immediately, and beat it about the fellow's head, and gave him one or two black eyes.[58]

There is also some evidence that boys in larger factories would occasionally turn the tables on unpopular or violent operatives by resorting to gang reprisals, though such revolts tended to occur in larger premises and would have been impossible for individual child workers or isolated apprentices.[59] Open resistance was generally practised by older children and court records show that older apprentices were more likely to be prosecuted for striking a master or a member of a master's family.[60] Some apprentices also practised sabotage, absenteeism or simply ran away.[61]

57   PP 1842 (381), p. 130.
58   PP 1831–2 (706), Q. 1150–1, pp. 46–7.
59   M. J. Childs, *Labour's Apprentices: Working-Class Lads in Late Victorian and Edwardian England* (Montreal and Kingston: McGill-Queen's University Press, 1992), p. 83.
60   Warner and Griller, p. 575. Levene has argued that relationships were perhaps more harmonious than has been supposed: A. Levene, '"Honesty, Sobriety and Diligence": Master–Apprentice Relations in Eighteenth- and Nineteenth-Century England', *Social History*, 33 (2008), 183–200.
61   See the exploration of such behaviours at the Greg enterprises in S. Peers, 'Power, Paternalism, Panopticism and Protest: Geographies of Power and Resistance in a Cotton Mill Community, Quarry Bank Mill, Styal, Cheshire, 1784–1860' (D.Phil. thesis, Oxford University, 2008), pp. 245–74.

Piece-work was almost always associated with higher levels of physical ill-treatment and the second report of the Children's Employment Commission in 1843 discovered that the highest incidence of cruelty occurred where men's wages were dependent on the pace of their child assistants.[62] The Factory Commission noted:

> The men do not practise the system of fining [towards scavengers]. The sum which they earn is so small it would be considered by many a shame to make it less. They do not, however, scruple to give them a good bobbying, as it is called, that is, beating them with a rope thickened at one end, or perhaps with a strap, or, in some few brutal instances, with the combined weapons of fist and foot.[63]

Punishments were meted out to the slowest, or least able, workers (a young Dent knitter opined that the slowest workers 'gat weel thumpt').[64] In the Derbyshire coalfield, meanwhile, young waggoners, behind with their work, would have their ears nipped by the loaders.[65] Much of the violence against young children therefore tended to arise from immediate situations on the shop floor, rather than from any specific industrial policies relating to corporal punishment. A piecer at Sadler's Committee recalled the unstructured mix of punishments and inducements adopted by operatives in the spinning factory where he had worked in the late eighteenth century, noting 'some have more humanity, and rather wish to encourage the children to attention ... Some of them who are kind have some rewards, such as some fruit; and others will keep beating the children, whether they are in fault or not.'[66] There is some evidence that children cooperated with one another to avoid beatings. A witness to the Factory Commission observed: 'If one piecer finishes piecing up his ends before another, he runs to his neighbour to help him, and thus may save him a scolding or a blow, and he may immediately after be indebted to his neighbour in return. This creates feelings of kindness'.[67]

---

62   PP 1843 [431], p. 87.
63   PP 1833 (450), pp. 45–6.
64   I. Pinchbeck, *Women Workers and the Industrial Revolution, 1750–1850* (London: Routledge, 1930), p. 234.
65   The ears of children were sometimes pierced through by the fingernails of their juvenile superiors (PP 1842 (382), pp. 284–5).
66   PP 1831–2 (706), p. 46.
67   PP 1833 (450), D1, p. 44, cited in M. Anderson, *Family Structure in Nineteenth-Century Lancashire* (Cambridge: Cambridge University Press, 1971), pp. 215–16, n. 9.

Nardinelli has argued that levels of corporal punishment against children were greater in factories and mines but that parents tolerated higher levels of physical violence because the superior wages achievable by factory children provided 'compensating differentials'. Corporal punishment, he claimed, raised the productivity and wages of industrial children by around 16–18 per cent.[68] Although such arguments have been regarded as lacking a moral dimension, a relationship between corporal punishment and productivity almost certainly existed in industrial situations and the obvious connection between the two requires at least some investigation beyond *a priori* claims of intrinsic industrial cruelty.[69] Nardinelli's analysis of industrial corporal punishment was important because it sought to explore the underlying economic motivations for much workplace violence. He posed the question of what inducements might be offered to a child who received little or no payment (or other reward) for her work and whose productivity was therefore not linked to remuneration. These are crucial questions that lie at the core of the analysis of industrial violence. However, having raised such issues, Nardinelli did not explore them thoroughly. His analysis did not investigate fully the evident variations in the severity of workplace punishments. Severe and moderate punishments are viewed equally as factors of production when it is clear from the broader body of evidence that more severe abuse probably had the least to do with the production process. Most punishments in the industrial workplace tended to be 'moderate' and not usually intended to cause any serious or permanent injury to children. Corporal punishment was also assumed to have been much more common in industrial employments, though it is clear that beatings could be equally severe in domestic workshops or in subcontracted work situations. This could be seen to be the case in agricultural gangs where wages were extremely low but where the earnings of gangmasters relied upon the piecework of child employees. Objections might also be raised about the dangers of attempting to rationalise forms of corporal

68   C. Nardinelli, *Child Labor and the Industrial Revolution* (Bloomington and Indianapolis: Indiana University Press, 1990), pp. 91–2; Nardinelli, 'Corporal Punishment', p. 289. Clark has suggested that many adult operatives 'effectively hired capitalists to make them work harder' and that the desire to do this arose because they 'lacked the self-control to achieve higher earnings on their own': G. Clark, 'Factory Discipline', *Journal of Economic History*, 3 (1994), 128–63 (p. 128).
69   Cunningham, for example, represented Nardinelli's original article as 'a spoof': H. Cunningham, 'Child Labour', *Labour History Review*, 56, 3 (1991), 48–51.

punishment. Chwe, for example, pointed out that it might 'be a justification bordering on an excuse … people hurt others because of their self-interests, and not because they are "evil" … [but] a person who hurts others might be more likely to stop if he could think of himself only as purely evil. Calling his act a rational choice allows him to say to himself, "I may be cruel, but at least I'm rational", or "It may be cruel, but at least it's effective"'. Southern plantation owners frequently stressed the efficiency and rationality of their slave-control practices, which often included beating and whipping.[70] Claims to rationality, therefore, may sometimes be used to negate claims that ill-treatment originates in cupidity or mental instability.[71] Such questions remain largely unexplored by social historians.

The corporal punishment of working children was also closely related to the maintenance of workplace safety and nowhere was this more apparent than in the coalmining industry. Throughout the first half of the nineteenth century, increases in demand for coal provided an impetus to the opening of more extensive collieries in which previously inaccessible seams were brought into production by the sinking of deeper shafts. As larger and more extensive underground workings were at greater risk of explosions as a result of accumulations of methane gas, mining engineers adopted increasingly complex methods of ventilation to purge gases from mines.[72] Underground ventilation currents were maintained by the installation of trapdoors that were frequently attended by young children. 'Trappers' were required to open such ventilation doors momentarily to allow the passage of coal tubs and then to ensure that they closed again to maintain the correct circulation of air currents. This was a simple procedure but was crucial to the safety of the entire workforce. Young trapdoor keepers would sometimes fall asleep in the warm, dark, atmosphere of the mine or would simply leave

70   The wide variety of humiliating punishments devised by leading educationists, such as 'weighting' naughty children, or forcing them to wear humiliating dress, were rationalised as being necessary to achieve desired ends: M. S. Y. Chwe, 'Why Were Workers Whipped? Pain in a Principal-Agent model', The Economic Journal, 100 (December 1990), 1109–21 (pp. 1117–8).

71   Chwe, p. 1118;

72   P. E. H. Hair, 'Mortality from Violence in British Coalmines, 1800–50', Economic History Review, 21 (1968), 545–61 (p. 549).

their doors unattended resulting in an interruption of ventilation.[73] The Durham Sub-Commissioner explained:

> In this state of sepulchral existence an insidious enemy gains upon him. His eyes are shut, and his ears fail to announce the approach of a tram. A deputy overman comes along, and a smart cut of his yard-wand at once punishes the culprit, and recalls him to his duty; and happy was it for him that he fell into the hands of the deputy overman, rather than one of the putters; for his fist would have inflicted a severer pain. The deputy overman moreover consoles him, by telling him that it was for his good that he punished him; and reminds him of boys well known to both, who when asleep had fallen down, and some had been severely wounded, and others killed. The little trapper believes that he is to blame, and makes no complaint.[74]

By the 1830s and 40s, the problem of inattentive trappers had resulted in regular patrolling of doors by overmen who inflicted regular, though moderate, corporal punishments and threats of violence. John Wilson, who began work in 1850 at the age of thirteen, noted that, 'it was considered part of the training of a boy to feel the weight of the overman's yard wand, just as there was the frequent and necessary use of the cane by the schoolmaster'.[75] George Parkinson, who began work at New Lambton in 1837 aged nine, described his first encounter with an overman, on his first day at work:

> Several men passing through my door at various times spoke kindly to the new 'trapper,' and told me to take care and keep in my hole. But one man came through, wearing blue clothes, a leather cap with a peak behind, and carrying a stick in his hand ... He looked very sternly at me, as he held up his stick in a threatening way, and said, 'Now mind, ef thoo gans to sleep and dizzent keep that door shut, thou'll get it!' ... I could not help wishing that the 'blue man' might not come through my door again, but that he might get out by some other way.[76]

---

73 Northumberland Record Office, Bell collection, *Coal Trade Office Statement*, 25 May 1842, Bell/9/122.
74 PP 1842 (381), pp. 129–30.
75 J. Wilson, *Memories of a Labour Leader* (London: T. Fisher Unwin, 1910), p. 69.
76 G. Parkinson, *True Stories of Durham Pit-Life* (2nd edn, London: Charles Kelly, 1912), pp. 20–1.

In the most advanced pits, punishments related to safety were moderate and highly regulated. The underviewer at Hetton Colliery stated that 'The overman may hit the boys gently with a bat; but nothing more is allowed'. Another testified that 'they are only corrected when they stand in need of it. The overman gives them a few strikes with a whip or stick, but not to hurt them at all badly. Boys are not beaten so as to make blood come. The beating is not more than a gentle correction'.[77] Overlookers and managers in technically advanced industrial enterprises therefore drew sharp distinctions between the requirement for moderate safety discipline and more serious violence.[78] The continuing presence of younger children in complex production situations led increasingly to a shift in employer attitudes and a desire to reduce the numbers of 'irresponsible' and inattentive child workers.[79]

In some industrial situations, the infliction of humiliation and shame was preferred to direct physical beating.[80] At the New Lanark mill, Robert Owen introduced the 'silent monitor' – a block of wood that could be placed on a machine and rotated to display a different colour according to the level of productivity or behaviour of a particular child.[81] In Bury, meanwhile, badges of disgrace were worn by recalcitrant factory children whilst those displaying good conduct and high productivity were rewarded with certificates, food and small monetary inducements.[82] Similarly, the Gregs maintained a savings scheme for their apprentices in which the sums accumulated over time and were thought to act as a disincentive for older apprentices to abscond.[83] Disobedient children were sometimes forced to hold up cards upon which their offences were written whilst others were made to wear degrading dress or forced to carry weights strapped to their bodies.[84] In some mills, the tethering or weighting of children seems to have been deployed and, during the factory debate, a witness to the Sadler Committee claimed that child doffers in Leeds had actually worked in chains. Such accounts were widely publicised by the leaders of the short

---

77   PP 1842 (380), p. 133.
78   PP 1842 (381), pp. 143, 150, 653.
79   See Kirby, 'Historic Viability of Child Labour'.
80   Peers, 'Power, Paternalism'.
81   G. D. H. Cole, *The Life of Robert Owen* (1925; 3rd edn, London: Frank Cass, 1965), pp. 104–5.
82   K. Honeyman, *Child Workers in England, 1780–1820: Parish Apprentices and the Making of the Early Industrial Labour Force* (Aldershot: Ashgate, 2007), p. 179.
83   Peers, 'Power, Paternalism'.
84   Pollard, p. 263.

time movement who were quick to draw parallels with the chaining of slaves. Although Richard Oastler claimed that children in a Wigan mill had worked whilst shackled with heavy weights, the practice was never proven.[85] One of the children said to have been chained by her overseer was subsequently examined by the Factory Commission:

> as far as my recollection goes it was a chain which belongs to the carding cans, that I spoke of; it might be taken off the cans; he would take the chain off, and put it round the waists of the children. He did not fasten them any where, nor do I know for what purpose he put the chain round their waists at all; perhaps it was to make a noise. He would tie it round their waists, but not have them held or confined by it in any manner whatever: it was more for a disgrace than anything else.[86]

The girl had later been shamed by her overseer by being forced to walk up and down 'with a bit of a Scotch cap, and a sword in her hand' as a punishment for attempting to run away.[87] The tethering of children was not peculiar to factories, however, and had long been practised in domestic situations, sometimes as a protection from domestic hazards or to ensure a child's attention to a given task. Social reformers of a later hue would have blanched at the account of the eighteenth-century Spitalfields silk weaver who recalled: 'father used to tie me down to the loom in the morning, before he went out, and dare me to leave it till he came back.'[88] Weighting had also been advocated by the leading educationist Joseph Lancaster as a punishment for idle or talkative school children and some workhouses adopted similar practices. Digby, for example, recorded the case of a twelve-year-old parish boy whose punishment for attempting to abscond from a Norfolk workhouse was to have an iron collar and a wooden yoke whilst chained by the leg to a large wooden weight.[89]

85   PP 1831–2 (706), p. 196; PP 1833 (450), D1, p. 104.
86   PP 1833 (450), C2, p. 39. There is evidence that both Oastler and Phillip Grant (another Ten Hours leader) visited the girl's mother prior to the allegations being made public: PP 1833 (450), D1, pp. 104–15; Pinchbeck and Hewitt, pp. 409–10.
87   PP 1833 (450), D1, pp. 104–15.
88   E. Kerridge, *Textile Manufacturers in Early Modern England* (Manchester: Manchester University Press, 1985), p. 209.
89   Chapman, *Early Factory Masters*, pp. 203–4; Rooke, 'Rewards and Punishments'; A. Digby, *Pauper Palaces* (London: Routledge & Kegan Paul, 1978), p. 182.

Severe violence and murder

Severe beating was rare and was generally frowned upon, not least because it was unlikely to promote greater efficiency. As Pressley pointed out, an apprentice 'was an investment in a piece of capital that if mistreated ceased to function to its maximum capacity.'[90] The majority of masters were aware that serious injuries would render a child incapable of productive labour and would be likely to lead to prosecution. Most severe punishments were therefore generally meted out by mentally ill or sadistic masters and usually had little to do with the occupation followed by child victims. Indeed, it is telling that in investigating cases of sudden and unnatural deaths amongst children in the mid-nineteenth century, the police almost always paid closest attention to circumstances such as illegitimacy or the presence of a stepfather. The occupation carried out by a deceased child was hardly ever considered to be a predisposition to violence or murder.[91] The murder of working children was, in fact, extremely rare and was almost always preceded by a history of escalating domestic abuse. Inquest juries often found it difficult to prove that ill-treatment had contributed directly to the death of a working child, however. In 1848 a seventeen-year-old London apprentice died after suffering a succession of abuses at the hands of a brutal master and mistress. The chief witness at the inquest noted that the boy, apprenticed at the age of twelve or thirteen,

> had never slept on a bedstead, and his principal food for dinner was boiled rice, and occasionally a couple of sausages and a bit of cabbage. He was worked from sixteen to eighteen hours a day, and also on the Sunday, until prevented by the magistrates at Clerkenwell Police Court. [The] witness spoke to his mistress about treating him better, when she replied, 'I will treat him worse than ever yet.' The master also said, 'That however be the treatment, it was good enough for a parish apprentice.'

The witness 'had frequently taken victuals to the deceased, for she knew

---

90   J. Pressley, 'Childhood, Education and Labour: Moral Pressure and the end of the Half-Time System' (Ph.D. thesis, Lancaster University, 2000), p. 34.
91   P. A. Sambrook, 'Childhood and Sudden Death in Staffordshire, 1851 and 1860', in *Staffordshire Histories: Essays in Honour of Michael Greenslade*, ed. P. Morgan and A. D. M. Phillips (Stafford: Staffordshire Record Society, 1999), pp. 216–52 (pp. 239–40).

he was half-starved. He had told her that his master was in the habit of beating him with a rope in the open yard, for which he was charged before the magistrates at Clerkenwell Police office on two occasions.' The cause of death was given by an apothecary as lung disease and, after long deliberation, the jury found that the boy had died from consumption 'but they considered the conduct of the master and mistress very reprehensible in keeping the deceased upon such short diet.'[92] Joseph Rae, meanwhile, was tried at Edinburgh in 1817 for the murder of his eleven-year-old apprentice following a lengthy period of cruel and sadistic treatment during which the child had been repeatedly stripped, beaten with ropes and forced to eat rotten offal. The verdict of the Court was *culpable homicide* since the proximate cause of death had been the child becoming stuck fast for several hours in a chimney whilst at work.[93] Meanwhile, the pattern of abuse and torture inflicted upon two servants bound from St Dunstan's parish between 1765 and 1767, which had been reported repeatedly and investigated by parish officers, nonetheless resulted in the death of one of the girls.[94]

Rumours about the murder of children stalked the factory debate, though little evidence was ever offered in support of such allegations. During the 1833 factory inquiry, placards proclaiming 'Child Murder no Crime!' were carried during street protests, whilst Oastler dubbed the Factory Commission 'the secret inquisition to perpetuate child murder'. Southey, too, condemned the 'soul-murder and infanticide' in factories.[95] The economic historian, Henry Gibbins, would claim that parish apprentices 'had irons riveted on their ankles with long links reaching up to the hips, and were compelled to work and sleep in these chains ... Many died and were buried secretly at night in some desolate spot, lest people

92   Anon., 'Alleged Death of a Parish Apprentice from Ill-Treatment', *The Examiner*, 22 January 1848, p. 60.

93   Anon., 'Trial of a Chimney-Sweeper for the Murder of his Apprentice', *Blackwoods Edinburgh Magazine*, August 1817, 547–8; Anon., *The Times*, 4 November 1817, p. 3.

94   Anon., 'An authentick Narrative of the many horrid Cruelties inflicted by Mrs. Elizabeth Brownrigg, upon her poor Apprentice girls', *Gentleman's Magazine*, September 1767, 433–7. The mistress was eventually hanged at Tyburn: Anon., *Genuine and Authentic Account of the Life, Trial, and Execution, of Elizabeth Brownrigg, who was Executed on Monday the 14th of September, 1767, for the Barbarous Murder of Mary Clifford, her Apprentice Girl* (London: R. Richards, 1767).

95   Ward, *Factory Movement*, pp. 24, 93; PP 1833 (450), D1, p. 104; Anon., 'Factory Children', *The Times*, 25 February, 1833, p. 3.

should notice the number of the graves'.[96] However, most deaths of child workers were said to have resulted from gross overwork. William Dodd reported in one of his letters to Lord Ashley, 'I have just heard of a girl who dropped down dead beside the frame she was working at, a few days ago; her disease was called palpitation of the heart ... it is called anything but its right name, which is neither more nor less than *murder*.'[97] There is little evidence to support allegations of child murder in the industrial workplace. An extensive survey of evidence to committees of inquiry on child labour between 1816 and 1832, reports of the 1833 Factory Commission and the Children's Employment Commission reports of 1842 and 1843, discloses no examples of the murder of children whilst at work. It is inconceivable that opponents of the factory system such as Oastler would have withheld evidence of the murder of industrial children from the major state inquiries had any existed.[98]

Accounts which describe the treatment of industrial children as intrinsically brutal, therefore, have mostly failed to take account of the historically specific circumstances under which such punishments occurred. The most serious physical violence was targeted at groups such as parish apprentices and illegitimate children who were put out to work at early ages and who generally had no protectors in the workplace.[99] The roots of severe physical violence against such children, therefore, lay chiefly in their social background rather than their occupation. It is significant that a decline in the numbers of pauper apprentices in the textiles labour force also presaged a fall in reports of factory beatings. As Robert Blincoe

96   H. de B. Gibbins, *The Industrial History of England* (London: Methuen, 1904), p. 180.

97   W. Dodd, *The Factory System Illustrated in a Series of Letters to the Right Hon. Lord Ashley* (London: John Murray, 1842), p. 226 (18 January 1842), emphasis in the original. One of Oastler's major witnesses to the Sadler Committee, Joseph Hebergam, claimed that 'about a dozen' children of the fifty he had worked with in the mill had subsequently died, though there was apparently no record of their deaths because they had already left the mill (PP 1831–2 (706), pp. 158–60).

98   PP 1816 (397); PP 1831–2 (706); PP 1833 (450), D1; PP 1834 (167); PP 1842 (380), PP 1842 (381), PP 1842 (382). The second report of the Children's Employment Commission in 1843 contains a report of the discovery of a skeleton suspected to have been that of an apprentice who had gone missing many years earlier and whose master (long since deceased) had been known to be brutal (PP 1843 [432], Q77).

99   Peter Laslett described them as 'the helpless victims of a powerful social and familial convention': P. Laslett, *Family Life and Illicit Love in Earlier Generations* (Cambridge: Cambridge University Press, 1977), p. 160.

himself stated in his testimony to the 1833 Factory Commission, his own gross ill-treatment thirty years earlier had occurred largely because 'we were apprentices, without father or mother to take care of us; I don't say that they often do that now … Not so much in Manchester, where justice is always at hand'.[100] Indeed, in many large urban mills, strapping child workers to elicit greater amounts of work had been prohibited as early as 1818 and the use of fines and dismissal had become the most common sanction for serious misbehaviour.[101] It is notable too, that the vast majority of nineteenth-century working-class autobiographers do not mention serious workplace punishments as a feature of their early working lives.[102] It must be concluded therefore that the lives of most industrially employed children were not dominated by what the Hammonds characterised as 'the driving power of terror'.[103] Piecework production and specialisation of function was certainly implicated in higher levels of violence, though such examples might be equally applied to high-pressure domestic production or agricultural harvesting situations. Where corporal punishment was practised in any systematic manner in industrial situations, it tended to be generally moderate and connected in highly complex ways with the needs of production or the maintenance of workplace safety. Most parents and managers accepted that moderate discipline had a utility in preventing serious injuries to children as well as preserving the safety of the labour force as a whole. By the time of the major factory debates of the early 1830s and 40s, the corporal punishment of children in mills and factories had become extremely rare. The eminent Scottish chemist and geologist Andrew Ure, whose treatise on manufacturing of 1835 required him to inspect a large number of textiles mills over several months, did not encounter a single case of violence against children.[104] By the early 1840s, moreover, William Dodd, the writer on factory health and one of the most vociferous of extra-governmental campaigners against child labour, hardly mentioned workplace violence in his extensive reports on

100   Chapman, *Early Factory Masters*, pp. 201–2; PP 1833 (519), D3, p. 18. Pollard thought that 'Blincoe's sadistic master was not typical and that large employers generally frowned on beatings' (p. 260).
101   PP 1818 (90), pp. 175, 176; PP 1818 (90), p. 193.
102   See Humphries, 'Childhood and Violence'.
103   Hammond and Hammond, *Town Labourer*, p. 160.
104   A. Ure, *Philosophy of Manufactures: or, an exposition of the scientific, moral, and commercial economy of the Factory System of Great Britain* (London: Charles Knight, 1835), p. 301.

the factory districts. Despite the claims of campaigning groups in the 1830s, therefore, the beating of child factory workers was extremely rare. Few people associated with industrial production reported widespread ill-treatment and by the 1840s the more tangible problems of industrial injuries and evasion of age and time regulations had become the major areas of interest for inspectors and operatives alike.

Conclusion

Relocating the Health of
Industrial Children, 1780–1850

The complex epidemiology of early manufacturing towns and the wide variety of industrial processes carried out by child workers preclude any generalised statements about the effects of industrial work upon child health. Despite such difficulties, however, it is clear from the diversity of children's occupational health experiences examined in this study that the enduring and often simplistic stereotype of the health-impaired and abused industrial child can no longer be sustained. Working children were prone to a wide range of exogenous factors such as the urban disease environment, social class, household poverty, pre-existing disability or orphanage, and such influences almost certainly proved more harmful to their health and welfare than discrete workplace factors.

This is not to say that early industrial work was not harmful. The complex and protracted entry of children into industrial work, often determined by a child's developing strength, skill and dexterity, involved an increasing engagement with the workplace over several years as well as an increasing exposure to risk. Industrial injuries sometimes permanently disabled children and rendered them incapable of future productive labour. The constantly changing biology of children's bodies also served to amplify the effects of specific chemicals, raw materials and pathogens in ways not fully understood by nineteenth-century medical commentators. Moreover, factors such as the onset of sexual maturity (which commonly took place during the early years of industrial employment) often had a profound influence upon children's work attendance patterns. For example, factory returns from 1818 suggest that indispositions relating to puberty were the most important reported cause of absenteeism amongst adolescent girls.[1] The health of child workers was therefore subject to a diverse range of work and non-work related influences. The complex

---

1   PP 1819 (24), App., p. 106; see chapter one.

relationships between a child's developing physical and mental capacities, the disease environment and the industrial workplace were almost universally overlooked and, prior to the 1840s and 50s, few medical specialists had made any serious efforts to understand the aetiology of ill-health among working children. Most contemporary medical commentary on child industrial health between 1780 and 1850 consisted of outlandish or theoretical assertions about the industrial or ergonomic origins of ailments such as bone deformities and a range of non-specific constitutional conditions that were supposed to be associated with industrial employment. Such theories were frequently highly unreliable and tended to conflate workplace risks with broader epidemiological influences. Indeed, many of the disabilities observed amongst child factory workers must have resulted from disease experiences which predated working life. As Chadwick pointed out, the vast majority of diseases to which children fell prey in manufacturing districts occurred in infancy or early childhood, long before children could be engaged in industrial work.[2]

Physical disabilities would also have been imparted by common conditions such as rickets or poliomyelitis that were little understood at that time. Historians have rarely tested or criticised the generalised explanations offered by early nineteenth-century medical men, though their opinions that deformities and stunted growth might result from unfavourable ergonomics or standing for long periods were frequently ridiculed by local observers who lived and worked in the factory districts.[3] The claim that stunted growth was common amongst factory children has also been largely refuted by surviving data on child heights, which suggests that the nutritional status of child factory workers was little different (and in some cases somewhat better) than that of the general urban child population. Nonetheless, the continued dominance of theoretical medical opinion about the causes of child industrial ill-health ensured that, until the mid-1830s, the views of medical pioneers such as Kay and Thackrah (who regarded child industrial ill-health as a function

2   E. Chadwick, *Report on the Sanitary Condition of the Labouring Population of Great Britain* (1842), ed. M. W. Flinn (Edinburgh: Edinburgh University Press, 1965), p. 223.
3   Although diseases such as scrofula were claimed to have a higher prevalence amongst factory workers, the disease was actually far less common amongst manufacturing populations than amongst the population as a whole: B. Phillips, *Scrofula; its Nature, its Causes, its Prevalence, and the Principles of Treatment* (Philadelphia: Lea & Blanchard, 1846), pp. 184–5.

of the wider problem of public health) would remain peripheral influences upon state inquiries.[4] It is notable that when Thackrah appeared as a witness at the Sadler Committee of 1831–32, he displayed a remarkable reluctance to agree with the specific aetiologies of factory ailments advanced by the Committee's supposed medical 'experts'. Crucially, the absence of any observational or longitudinal studies of industrial health during the early factory debates meant that injuries to the upper limbs (the most common threat to the health of factory children) were still largely overlooked until the late 1840s, even by the most vociferous of factory reformers. As late as the 1860s, machinery injuries remained the largest cause of accidental death amongst workers aged eleven to fifteen in industrial districts.[5] It is clear, therefore, that the medical profession played no appreciable role in identifying or removing any of the major causes of child industrial ill-health between 1780 and 1850 and were often responsible for diverting attention away from the major risks facing working children.

Medical commentators also displayed a profound ignorance of industrial processes themselves. It was frequently claimed by doctors that children in mills and factories suffered from the longest hours and worst working conditions. However, comparative evidence suggests strongly that labour intensity in large textiles mills and factories was considerably lower than amongst children in other urban occupations. As early as 1819,

4   J. V. Pickstone, 'Ferriar's Fever to Kay's Cholera: Disease and Social Structure in Cottonopolis', *History of Science*, 22 (1984), 401–19 (pp. 415–16).

5   The most recent history of medical practitioners contains not a single index entry for 'children' or 'childhood' for a period in which children below fourteen accounted for 35–40 per cent of the population: M. Brown, *Performing Medicine: Medical Culture and Identity in Provincial England, c.1760–1850* (Manchester: Manchester University Press, 2011). A lack of accurate studies or diagnosis of child occupational health was matched by an absence of therapeutic remedies offered for supposed industrial ailments or deformities. As Smith pointed out, the 'selfish professionalism' of medical practitioners left occupational health conditions unheeded and untreated: F. B. Smith, *The People's Health, 1830–1910* (London: Weidenfeld & Nicholson, 1979), p. 188. See Robert Baker's report for 1840 which showed that 97 per cent of injuries to Leeds mill workers involved the upper limbs: W. R. Lee, 'Robert Baker: the First Doctor in the Factory Department, Part 1. 1803–1858', *British Journal of Industrial Medicine*, 21 (1964), 85–93 (p. 89); P. A. Sambrook, 'Childhood and Sudden Death in Staffordshire, 1851 and 1860', in *Staffordshire Histories: Essays in Honour of Michael Greenslade*, ed. P. Morgan and A. D. M. Phillips (Stafford: Staffordshire Record Society, 1999), pp. 216–52 (p. 226).

Table 8: Hours of work of children in selected industries, 1819

Industry	Hours
Collieries (underground), Lancashire	11
Silk Mills, Derby	12
Silk Mills, Congleton	12
Silk Mills, Macclesfield	12.5
Hosiery, Leicester	12–13
Silk Mills, Nottingham	13
Watchmakers, Coventry	12–14
Pin Making, Warrington	14
Earthenware, Staffordshire	12–15
Hosiery, Nottingham	15
Drawboys in Weaving, Paisley	15
Cotton Hand Weavers, Lancs, Yorks, Cheshire	14–16
Drawboys in Weaving, Glasgow	16–17*

Source: PP 1819 (24), App., pp. 112–14.
Notes: * The report noted 'very irregular; not uncommon for them to work as late as 11 or 12 at Night, and even to 1 o'clock in the Morning'.

the average twelve-hour days worked by children in textiles mills were generally less than those in heavier domestic manufactures (Table 8).[6]

The children of domestic weavers who gained employment in mills often complained that they found hand weaving too heavy and preferred the lighter ancillary tasks associated with spinning. Mrs Cooke Taylor interviewed a number of mill boys whose parents were hand weavers, asking them if they would not rather be working at home. Their response was that in the mill they at least knew what their hours would

6   P. Kirby, *Child Labour in Britain, 1750–1870* (Basingstoke: Palgrave, 2003), p. 52, tab. 3.1; Kirby and Musson, *Voice of the People*, p. 12; PP 1819 (24), App., pp. 112–14. Working hours in factories would often also include breaks for meals and cleaning. Kay suggested that cotton factory workers commenced work at six in the morning, returning home for thirty or forty minutes to eat breakfast. They would then return to the mills and workshops until twelve o'clock when they would take an hour for dinner, working thereafter until seven in the evening: J. P. Kay, *The Moral and Physical Condition of the Working Classes Employed in the Cotton Manufacture in Manchester* (London: James Ridgway, 1832, pp. 23–5.

be whereas at home they would be expected to work longer hours with little pay.[7] During the hand-loom weavers' distress of the early 1840s, child workers drafted in to the less skilled parts of the trade were said to have worked 'from five in the morning till twelve at night for many days without intermission'.[8] Larger and more highly capitalised mills also became progressively less labour intensive throughout the first half of the nineteenth century as new advances were developed in spinning technology. Numerous cotton operatives who had commenced work as children around 1780 claimed that jenny spinning – which had been common in the late eighteenth century but which had all but disappeared in the major textiles centres by the 1820s – had been much more arduous and damaging to children's health compared with the lighter work of piecing, cleaning or doffing.[9] Honeyman noted, too, that the overworking of children in factories was largely 'a minority opinion in early nineteenth century public documents.'[10] The summary report of the Factory Commission of 1833 considered in detail the matter of labour intensity across a variety of child textiles occupations and concluded that:

of all employments to which children are subjected, those carried on in the factories are amongst the least laborious and of all departments of indoor labour amongst the least unwholesome. Handloom weavers, frame work knitters, lace runners, and work people in other lines of domestic manufacture are in most cases worked at an earlier age for longer hours and for less wages than the body of children employed in factories.[11]

7   R. Boyson, 'Industrialisation and the Life of the Lancashire Factory Worker', in *The Long Debate on Poverty* (London: Institute of Economic Affairs, 1972), pp. 61–87 (pp. 66–7).

8   PP 1843 [431], B40–1, cited in A. H. Robson, *The Education of Children Engaged in Industry in England, 1833–1876* (London: Kegan Paul, 1931), p. 2, n. 2.

9   PP 1818 (90), p. 111; PP 1819 (24), pp. 347–8, 377. Smelser suggested that '[factory] working conditions in a physical sense were probably improving in the 1820s and 1830s': N. J. Smelser, *Social Change in the Industrial Revolution: An application of theory to the Lancashire Cotton Industry, 1770–1840* (London: Routledge & Kegan Paul, 1959), pp. 265–6.

10   K. Honeyman, *Child Workers in England, 1780–1820: Parish Apprentices and the Making of the Early Industrial Labour Force* (Aldershot: Ashgate, 2007), p. 135.

11   Cited in I. Pinchbeck and M. Hewitt, *Children in English Society, vol. 2, From the eighteenth century to the Children Act 1948* (London: Routledge, 1973), p. 403. As Pinchbeck pointed out, children in domestic industry had long been '[h]idden away in cottages, where they attracted no attention, thousands of children ... worked factory

The relative lightness of mill work also appeared to have opened up new work opportunities for disabled children and adolescents. Whilst it is impossible to gauge accurately the number of disabled children employed, it is likely that they had a heightened presence in mills and factories and that this resulted from their inability to take part in many heavier agricultural or labouring jobs. The increasing availability of light ancillary tasks in textiles mills, therefore, may have served as a form of social inclusion for many disabled children and young adults, presenting novel opportunities for them to engage profitably with the emergent new industrial enterprises. Disabled workers themselves commented on the relative ease with which they could perform industrial work. William Dodd (the self-styled 'factory cripple'), for example, argued that the low intensity of factory work provided his only practical means of earning a living.[12]

Curiously, the rising tide of complaints about ill-health and long hours amongst working children also coincided with a protracted decline in the proportions of young children in large factories. The percentage of factory workers aged below ten fell from around 4.5 per cent in 1818 to 1.0 per cent in 1833–35 whilst those below thirteen declined from 21.5 to 13.1 per cent over the same period.[13] This tendency was supported by the evidence of many operative witnesses. Older spinners who gave evidence to the Kenyon Committee observed that the average age at recruitment in spinning had increased significantly during the first two decades of the nineteenth century and in 1818 the large McConnell and Kennedy enterprise in Manchester employed only four children aged below nine in

hours every day, under conditions which were often no better than those which aroused so much feeling in industrial centres': I. Pinchbeck, *Women Workers and the Industrial Revolution, 1750–1850* (London: Routledge, 1930), p. 232. Child labour in factories often included long periods of play (Honeyman, p. 135).

12   W. Dodd, *A Narrative of the Experiences and Sufferings of William Dodd, a Factory Cripple, Written by Himself* (2nd edn, London: L. & G. Seeley, 1841), pp. 281, 284. Dodd pointed out that factory work was lighter than shop work with which he had been unable to cope.

13   H. Freudenberger, F. J. Mather and C. Nardinelli, 'A New Look at the Early Factory Labor Force', *Journal of Economic History*, 44 (1984), 1085–90 (p. 1087). Over the longer term, an industry estimate from 1790 suggested that there had been 100,000 children employed in cotton – nearly four times the number recorded at the census of 1851: Anon., *Case of the British cotton spinners and manufacturers of piece goods, similar to the importations from the East Indies* (London: P. Colquhoun, 1790), App., p. 7. Child labour in large factories and mines probably never accounted for more than a quarter of working children (Kirby, *Child Labour in Britain*, p. 52, tab. 3.1).

a labour force of 1,125.[14] The decline in industrial child labour therefore occurred earliest in the most highly capitalised urban enterprises whereas technologically backward rural and semi-rural enterprises continued to harbour the worst working conditions, greater proportions of young workers and higher levels of pauper apprenticeship.[15] It is also clear that urban and industrial families during the Industrial Revolution tended to place their children into work at much later ages compared with relatively poorer rural and semi-rural households.[16] Records of child applications for factory work in northern counties from the later 1830s show that the peak in applications to rural mills occurred at the age of nine whereas in large factory towns it occurred at the later age of thirteen.[17] The emergence of large complex industrial production was therefore crucial to the secular fall in the viability of industrial child labour and to a rise in the age at recruitment. Technological change, a shift to larger urban mills and increasing concerns for workplace safety served to reduce industrial demand for child labour whilst rising real incomes amongst industrial families reduced the burden of poverty which had hitherto forced them to depend upon the subsidiary incomes of their children.[18] Surviving quantitative evidence underpins this shift. At the high point of the Industrial Revolution, the major industrial counties and urban centres harboured concentrations of child labour similar to or below those of the national average. Recorded employment among

14 PP 1818 (90), p. 156. Though the firm continued to rely upon older children with 40 per cent of its labour force aged between nine and sixteen (with the majority of these at older ages).

15 H. P. Marvel, 'Factory Regulation: A Reinterpretation of Early English Experience', *Journal of Law and Economics*, 20 (1977), 379–402, p. 380.

16 P. Kirby, 'A Brief Statistical Sketch of the Child Labour Market in Mid-Nineteenth Century London', *Continuity and Change*, 20 (2005), 229–45. The retention of adolescents and young adults within the urban industrial family led to the establishment of the general custom of children remaining in the parental home until marriage: R. Burr Litchfield, 'The Family and the Mill: Cotton Mill Work, Family Work Patterns, and Fertility in Mid-Victorian Stockport', in *The Victorian Family: Structure and Stresses*, ed. A. S. Wohl (London: Croom Helm, 1978), pp. 180–96 (p. 192). In rural society, large numbers left home to start work several years before marriage. In 1861, 98 per cent of Preston children in the 15–19 age-group resided with their parents, compared with only 62 per cent in the rural parish of Colyton in 1841: R. Wall, 'The Age at Leaving Home', *Journal of Family History*, 3 (1978), 181–202 (pp. 190, 193, 197).

17 PP 1837 (99), pp. 6–11.

18 C. Nardinelli, 'Child Labor and the Factory Acts', *Journal of Economic History*, 40 (1980), 739–55 (p. 739).

children in England and Wales in 1851 accounted for just 2.0 per cent of all children aged 5–9 and 30.0 per cent of those aged 10–14, whilst in industrialised Lancashire the proportions were only slightly greater at 2.2 and 39.0 per cent respectively. In the London conurbation, however, the incidence of child employment amongst ten to fourteen-year-olds was exceptionally low at around half the national average. There was also a tendency amongst the metropolitan poor towards smaller families which further reduced child dependency. Factors associated with urbanisation and industrialisation were therefore crucial in the decline of child labour and by the mid-to-late nineteenth century the employment of young children in urban districts had become a highly marginal and casual activity associated chiefly with severe household poverty. In rural districts, by contrast, child employment in casual agricultural work continued to prove problematical for educational reformers throughout the second half of the nineteenth century.[19]

For much of the period 1780–1850, the social position of children, rather than their occupations, also appears to have been the decisive factor in determining levels of ill-treatment and corporal punishment. The historical assumption that ill-treatment was somehow more intense in the industrial workplace seems largely to have stemmed from misleading and exaggerated claims made by reformers during the factory debates of the 1830s. In fact, there is little evidence of widespread cruelty against industrial children and such claims tend to rest upon a small number of unrepresentative accounts of excessive violence against vulnerable groups of child workers. Thus, a handful of reports of late eighteenth-century brutality against pauper apprentices re-emerged in the polemical literature of the 1830s to promote the view that beatings were widespread in factory production. By that time, the proportions of such children in the factory labour force had fallen to almost insignificant levels. Unfortunately, few comparative studies of ill-treatment were conducted across occupations and it is often impossible to show (other than through

19   See, for example, P. Kirby, 'The Transition to Working Life in Eighteenth and Nineteenth-Century England and Wales', in *Child Labour's Global Past: 1650–2000*, ed. K. Lieten and E. van Nederveen Meerkerk (Amsterdam: International Institute for Social History, 2011), pp. 119–36 (pp. 128–33); A. Levene, *The Childhood of the Poor: Welfare in Eighteenth-Century London* (Basingstoke: Palgrave, 2012), p. 42; Kirby, 'Brief Statistical Sketch'. A mixture of agricultural labour, domestic work and cottage industry ensured that in 1851 the highest rate of child labour existed not in industrial counties but in rural Bedfordshire (Kirby, *Child Labour in Britain*, pp. 61–2).

an injudicious selection of anecdotes) whether the physical ill-treatment of children in textiles factories was any more frequent or intense than those in other settings. It is likely, however, that the greater publicity given to industrial violence in the 1830s brought to public view and disapprobation such forms of ill-treatment that had long been practised in domestic production. The increasing level of surveillance on the factory floor almost certainly led to rising disapproval of workplace violence and to a progressive decline in ill-treatment.[20] Robert Blincoe, who had himself suffered serious abuse as a parish apprentice, offered precisely that explanation when he argued in the 1830s that the beating of children in large urban factories had largely disappeared. It is notable, too, that the framers of child labour laws of the 1830s and 40s did not consider violence against working children to be a major problem. None of the early factory and mines legislation contained any provision to outlaw or even limit the physical abuse of children in the industrial workplace.[21]

Finally, despite the implicit emphasis in traditional accounts on the effectiveness of child labour laws in improving the overall welfare of child workers, such legislation in reality had little effect upon either health or working conditions. The early stress on health improvements embodied in legislation such as the 1802 Health and Morals of Apprentices Act was not revisited until the introduction of limited workplace safety clauses of the Factory Act of 1844.[22] Indeed, the faulty framing of legislation and the inability of law-makers to understand industrial processes often resulted in laws which were unworkable and unenforceable. For much of the decade following the 1833 Act, the inability of the factory inspectorate to secure compliance with age regulations meant that hundreds

---

20   Pinchbeck, p. 232; M. D. George, *London Life in the Eighteenth Century* (London: London School of Economics, 1997), p. 261. Even the Hammonds were forced to admit that many of the abuses that beset the labour market generally 'were at once more evident and manageable in the factory than in the domestic workshop': J. L. Hammond and B. Hammond, 'Preface', in *The Town Labourer, 1760–1832: The New Civilisation* (1917; London: Longmans, Green & Company, 1966), pp. vii–xi (p. viii).

21   PP 1833 (519), D3, p. 18.

22   7 Vict., c. 15, ss. xx–xxiii. The 1833 Factory Act delayed the entry of children to the factory labour force by only about a year and children as young as eight were permitted to work half time in textiles as late as 1874 (the half-time system itself was not discontinued until the early 1920s): M. Anderson, 'Sociological History and the Working-Class Family, Smelser Revisited', *Social History*, 1 (1976), 317–34 (p. 323); Kirby, *Child Labour in Britain*, p. 94; J. Pressley, 'Childhood, Education and Labour: Moral Pressure and the end of the Half-Time System' (Ph.D. thesis, Lancaster University, 2000), p. 1.

of appointed certifying factory surgeons were occupied chiefly in the assessment of the ages of child applicants rather than in the promotion of their health. It was only after 1844 that factory surgeons began to take on a limited role in examining the health of child applicants for work.[23] However, formal medical inspection of child factory workers did not commence until 1867 and child labourers in workshops escaped medical examinations altogether until 1906.[24] Many harsh working conditions continued unabated into the twentieth century – even in the most heavily regulated of industries. In coalmining, the use of leather belts and chains to drag coal sledges through narrow seams, described in the 1840s as 'a wretched and slave-like mode of labour', was still in use by adolescents in some English mines as late as the 1920s, despite many decades of mines regulation.[25] Similarly, there were few legislative attempts to deal with the problems of dust and other suspended contaminants in the factory workplace, and preventable pulmonary diseases continued to injure the health of both child and adult textiles workers well into the twentieth century. Child labour laws also frequently compounded the problems of family poverty that gave rise to child labour. The most common reaction amongst employers to the introduction of age regulations was to dismiss all the young children who fell within the new restrictions.[26] Since laws prohibiting children from labour never contained provisions to compensate poor families for the loss of their children's incomes, the child workers excluded from regulated factory jobs might simply be transferred to more hazardous and often lower-paid unregulated trades.[27] Years after the factory debate, a leading factory inspector

23   S. Huzzard, 'The Role of the Certifying Factory Surgeon in the State Regulation of Child Labour and Industrial Health' (MA thesis, University of Manchester, 1976), pp. 38–45.

24   F. Keeling, *Child Labour in the United Kingdom: A Study of the Development and Administration of the Law Relating to the Employment of Children* (London: International Association for Labour Legislation, 1914), pp. xi–xii.

25   PP 1928–9 [Cmd. 3200]; P. Kirby, 'The Historic Viability of Child Labour and the Mines Act of 1842', in *A Thing of the Past? Child Labour in Britain in the Nineteenth and Twentieth Centuries*, ed. M. Lavalette (Liverpool: Liverpool University Press, 1999), pp. 101–17 (p. 116).

26   The factory inspectors claimed that the only objections received to the practice of using surgeons to certify the ages of child applicants for factory work came from workpeople themselves who complained mainly about the fee of 6d (PP 1834 (596), p. 9).

27   As one Yorkshire commentator observed, 'It has long been a grievance in this Riding that whilst the Factory Act prohibits a class of children from working in Factories ...

admitted candidly that the exclusion of young children by the early factory acts had been 'the open sesame to any kind of other work either not controlled by the Legislature at all, or not subject to the supervision of our department'.[28] Given the limited reach of early child labour laws, the absence of workplace safety clauses and the general lack of regard amongst legislators for the economic plight of poor families, it would be extremely unwise to attribute to early nineteenth-century child labour legislation any measurable advancement in the physical health or general well-being of industrially employed children.

Ultimately, the absence of a coherent body of medical evidence relating to the causes of occupational ill-health together with the deficiency of longitudinal statistical series of occupational mortality and morbidity during the Industrial Revolution render simplistic assumptions about the health of early industrial child workers untenable. However, as early as the second decade of the nineteenth century, factory-employed children were clearly better off in terms of both income and overall health compared with child workers in domestic occupations and by contrast with the average urban child dweller. This may well have been a result of their higher industrial earnings which allowed them to command a greater share of food and other household resources. With the important exception of industrial injuries, the child workers who staffed the mills and factories of the Industrial Revolution were at no greater risk of poor health than those in other occupations.[29] Such a conclusion clearly presents a major challenge to the predominantly pessimistic historiography of industrial child employment.

This study has concentrated chiefly on the experiences of children in large industrial processes and it is lamentable that the comparative health of child workers in areas such as domestic service, workshop production and agriculture has remained so little explored. Many questions remained unanswered. The connections between the declining economic value of

those very children so discharged from factories are ... transferred to the mines of the neighbourhood (to the great annoyance, as well as to the prejudice of the millowners, for whose operations these little workers were best calculated)': Anon., 'Lord Ashley's Bill', *Leeds Mercury*, 18 June 1842; F. Horner, *On the Employment of Children in Factories and Other Works in the United Kingdom and in some Foreign Countries* (London: Longman, 1840), p. 122. See also Nardinelli, 'Child Labor and the Factory Acts', p. 752; Kirby, *Child Labour in Britain*, pp. 131–3.

28   Quoted in Nardinelli, 'Child Labour and the Factory Acts', p. 751.

29   The relationship between child age and risk in the production of industrial injuries prior to 1850 awaits a detailed investigation.

child labour and a decrease in marital fertility during the second half of the nineteenth century, or the effects of a falling age of physical maturity coupled with a rising age at starting work, remain largely unaddressed. Crucially, the complex and universal transition from child dependency to relative economic independence experienced by almost all working-class people between the ages of ten and twenty remains a process little understood.[30] Social historians will need to discover new ways of investigating such historical problems through a closer understanding of the relationship between the stages of child development, the changing industrial workplace and the evolving urban environment. The current methodological shift towards framing the analysis of modern child labour more firmly as a public health issue, together with innovations in occupational medicine, are likely to provide valuable new understandings of the effects of hazardous historic working environments and materials on child workers.[31] Further research into the health histories of employed children will require an increasingly interdisciplinary approach to the study of causation, a more critical attitude to medical theory and a readiness to challenge ingrained attitudes to child labour, both past and present.[32]

30   See the discussion in Kirby, 'Transition to Working Life'.
31   A. G. Fassa, D. L. Lewis and T. J. Scanlon (eds.), *Child Labour: A Public Health Perspective* (Oxford: Oxford University Press, 2010).
32   See V. Goddard and B. White, 'Child Workers and Capitalist Development', *Development and Change*, 13 (1982), 465–78 (p. 466).

Appendix

A.1. Numbers of children in Horner's 1837 survey by age and place of residence

	age	8	9	10	11	12	13	14	Total
Males	Large towns	146	171	193	221	254	467	207	1659
	Small towns	230	304	378	415	489	858	389	3063
	Rural districts	290	470	444	586	685	808	356	3639
	Total	666	945	1015	1222	1428	2133	952	8361
Females	Large towns	131	149	167	180	243	537	246	1653
	Small towns	181	323	408	389	479	877	402	3059
	Rural districts	227	341	461	485	608	826	381	3329
	Total	539	813	1036	1054	1330	2240	1029	8041

Source: PP 1837 (99), pp. 6–11; P. Kirby, *The Physical Stature of 16,402 Children in Northern English Factory Districts, 1837* (database), UK Data Archive, University of Essex (2010), http://www.esds.ac.uk/findingData/snDescription.asp?sn=6426.

A.2. Mean heights (inches) of 16,402 children in the north of England, 1836–37

Age	Sex	Large towns			Rural districts			Smaller towns			All districts		
		Mean	SD	N	Mean	SD	N	Mean	SD	N	Mean	SD	N
8	M	45.76	1.89	74	45.37	2.56	138	45.77	2.37	115	45.60	2.36	327
	F	45.69	1.67	64	45.01	2.59	109	44.76	2.45	94	45.08	2.37	267
8.5	M	47.00	1.57	72	47.04	2.18	152	46.74	2.46	115	46.93	2.17	339
	F	46.76	1.67	67	46.60	2.22	118	45.56	2.26	87	46.31	2.17	272
9	M	47.51	1.95	85	47.75	2.02	247	47.58	2.41	195	47.65	2.16	527
	F	47.29	1.57	76	47.27	2.21	182	47.58	1.85	180	47.40	1.97	438
9.5	M	48.46	1.76	86	48.59	2.15	223	47.06	2.09	109	48.17	2.16	418
	F	48.18	1.65	73	47.93	2.09	159	47.89	2.22	143	47.96	2.06	375
10	M	49.08	2.12	92	49.30	2.09	255	48.74	2.21	227	49.04	2.15	574
	F	48.87	1.57	87	49.38	2.22	195	48.78	2.07	225	49.03	2.07	507
10.5	M	49.61	1.81	101	49.99	1.98	189	49.33	2.13	151	49.68	2.01	441
	F	49.39	1.45	80	50.19	2.12	266	49.46	2.25	183	49.82	2.11	529
11	M	49.61	1.94	110	50.79	2.10	312	50.02	2.10	242	50.31	2.12	664
	F	49.82	1.86	94	50.36	2.24	259	50.27	2.19	223	50.24	2.17	576
11.5	M	50.38	1.77	111	51.62	2.01	274	51.04	2.40	173	51.19	2.15	558
	F	51.05	2.19	86	51.54	2.10	226	50.85	2.15	166	51.21	2.16	478
12	M	50.88	1.81	133	52.14	2.10	374	51.69	2.43	260	51.77	2.22	767
	F	51.05	2.01	122	52.32	2.39	317	51.80	2.13	273	51.90	2.27	712

Age	Sex	Large towns			Rural districts			Smaller towns			All districts		
		Mean	SD	N	Mean	SD	N	Mean	SD	N	Mean	SD	N
12.5	M	51.40	1.99	121	52.78	2.29	311	52.56	2.20	229	52.45	2.26	661
	F	52.15	2.15	121	53.09	2.13	291	52.29	1.86	206	52.64	2.09	618
13	M	52.55	1.63	243	53.19	1.90	517	53.29	2.14	509	53.11	1.97	1269
	F	52.81	1.98	293	53.68	2.40	485	53.48	2.11	482	53.40	2.22	1260
13.5	M	53.48	1.76	224	54.46	2.11	291	54.41	2.12	349	54.18	2.07	864
	F	53.93	2.24	244	55.00	2.38	341	54.70	2.43	395	54.61	2.40	980
14	M	55.11	2.21	207	55.73	2.60	356	56.11	2.38	389	55.75	2.46	952
	F	55.68	2.15	246	55.87	2.49	381	56.26	2.09	402	55.98	2.27	1029

Notes: SD = Standard deviation. N = Number of observations.
Source: PP 1837 (99), pp. 6–11.

A.3. Places of residence of the children

Large towns
Bolton
Halifax
Leeds
Manchester
Preston
Stockport

Smaller towns
Bingley
Blackburn
Burnley
Cheadle
Chorley
Clitheroe
Colne
Dewsbury
Huddersfield
Knutsford
Middleton
Mold
Nantwich
Newcastle [Staffs]
Oldham
Otley
Rochdale
Sandbach
Selby
Settle
Skipton
Ulverston

Rural districts
Accrington
Addingham

Batley
Burton
Cleckheaton
Grassington
Great Horton
Guiseley
Hampsthwaite
Hebden Bridge
Heckmondwike
Heywood
Hipperholme
Holmfirth
Kettlewell
Kirkham
Kirkland
Lees-in-Oldham
Leyland
Linthwaite
Marple Bridge
Marsden
Meltham
Mirfield
Morley
New Mills
Ossett
Pateley Bridge
Pudsey
Radcliffe
Ramsbottom
Rothwell
Royton
Sedbergh
Skelmanthorpe
Sowerby Bridge
Stainland

Source: PP 1837 (99), pp. 6–11.

Bibliography

Statutes

20 Geo. II, c. 19, *An Act for the Recovery of the Wages of Servants* (1747).

32 Geo. III, c. 57, *An Act for the further Regulation of Parish Apprentices* (1792).

42 Geo. III, c. 73, *An Act for the Preservation of the Health and Morals of Apprentices and others, Employed in Cotton and Other Mills, and Cotton and Other Factories* (1802).

59 Geo. III, c. 66, *An Act to make further Provisions for the Regulation of Cotton Mills and Factories, and for the better Preservation of the Health of Young Persons employed therein* (1819).

60 Geo. III, c. 5, *An Act to amend and Act of the last Session of Parliament to make further Provision for the Regulation of Cotton Mills and Factories, and for the Preservation of the Health of Young Persons employed therein* (1819).

6 Geo. IV, c. 63, *An Act to make further Provision Provisions for the Regulation of Cotton Mills and Factories, and for the better Preservation of the Health of Young Persons employed therein* (1825).

1 & 2 Will. IV, c. 39, *An Act to repeal the Laws relating to Apprentices and other Young Persons employed in Cotton Factories and Cotton Mills, and to make further Provisions in lieu thereof* (1831).

3 & 4 Will. IV, c. 103, *An Act to regulate the Labour of Children and Young Persons in the Mills and Factories of the United Kingdom* (1833).

6 & 7 Will. IV, c. 86, *An Act for registering Births, Deaths, and Marriages in England* (1836).

5 & 6 Vict., c. 99, *A Bill To prohibit the Employment of Women and Girls in Mines and Collieries, to regulate the Employment of Boys, and make Provisions for the Safety of Persons working therein* (1842).

7 Vict., c. 15, *An Act to amend the Laws relating to Labour in Factories* (1844).

13 & 14 Vict., c. 100, *An Act for Inspection of Coal Mines in Great Britain* (1850).

17 & 18 Vict., c. 80, *An Act to provide for the better regulation of Births, Deaths, and Marriages in Scotland* (1854).

37 & 38 Vict., c. 88, *An Act to amend the Law relating to the Registration of Births and Deaths in England, and to consolidate the Law respecting the Registration of Births and Deaths at Sea* (1874).

Official publications

PP = parliamentary papers

Health and Safety Executive, *Reporting of Injuries, Diseases and Dangerous Occurrences Regulations* 1995 (RIDDOR) statistics, http://www.hse.gov.uk/statistics/demographic.htm, Excel files: ridagegen1 (Injuries to men employees by age of injured person and severity of injury') and ridagegen2 (Injuries to women employees by age of injured person and severity of injury').

PP 1814–15 (304), *Report from the Select Committee on Parish Apprentices.*

PP 1816 (397), *Report of the minutes of evidence, taken before the Select Committee on the State of the Children Employed in the Manufactories of the United Kingdom.*

PP 1817 (400), *Report from the Committee on Employment of Boys in Sweeping of Chimnies: together with the minutes of the evidence taken before the committee, and an appendix.*

PP 1818 (61), *A Bill [as amended by the committee] to amend and extend an Act, made in the 42d year of His Present Majesty, for the Preservation of the Health and Morals of Apprentices, and others, employed in Cotton and other mills, and Cotton and other Factories.*

PP 1818 (90), *Evidence of Committee on Health and Morals of Apprentices.*

PP 1819 (24), *Minutes of Evidence taken before The Lords Committee appointed to enquire into the State and Condition of the Children Employed in the Cotton Manufactories of the United Kingdom.*

PP 1819 (108), *An Account of the Cotton and Woollen Mills and Factories ... From the Year 1803 to the Last Year Inclusive.*

PP 1819 (247), *A bill for the promotion of the education and morals of children, in cotton and other factories in Ireland.*

PP 1819 (449), *Report from the select committee appointed to consider the validity of the doctrine of contagion in the plague.*

PP 1825 (382), *A Bill [as amended by the committee] to make further Provisions for the Regulation of Cotton Mills and Factories, and for the better Preservation of the Health of Young Persons employed therein.*

PP 1831–2 (706), *Report from the Committee on the 'Bill to Regulate the Labour of Children in the Mills and Factories of the United Kingdom' with minutes of evidence, appendix and index.*

PP 1833 (450), *Factories Inquiry Commission. First report of the Central Board of His Majesty's commissioners appointed to collect information in the manufacturing districts, as to the employment of children in factories, and as to the propriety and means of curtailing the hours of their labour: with minutes of evidence, and reports by the district commissioners.*

PP 1833 (519), *Factories Inquiry Commission. Second report of the Central Board of His Majesty's commissioners appointed to collect information in the manufacturing districts, as to the employment of children in factories, and as to the propriety and means of curtailing the hours of their labour: with minutes of evidence, and reports by the Medical Commissioners.*

PP 1834 (167), *Factories Inquiry Commission. Supplementary report of the Central Board of His Majesty's commissioners appointed to collect information in the manufacturing districts, as to the employment of children in factories, and as to the propriety and means of curtailing the hours of their labour. Part I.*

PP 1834 (596), *Reports of inspectors of factories to the Secretary of State; presented according to the provisions of the act of Parliament.*

PP 1835 (156), *Return of the number of surgeons appointed by the Inspectors of Factories; specifying the number of certificates granted by each of the said surgeons.*

PP 1835 (342), *Factories regulation. Reports made to the Secretary of State by the Inspectors of Factories, in pursuance of the 45th section of the Factories Regulation Act.*

PP 1837 (546), *Third annual report of the Poor Law Commissioners for England and Wales; together with appendices.*

PP 1837 [73], *Reports of the inspectors of factories to His Majesty's Principal Secretary of State for the Home Department.*

PP 1837 (99), *Factory children. A return of the number and names of the surgeons who have furnished the inspectors of factories with tables containing the stature of children measured by them, &c.*

PP 1837–8 (119), *Reports of the inspectors of factories to Her Majesty's Principal Secretary of State for the Home Department, for the year ending 31st December, 1837.*

PP 1837–8 (292), *A bill for regulating the employment of children and young persons in factories.*

PP 1837–8 (399), *Second memorial of the Short-Time Committee of Manchester and report thereupon by Leonard Horner, Esq.*

PP 1839 [159], *Reports of the inspectors of factories to Her Majesty's Principal Secretary of State for the Home Department.*

PP 1839 (434), *A bill for regulating the employment of children and young persons in factories.*

PP 1840 (203), *First report from the Select Committee on the Act for the Regulation of Mills and Factories; together with the minutes of evidence, taken before them, and an appendix.*

PP 1841 (1), *Report to the Secretary of State for the Home Department, from the Poor Law Commissioners, on the Training of Pauper Children.*

PP 1841 [311], *Special reports of the inspectors of factories to Her Majesty's Principal Secretary of State for the Home Department, on the practicability of legislative interference, to diminish the frequency of accidents to the children and young persons employed in factories, arising from machinery being cleaned while in motion, and from dangerous parts of the machinery being left unguarded.*

PP 1842 (380), *Commission for Inquiring into the Employment and Condition of Children in Mines and Manufactories, First Report of the Commissioners.*

PP 1842 (381), *Appendix to First Report of the Commissioners, Part I.*

PP 1842 (382), *Appendix to First Report of the Commissioners, Part II.*

PP 1842 (551), *Report from the Select Committee on the West Coast of Africa, Part II.*

PP 1843 [431], *Children's Employment Commission. Second Report of the commissioners. Trades and manufactures.*

PP 1843 [432], *Children's Employment Commission. Second Report of the commissioners. Trades and manufactures. Appendix to 2nd rep., Pt. I.*

PP 1843 [510], *Reports of Special Assistant Commissioners on the Employment of Women and Children in Agriculture.*

PP 1847 [870], *Reports of the Commissioners of Inquiry into the state of education in Wales, Appointed by the Committee of the Council on Education., in three parts, Part II.*

PP 1854 (523), *Assaults on women and children (metropolis).Return relating to charges preferred against male persons for assaults on women and children, at each court within the Metropolitan Police district, from 1 June 1850 to 1 June 1853.*

PP 1863 [3221], Part I.1, *Census of England and Wales 1861: General Report; Summary Tables, Abstracts of Ages, Occupations and Birthplaces of People, Division I. to Division III.*

PP 1864 [3309], *Reports of the inspectors of factories to Her Majesty's Principal Secretary of State for the Home Department for the half year ending 31st October 1863.*

PP 1868–9 [4093-1], *Reports of the inspectors of factories to Her Majesty's principal secretary of state for the Home Department for the half year ending 31st October 1868.*

PP 1928–9 [Cmd. 3200], *Report of the Departmental Committee on the Use of the Guss in Somerset Mines.*

Primary and Secondary Sources

Abrams, H. K., 'A Short History of Occupational Health', *Journal of Public Health Policy*, 22 (2001), 34–80.

'Agonistes', 'Defence of the Payment for Medical Replies by the Life-Assurance Companies instead of the Party Petitioning to Assure', *The Lancet*, 38, 30 April 1842, 164–5.

Aitchison, J., *Servants in Ayrshire, 1750–1914* (Ayr: Ayrshire Archaeological & Natural History Society, 2001).

'Alfred' [S. Kydd], *The History of the Factory Movement from the Year 1802 to the Enactment of the Ten Hours Bill In 1847* (London: Simpkin, Marshall & Co, 1857).

Altin, R., S. Ozkurt, F. Fisekci, A. H. Cimrin, M. Zencir and C. Sevinc, 'Prevalence of Byssinosis and Respiratory Symptoms among Cotton Mill Workers', *Respiration*, 69 (2002), pp. 52–6.

Amussen, S. D., 'Punishment, Discipline, and Power: The Social Meanings of Violence in Early Modern England', *Journal of British Studies*, 34 (January 1995), 1–34.

Anderson, A. M., 'Historical Sketch of the Development of Legislation for Injurious and Dangerous Industries in England', in *The Dangerous Trades: the Historical, Social and Legal Aspects of Industrial Occupations as Affecting Health*, ed. T. Oliver (London: John Murray, 1902), pp. 24–43.

Anderson, M., *Family Structure in Nineteenth-Century Lancashire* (Cambridge: Cambridge University Press, 1971).

——, 'The Social Implications of Demographic Change', in *Cambridge Social History of Britain, 1750–1950*, ed. F. M. L. Thompson (Cambridge: Cambridge University Press, 1990), vol. 2, pp. 1–70.

——, 'Sociological History and the Working-Class Family, Smelser Revisited', *Social History*, 1 (1976), 317–34.

Andrews, J. P., *An appeal to the humane, on behalf of the most deplorable class of society, the climbing boys, employed by the chimney-sweepers* (London: John Stockdale, 1788).

Andrews, T., *The miseries of the miserable or, an essay towards laying open the decay of the fine woollen trade and the unhappy condition of the poor Wiltshire manufacturers* (n.p., 1739).

Anon., 'Accident by Machinery – Liability of Mill-Owners', *The Manchester Times and Gazette*, 22 August 1840, p. 3.

——, 'Accidents by Machinery', *The Manchester Times and Gazette*, 7 February 1835, p. 2.

——, 'Agricultural Gangs', *Quarterly Review*, 123 (1867), 173–90.

——, 'Alleged Death of a Parish Apprentice from Ill-Treatment', *The Examiner*, 22 January 1848, p. 60.

——, 'An authentick Narrative of the many horrid Cruelties inflicted by Mrs. Elizabeth Brownrigg, upon her poor Apprentice girls', *Gentleman's Magazine*, September 1767, 433–7.

——, 'Another Fatal Accident', *The Manchester Times and Gazette*, 18 June 1836, p. 3.

——, 'Awful Death', *Blackburn Standard*, 22 July 1840, p. 2.

——, 'A Bill to Amend the Laws Relating to Parish Apprentices', *Bradford Observer*, 10 July 1834, p. 181.

——, *Bolton Free Press*, 19 February 1836, p. 2.

——, *Caledonian Mercury*, 21 March 1836, p. 3.

——, *Case of the British cotton spinners and manufacturers of piece goods, similar to the importations from the East Indies* (London: P. Colquhoun, 1790).

——, 'The Collieries, No. 1', *Penny Magazine Monthly Supplement*, 28 February–31 March 1835, 121–8.

——, *The Commissioners' Vade Mecum whilst engaged in collecting evidence for the Factory Masters* (Leeds: n.p., 1833).

——, 'Coroner's Inquest – Child Drowned', *The Manchester Times and Gazette*, 31 July 1841, p. 3.

——, 'Death by Falling Down a Coal Pit', *The Manchester Times and Gazette*, 12 April 1834, p. 2.

——, *Exposition of the Factory Question* (Manchester: T. Sowler, 1832).

——, 'Factory Children', *The Times*, 25 February, 1833, p. 3.

——, 'Fatal Accident', *Blackburn Standard*, 11 December 1839, p. 2.

——, 'Fatal Accident', *The Manchester Times and Gazette*, 11 June 1836, p. 2.

——, *Genuine and Authentic Account of the Life, Trial, and Execution, of Elizabeth Brownrigg, who was Executed on Monday the 14th of September, 1767, for the Barbarous Murder of Mary Clifford, her Apprentice Girl* (London: R. Richards, 1767).

——, 'Information Under the Factory Act', *Preston Chronicle*, 30 April 1842, p. 4.

——, 'Lord Ashley's Bill', *Leeds Mercury*, 18 June 1842.

——, *Medico-Chirurgical Review*, 20, 31 (1832), 77–83.

——, 'Mr Fielden, MP, and the Factory Inspector', *The Champion*, 16 October 1836.

——, 'The Piecener's Complaint', *Short Time Tracts*, no. 4 (November 1835), 2 (Goldsmiths' Library, University of London).

——, *Preston Chronicle*, 22 August 1840, p. 2.

——, 'The Putrid Fever at Robert Peel's Radcliffe Mills', *Notes and Queries*, January 1958, 26–35.

——, *A Short Essay written for the Service of the Proprietors of Cotton-Mills and the Persons employed in Them* (Manchester: C. Wheeler, 1784).

——, 'The Ten Hours' Labour Bill', *London Medical Gazette*, 26 January 1833, pp. 562–6.

——, *The Times*, 4 November 1817, p. 3.

——, 'Trial of a Chimney-Sweeper for the Murder of his Apprentice', *Blackwoods Edinburgh Magazine*, August 1817, 547–8.

——, 'Violation of the Factory Act', *The Charter*, 24 March 1839, p. 137.

Arch, J., *From Ploughtail to Parliament: An Autobiography* (1897–8; London: Ebury Press, 1986).

Ashton, T. S., 'Frances Collier, 1889–1962: A Memoir', in F. Collier, *The Family Economy of the Working Classes in the Cotton Industry, 1784–1833*, ed. R. S. Fitton (Manchester: Manchester University Press, 1964), pp. v–x.

Bailey, F. A., 'Coroner's Inquests held in the Manor of Prescot, 1746–89', *Transactions of the Historic Society of Lancashire and Cheshire*, 86 (1934), 21–39.

Baines, E., *History of the cotton manufacture in Great Britain: with a notice of its early history in the East and in all the quarters of the globe: a description of the great mechanical inventions which have caused its unexampled extension in Britain: and a view of the present state of the manufacture and the condition of the classes engaged in its several departments* (London: H. Fisher, R. Fisher & P. Jackson, 1835).

Barker, D. J. P., 'The Foetal and Infant Origins of Inequalities in Health in Britain', *Journal of Public Health Medicine*, 13 (1991), 64–8.

Barnes, E., *Diseases and Human Evolution* (Albuquerque: University of New Mexico, 2005).

Bartrip, P. W. J., 'British Government Inspection, 1832–1875: Some Observations', *Historical Journal*, 25 (1982), 605–26.

——, *The Home Office and the Dangerous Trades: Regulating Occupational Disease in Victorian and Edwardian Britain* (Amsterdam: Rodopi, 2002).

——, 'Success or Failure? The Prosecution of the Early Factory Acts', *Economic History Review*, 38 (1985), 423–7.

—— and S. B. Burman, *The Wounded Soldiers of Industry: Industrial Compensation Policy, 1833–1897* (Oxford: Oxford University Press, 1983).

—— and P. T. Fenn, 'The Administration of Safety: the Enforcement of the Early Factory Inspectorate, 1844–1864', *Public Administration*, 58 (1980), 87–107.

—— and P. T. Fenn, 'The Conventionalization of Early Factory Crime: A Re-assessment', *International Journal of the Sociology of Law*, 8 (1980), 175–86.

—— and P. T. Fenn, 'The Evolution of Regulatory Style in the Nineteenth-Century British Factory Inspectorate', *Journal of Law and Society*, 10 (1983), 201–22.

Beattie, J. M., *Crime and the Courts in England, 1660–1800* (Oxford: Oxford University Press, 1986).

Benson, J., *British Coalminers in the Nineteenth Century: A Social History* (Dublin: Gill & Macmillan, 1980).

Bernard, T., 'Extract from a further account of the House of Recovery at Manchester', *Reports of the Society for Bettering the Condition and Increasing the Comforts of the Poor*, 2 (1800), 158–64.

——, 'Extract from an Account of a Chimney Sweeper's Boy, with Observations and a Proposal for the Relief of Chimney Sweepers', *Reports of the Society for Bettering the Condition and Increasing the Comforts of the Poor*, 1 (1798), 108–14.

——, 'Extract from an Account of Mr Dale's Cotton Mills at New Lanerk, in Scotland', *Reports of the Society for Bettering the Condition and Increasing the Comforts of the Poor*, 2 (1800), 250–7.

Black, J., 'A Medico-Topographical, Geological, and Statistical Sketch of Bolton and its Neighbourhood', *Transactions of the Provincial Medical and Surgical Association*, 5 (1837), 125–224.

——, 'Remarks on the Influence of Physical Habits and Employment', *London Medical Gazette*, 2, 12 (1833), 143–8.

Blanc, P. D., *How Everyday Products Make People Sick: Toxins at Home and in the Workplace* (Berkeley: University of California Press, 2009).

——, 'Inhalation Fever', in *Environmental and Occupational Medicine*, ed. W. N. Rom and S. B. Markowitz (Philadelphia: Lippincott, Williams & Wilkins, 2007), pp. 402–17.

Blaug, M., 'The Classical Economists and the Factory Acts – a Re-Examination', *Quarterly Journal of Economics*, 72 (1958), 211–26.

Bolin-Hort, P., *Work, Family and the State: Child Labour and the Organisation of Production in the British Cotton Industry, 1780–1920* (Lund: Lund University Press, 1989).

Borsay, A., 'Deaf Children and Charitable Education in Britain, 1790–1944', in *Medicine, Charity and Mutual Aid: The Consumption of Health and Welfare, c.1550–1950*, ed. A. Borsay and P. Shapely (Aldershot: Ashgate, 2007), pp. 71–90.

——, *Disability and Social Policy in Britain since 1750: a history of exclusion* (Basingstoke: Palgrave Macmillan, 2005).

Bowden, S. and G. Tweedale, 'Mondays without Dread: The Trade Union Response to Byssinosis in the Lancashire Cotton Industry in the Twentieth Century', *Social History of Medicine*, 16, 1 (2003), 79–95.

—— and G. Tweedale, 'Poisoned by the Fluff: Compensation and Litigation for Byssinosis in the Lancashire Cotton Industry', *Journal of Law and Society*, 29, 4 (2002), 560–79.

Boyson, R., 'Industrialisation and the Life of the Lancashire Factory Worker', in *The Long Debate on Poverty* (London: Institute of Economic Affairs, 1972), pp. 61–87.

Brachman, P. S., 'Inhalation Anthrax', *Annals of the New York Academy of Sciences*, 353 (1980), 83–93.

Brandon, S., 'The Early History of Psychiatric Care of Children', in *Child Care Through the Centuries: An Historical Survey from Papers Given at the Tenth British Congress on the History of Medicine*, ed. J. Cule and T. Turner (Cardiff: British Society for the Social History of Medicine, 1986), pp. 61–78.

Bray, W., *Sketch of a Tour into Derbyshire and Yorkshire, including part of Buckingham, Warwick, Leicester, Nottingham, Northampton, Bedford* (London: B. White, 1778).

British Association for the Advancement of Science, *Final report of the anthropometric committee* (London: J. Murray, 1884).

Brockliss, L., 'Apprenticeship in Northwest Europe, 1300–1850', in *Childhood and Violence in the Western Tradition*, ed. L. Brockliss and H. Montgomery (Oxford: Oxbow Press, 2010), pp. 171–80.

Brockliss, L. and H. Montgomery (eds), *Childhood and Violence in the Western Tradition* (Oxford: Oxbow Press, 2010).

Bronstein, J. L., *Caught in the Machinery: Workplace Accidents and Injured Workers in Nineteenth-Century Britain* (Stanford: Stanford University Press, 2008).

Brown, E., 'On the quicksilver mines in Friuli', *The Philosophical Transactions of the Royal Society of London* (1672–83; abridged, London: C. & R. Baldwin, 1809), vol. 1, pp. 407–9.

Brown, J., 'The Condition of England and the Standard of Living: Cotton Textiles in the Northwest, 1806–1850', *Journal of Economic History*, 50 (1990), 591–614.

—— (ed.), *A Memoir of Robert Blincoe, an orphan boy* (Manchester: J. Doherty, 1832).

Brown, M., *Performing Medicine: Medical Culture and Identity in Provincial England, c.1760–1850* (Manchester: Manchester University Press, 2011).

Buchanan, I., 'Infant Feeding, Sanitation and Diarrhoea in Colliery Communities, 1880–1911', in *Diet and Health in Modern Britain*, ed. D. J. Oddy and D. S. Miller (Beckenham: Croom Helm, 1985), pp. 148–77.

Buer, M. C., *Health, Wealth, and Population in the early days of the Industrial Revolution* (London: Routledge, 1926).

Burnett, J. (ed.), *Destiny Obscure: Autobiographies of Childhood, Education and Family from the 1820s to the 1920s* (London: Allen Lane, 1982).

——, *Plenty and Want: A Social History of Diet in England from 1815 to the Present Day* (London: Scholar Press, 1979).

Burr Litchfield, R., 'The Family and the Mill: Cotton Mill Work, Family Work Patterns, and Fertility in Mid-Victorian Stockport', in *The Victorian Family: Structure and Stresses*, ed. A. S. Wohl (London: Croom Helm, 1978), pp. 180–96.

Buxton, N. K., *The Economic Development of the British Coal Industry from Industrial Revolution to the Present Day* (London: Batsford, 1978).

Carson, W. G., 'The Conventionalization of Early Factory Crime', *International Journal of the Sociology of Law*, 7 (1979), 37–60.

——, 'White-Collar Crime and the Enforcement of Factory Legislation', *British Journal of Criminology*, 10 (1970), 383–98.

Carter, T., 'British Occupational Hygiene Practice, 1720–1920', *Annals of Occupational Hygiene*, 48 (2004), 299–307.

Chadwick, E., *Report on the Sanitary Condition of the Labouring Population of Great Britain* (1842), ed. M. W. Flinn (Edinburgh: Edinburgh University Press, 1965).

Chaloner, W. H., 'Mrs Trollope and the Early Factory System', *Victorian Studies*, 4, 2 (December 1960), 159–66.

——, 'New Introduction', in W. Dodd, *The Factory System Illustrated* (London: Frank Cass, 1968), pp. v–xiii.

——, 'Robert Owen, Peter Drinkwater and the Early Factory System in Manchester, 1788–1800', *Bulletin of the John Rylands Library Manchester*, 37 (1954/5), 78–102.

Chapman, S. D., 'Cressbrook and Litton Mills: An Alternative View', *Derbyshire Archaeological Journal*, 139 (1969), 86–90.

——, *The Early Factory Masters: the Transition to the Factory System in the Midlands Textile Industry* (Newton Abbot: David & Charles, 1967).

Childs, M. J., *Labour's Apprentices: Working-Class Lads in Late Victorian and Edwardian England* (Montreal and Kingston: McGill-Queen's University Press, 1992).

Church, R., *The history of the British Coal Industry, vol. 3: 1830–1913, Victorian Pre-eminence* (Oxford: Oxford University Press, 1986).

Chwe, M. S. Y., 'Why Were Workers Whipped? Pain in a Principal-Agent model', *The Economic Journal*, 100 (December 1990), 1109–21.

Clapham, J. H., *An Economic History of Modern Britain: The Early Railway Age, 1820–1850* (1926; Cambridge: Cambridge University Press, 1950).

Clark, G., 'Factory Discipline', *Journal of Economic History*, 3 (1994), 128–63.

Clerke, W., *Thoughts upon the Means of Preserving the Health of the Poor, by Prevention and Suppression of Epidemic Fevers, Addressed to the Inhabitants of Manchester* (London: J. Johnson, 1790).

Cobden, J. C., *The White Slaves of England, Compiled from Official Documents* (Cincinnati: Derby, 1853; 2nd edn, New York: Saxton, Barker & Co., 1860).

Cockayne, E., *Hubbub: Filth, Noise and Stench in England, 1600–1770* (New Haven: Yale University Press, 2007).

Cockburn, J. S., 'Patterns of Violence in English Society: Homicide in Kent, 1560–1985', *Past & Present*, 130 (1991), 70–106.

Cole, G. D. H., *The Life of Robert Owen* (1925; 3rd edn, London: Frank Cass, 1965).

Collier, F., *The Family Economy of the Working Classes in the Cotton Industry, 1784–1833*, ed. R. S. Fitton (Manchester: Manchester University Press, 1964).

Combe, A., *Principles of Physiology* (New York: Harper & Brothers, 1834).

Cooke Taylor, W., *Factories and the Factory System; from Parliamentary Documents and Personal Examination* (London: Jeremiah How, 1844).

Cooper, B. B., *The Life of Sir Astley Cooper, Bart: Interspersed with Sketches from his Note-Books of Distinguished Contemporary Characters*, vol. 2 (London: John W. Parker, 1843).

Cooper, L., *Radical Jack* (London: Cresset Press, 1959).

Cooter, R. and W. Luckin (eds), *Accidents in History* (Atlanta: Rodopi, 1997).

Corfield, P. J., *The Impact of English Towns, 1700–1800* (Oxford: Oxford University Press, 1982).

Crafts, N. F. R., *British Economic Growth during the Industrial Revolution* (Oxford: Clarendon Press, 1985).

Crawford, P., 'Attitudes to Menstruation in Seventeenth-Century England', *Past & Present*, 91 (May 1981), 47–73.

Cretney, S., 'Children, Cruelty and Corporal Punishment in Twentieth-Century England: the Legal Framework', in *Childhood and Violence in the Western Tradition*, ed. L. Brockliss and H. Montgomery (Oxford: Oxbow Press, 2010), pp. 151–8.

Crowther, M. A., *The Workhouse System, 1834–1929: The History of an English Social Institution* (London: Methuen, 1983).

Cruickshank, M., *Children and Industry: Child Health and Welfare in North-West Textile Towns during the Nineteenth Century* (Manchester: Manchester University Press, 1981).

Cule, J. and T. Turner (eds), *Child Care Through the Centuries: An Historical Survey from Papers Given at the Tenth British Congress on the History of Medicine* (Cardiff: British Society for the Social History of Medicine, 1986).

Cunningham, H., 'Child Labour', *Labour History Review*, 56, 3 (1991), 48–51.

——, *The Children of the Poor: Representations of Childhood since the Seventeenth Century* (Oxford: Blackwell, 1991).

——, 'The Employment and Unemployment of Children in England c.1680–1851', *Past & Present*, 126 (1990), 115–50.

Davenport, R., L. Schwarz and J. Boulton, 'The Decline of Adult Smallpox in Eighteenth-Century London', *Economic History Review*, 64, 4 (2011), 1289–314.

Davin, A., 'Child Labour, the Working-Class Family, and Domestic Ideology in Nineteenth-Century Britain', *Development and Change*, 13 (1982), 633–52.

Davis, L. J., *Enforcing Normalcy: Disability, Deafness and the Body* (London: Verso, 1995).

Davis, R., *The Industrial Revolution and British Overseas Trade* (Leicester: Leicester University Press), 1979.

De Sanjose, S. and E. Roman, 'Low Birthweight, Preterm and Small for Gestational Age Babies in Scotland, 1981–1984', *Journal of Epidemiology and Community Health*, 45 (1991), 207–10.

Digby, A., *Making a Medical Living: Doctors and Patients in the English Market for Medicine, 1720–1911* (Cambridge: Cambridge University Press, 2002).

——, *Pauper Palaces* (London: Routledge & Kegan Paul, 1978).

Djang, T., *Factory Inspection in Great Britain* (London: Allen & Unwin, 1942).

Dodd, G., *The Textile Manufacturers of Great Britain* (London: Charles Knight & Co., 1844).

Dodd, W., *The Factory System Illustrated in a Series of Letters to the Right Hon. Lord Ashley* (London: John Murray, 1842).

——, *The Factory System Illustrated*, intro. W. H. Chaloner (London: Frank Cass, 1968).

——, *A Narrative of the Experiences and Sufferings of William Dodd, a Factory Cripple, Written by Himself* (2nd edn, London: L. & G. Seeley, 1841).

Duffy, B., 'Coal, Class and Education in the North-East', *Past & Present*, 90 (1981), 142–51.

Dupree, M. W., *Family structure in the Staffordshire potteries, 1840–1880* (Oxford: Clarendon Press, 1995).

Dyhouse, C., 'Working-Class Mothers and Infant Mortality in England, 1895–1914', *Journal of Social History*, 12, 2 (1978), 248–67.

Edmonds, E. V., 'Public Health in the Economics of Child Labour', in

Child Labour: A Public Health Perspective, ed. A. G. Fassa, D. L. Lewis and T. J. Scanlon (Oxford: Oxford University Press, 2010), pp. 45–54.

Edwards, M. M., *The Growth of the British Cotton Trade, 1780–1815* (Manchester: Manchester University Press, 1967).

Eijkemans, G. and A. G. Fassa, 'An Introduction to the Topic', *Global Occupational Health Network Newsletter* (Child Labour and Adolescent Workers), 9 (Summer 2005), 1–3.

Engels, F., *The Condition of the Working Class in England in 1844* (1845; Oxford: Oxford University Press, 1993).

Eveleth, P. B. and J. M. Tanner, *Worldwide Variations in Human Growth* (Cambridge: Cambridge University Press, 1976).

Falconer, W., *An Essay on the Preservation of the Health of Persons Employed in Agriculture* (Bath: n.p., 1789).

——, *Remarks on the Influence of Climate, Situation, Nature of Country, Population, Nature of Food and Way of Life* (London: n.p., 1781).

Falkner, F. and J. M. Tanner (eds), *Human growth* (London: Plenum Press, 1979).

Farrer, W., *A Particular Account of the Rickets in Children; and Remarks on its Analogy to the King's Evil* (London: J. Johnson, 1773).

Fassa, A. G., D. L. Lewis and T. J. Scanlon (eds.), *Child Labour: A Public Health Perspective* (Oxford: Oxford University Press, 2010).

——, D. L. Parker and T. J. Scanlon, 'A Rights-Oriented, Public Health Model of Child Labour' in *Child Labour: A Public Health Perspective*, ed. A. G. Fassa, D. L. Lewis and T. J. Scanlon (Oxford: Oxford University Press, 2010), pp. 37–43.

Fekkes, M., F. I. M. Pijpers, M. Fredriks, T. Vogels and S. P. Verloove-Vanhorick, 'Do Bullied Children get Ill, or do Ill Children get Bullied? A Prospective Cohort Study on the Relationship between Bullying and Health-Related Symptoms', *Pediatrics*, 117 (May 2006), 1568–74.

Ferguson, F., 'The Degeneracy of the Factory Population', *Sanitary Record*, 25 September 1875, 211–12.

——, 'Factory Children', *Sanitary Record*, 24 July 1875, 52–7.

Ferriar, J., 'Advice to the Poor', in *Medical Histories and Reflections* (London: W. Bulmer & Co., 1810), vol. 3, p. 281.

——, 'Origin of Contagious and New Diseases', in *Medical Histories and Reflections* (London: W. Bulmer & Co., 1810), vol. 1, 261–92.

——, 'Prevention of Fevers in Great Towns', *Medical Histories and Reflections* (London: W. Bulmer & Co., 1810), vol. 2, 213–47.

——, *To the Committee for the Regulation of the Police in the Towns of Manchester and Salford* (Manchester: n.p., 1792).

Fielden, J., *The Curse of the Factory System* (1836), ed. J. T. Ward (New York: A. M. Kelley, 1969).

Figlio, K., 'Chlorosis and Chronic Disease in Nineteenth-Century Britain: The Social Constitution of Somatic Illness in a Capitalist Society', *Social History*, vol. 3 (1978), 167–97.

Fildes, V. A., 'The English Disease: Infantile Rickets and Scurvy in Pre-Industrial England', in *Child Care Through the Centuries: An Historical Survey from Papers Given at the Tenth British Congress on the History of Medicine*, ed. J. Cule and T. Turner (Cardiff: British Society for the Social History of Medicine, 1986), pp. 121–34.

Finer, S. E., *The Life and Times of Sir Edwin Chadwick* (1952; London: Methuen, 1980).

Fisher, P. J., 'The Politics of Sudden Death: The Office and Role of the Coroner in England and Wales, 1726–1888' (Ph.D. thesis, University of Leicester, 2007).

Floud, R., K. Wachter and A. Gregory, *Height, Health and History: Nutritional Status in the United Kingdom, 1750–1980* (Cambridge: Cambridge University Press, 1990).

——, R. W. Fogel, B. Harris and S. C. Hong, *The Changing Body: Health, Nutrition, and Human Development in the Western World since 1700* (Cambridge: Cambridge University Press, 2011).

Fowler, A. and T. Wyke (eds), *The Barefoot Aristocrats: A History of the Amalgamated Association of Operative Cotton Spinners* (Littleborough: George Kelsall, 1987).

Freudenberger, H., F. J. Mather and C. Nardinelli, 'A New Look at the Early Factory Labor Force', *Journal of Economic History*, 44 (1984), 1085–90.

Garner, A. D. and E. W. Jenkins, 'The English Mechanics Institutes: The Case of Leeds, 1824–42', *History of Education*, 13:2 (1984), 139–52.

Gaskell, P., *The manufacturing population of England: its moral, social, and physical conditions, and the changes which have arisen from the use of steam machinery; with an examination of infant labour* (London: Baldwin & Cradock, 1833).

George, M. D., *London Life in the Eighteenth Century* (London: London School of Economics, 1997).

Gibbins, H. de B., *The Industrial History of England* (London: Methuen, 1904).

Gochfeld, M., 'Chronologic History of Occupational Medicine', *Journal of Occupational and Environmental Medicine*, 47, 2 (February 2005), 96–114.

Goddard, V. and B. White, 'Child Workers and Capitalist Development', *Development and Change*, 13 (1982), 465–78.

Goldsmith, O., Letter to *The Bee*, 10 November 1759, in *The Miscellaneous works of Oliver Goldsmith: with an Account of his Life and Writings*, ed. W. Irving (Philadelphia: J. Crissy & J. Grigg, 1830), pp. 454–8.

Goldwater L. J., 'The History of Occupational Medicine', *Clinics in Podiatric Medicine and Surgery*, 4 (1987), 523–7.

Gray, D. D., 'The Regulation of Violence in the Metropolis: The Prosecution of Assault in the Summary Courts, c.1780–1820', *London Journal*, 32 (2007), 75–87.

Gray, R., 'The Languages of Factory Reform in Britain, c.1830–1860', in *The Historical Meanings of Work*, ed. P. Joyce (Cambridge: Cambridge University Press, 1987), pp. 143–79.

——, 'Medical Men, Industrial Labour and the State in Britain, 1830–50', *Social History*, 16 (January 1991), 19–43.

Greenlees, J., *Female Labour Power: women workers' influence on business practices in the British and American cotton industries, 1780–1860* (Aldershot: Ashgate, 2007).

——, '"Stop Kissing and Steaming!": Tuberculosis and the Occupational Health Movement in Massachusetts and Lancashire, 1870–1918', *Urban History*, 32 (2005), 223–46.

Greg, S., *Two Letters to Leonard Horner Esq., on the Capabilities of the Factory System* (n.p., 1840).

Greg, W. R., 'Protection of Children in Mines and Collieries', *Westminster Review*, 38 (July 1842), 86–139.

Hair, P. E. H., 'Bridal Pregnancy in Rural England in Earlier Centuries', *Population Studies*, 20.2 (1966), 233–43.

—— (ed.), *Coals on Rails or the Reason of my Wrighting: the Autobiography of Anthony Errington, a Tyneside Colliery Waggon and Waggonway Wright, from his Birth in 1778 to Around 1825* (Liverpool: Liverpool University Press, 1988).

——, 'Mortality from Violence in British Coalmines, 1800–50', *Economic History Review*, 21 (1968), 545–61.

——, 'The Social History of British Coalminers' (D.Phil. thesis, University of Oxford, 1955).

Hales, S., *A Description of Ventilators: Whereby Great Quantities of Fresh Air May With Ease be Conveyed into Mines, Gaols, Hospitals, Work-Houses and Ships, in Exchange for their Noxious Air* (London: W. Innys, 1743).

Hamlin, C., 'Predisposing Causes and Public Health in Early-Nineteenth-Century Medical Thought', *Social History of Medicine*, 5 (1992), 43–70.

——, *Public Health and Social Justice in the Age of Chadwick: Britain, 1800–1854* (Cambridge: Cambridge University Press, 1998).

Hammel, E. A., S. R. Johansson and C. A. Ginsberg, 'The Value of Children during Industrialization: Sex Ratios in Childhood in Nineteenth-Century America', *Journal of Family History*, 8 (1983), 346–66.

Hammond, J. L. and B. Hammond, *Lord Shaftesbury* (London: Constable & Company, 1923).

—— and B. Hammond, *The Town Labourer, 1760–1832: The New Civilisation* (1917; London: Longmans, Green & Company, 1966).

Hanawalt, B. A., 'Childrearing among the Lower Classes of Late Medieval England', *Journal of Interdisciplinary History*, 8 (1977), 1–22.

——, *The Ties that Bound: Peasant Families in Medieval England* (Oxford: Oxford University Press, 1986).

Hardy, A., 'Cholera, Quarantine and the English Preventive System', *Medical History*, 37 (July 1993), 250–69.

——, *The Epidemic Streets: Infectious disease and the rise of preventive medicine, 1856–1900* (Oxford: Clarendon Press, 1993).

——, 'Rickets and the Rest: Child-care, Diet and the Infectious Children's Diseases, 1850–1914', *Social History of Medicine*, 5 (1992), 389–412.

Harris, B., M. Gorsky, M. Guntupalli and A. Hinde, 'Long-term Changes in Sickness and Health: Further Evidence from the Hampshire Friendly Society', *Economic History Review*, 65 (2012), 719–45.

Harrison, J., 'Extracts from the Report of the Inspectors of Factories, Illustrating the State of Health in the Different Factories', *Edinburgh Medical and Surgical Journal*, 44 (1835), 425–32.

Harrison, M., *Disease and the Modern World: 1500 to the Present Day* (Cambridge: Polity Press, 2004).

Hartwell, R. M., 'Children as Slaves', in *The Industrial Revolution and Economic Growth* (London: Methuen, 1971), pp. 390–408.

Hayek, F. A. (ed.), *Capitalism and the Historians* (Chicago: University of Chicago Press, 1954).

Heesom, A. J., 'The Coal Mines Act of 1842, Social Reform, and Social Control', *Historical Journal*, 24 (1981), 69–88.

——, 'The Northern Coal-Owners and the Opposition to the Coal Mines Act of 1842', *International Review of Social History*, 25 (1980), 236–71.

Hennock, E. P., 'Socialization and Working-Class Childhood in Nineteenth-Century England' (mimeo., University of Liverpool, 1989).

Henriques, U. R. Q., *Before the Welfare State: Social Administration in Early Industrial Britain* (London: Longman, 1979).

Hewitt, M., *Wives and Mothers in Victorian Industry* (London: Rockliff, 1958).

Hicks, W. C. R., 'The Education of the Half-Timer', *Economic History: A Supplement of the Economic Journal*, 3 (1939), 222–39.

Higgs, E., 'Disease, Febrile Poisons, and Statistics: the Census as a Medical Survey, 1841–1911', *Social History of Medicine*, 4 (1991), 465–78.

——, *Domestic Servants and Households in Rochdale, 1851–1871* (New York: Garland, 1986).

Hitchcock, M., '*In Vitro* Histamine Release from Human Lung as a Model for the Acute Response to Cotton Dust', *Annals of the New York Academy of Sciences*, 221 (1974), 124–31.

Hobbs, S., J. McKechnie and M. Lavalette, *Child Labor: a World History Companion* (Santa Barbara: ABC-Clio, 1999).

Hobcraft, J. and P. Rees (eds), *Regional Demographic Development* (London: Croom Helm, 1977).

Holdsworth, C., 'Dr John Thomas Arlidge and Victorian Occupational Medicine', *Medical History*, 42 (1998), 458–75.

——, 'Potters' Rot and Plumbism: Occupational Health in the North Staffordshire Pottery Industry' (Ph.D. thesis, University of Liverpool, 1995).

Holland, G. C., *Diseases of the Lungs from Mechanical Causes* (London: John Churchill, 1843).

Holyoake, G. J., *History of Cooperation*, vol. 2 (London: T. Fisher Unwin, 1908).

Honeyman, K., *Child Workers in England, 1780–1820: Parish Apprentices and the Making of the Early Industrial Labour Force* (Aldershot: Ashgate, 2007).

Hope, R. B., 'Dr Thomas Percival, a Medical Pioneer and Social Reformer, 1740–1804' (MA thesis, University of Manchester, 1947).

Hopkins, E., *Childhood Transformed: Working-Class Children in Nineteenth-Century England* (Manchester: Manchester University Press, 1994).

Horler, M., *The Early Recollections of Moses Horler*, ed. M. F. and H. Coombs (Radstock: n.p., 1900).

Horn, P., 'Child Workers in the Pillow Lace and Straw Plait Trades of

Victorian Buckinghamshire and Bedfordshire', *Historical Journal*, 17 (1974), 779–96.

——, 'The Traffic in Children and the Textile Mills, 1780–1816', *Genealogists' Magazine*, 24, 5 (March 1993), 177–85.

Horner, F., *On the Employment of Children in Factories and Other Works in the United Kingdom and in some Foreign Countries* (London: Longman, 1840).

Horrell, S. and J. Humphries, '"The Exploitation of Little Children": Child Labor and the Family Economy in the Industrial Revolution', *Explorations in Economic History*, 32 (1995), 485–516.

——, J. Humphries and H-J. Voth, 'Stature and Relative Deprivation: Fatherless Children in Early Industrial Britain', *Continuity and Change*, 13.1 (1998), 73–115.

Howard, J., *An Account of the Principal Lazarettos in Europe* (London: J. Johnson, 1791).

Howlett, J., 'Defence of his Pamphlet on Population', *Gentleman's Magazine*, 52 (1792), 525–6.

Huck, P., 'Infant Mortality and Living Standards of English Workers during the Industrial Revolution', *Journal of Economic History*, 55 (1995), 528–50.

Hudson, P., *The Industrial Revolution* (London: Edward Arnold, 1992).

Humphries, J., *Childhood and Child Labour in the British Industrial Revolution* (Cambridge: Cambridge University Press, 2010).

——, 'Childhood and Violence in Working-Class England, 1800–1870', in *Childhood and Violence in the Western Tradition*, ed. L. Brockliss and H. Montgomery (Oxford: Oxbow Press, 2010), pp. 135–40.

——, 'Short Stature among Coalmining Children: A Comment', *Economic History Review*, 50 (1997), 531–7.

—— and T. Leunig, 'Cities, Market Integration and Going to Sea: Stunting and the Standard of Living in Early Nineteenth-Century England and Wales', *Economic History Review*, 62 (2009), 458–78.

Hunter, D., *The Diseases of Occupations* (1955; London: Hodder & Stoughton, 1978).

Hutchins, B. L. and S. Harrison, *A History of Factory Legislation* (London: P. S. King & Son, 1903; 3rd edn, 1926).

Hutt, W. H., 'The Factory System of the Early Nineteenth Century', in *Capitalism and the Historians*, ed. F. A. Hayek (Chicago: University of Chicago Press, 1954), pp. 160–88.

Hutton, W., *History of Derby* (London: Nichols, Son & Bentley, 1791).

Huzzard, S., 'The Role of the Certifying Factory Surgeon in the State

Regulation of Child Labour and Industrial Health' (MA thesis, University of Manchester, 1976).

Ikin, J. I., 'Appointment of Certifying Surgeons under the New Factory Bill', *Provincial Medical and Surgical Journal*, 6, 15 April 1843, 56–7.

——, 'Certifying Surgeons under the Factory-Amendment Bill', letter to *The Lancet*, 38, 30 April 1842, 165–7.

Ingram, D., *An Historical Account of the Several Plagues that have Appeared in the World since the Year 1346* (London: R. Baldwin, 1755).

Inkster, I., 'Marginal Men: Aspects of the Social Role of the Medical Community in Sheffield, 1790–1850', in *Health Care and Popular Medicine*, ed. J. H. Woodward and D. Richards (London: Croom Helm, 1977), pp. 128–63.

Innes, J., 'Origins of the Factory Acts: the Health and Morals of Apprentices Act, 1802', in *Law, Crime and English Society, 1660–1830*, ed. N. Landau (Cambridge: Cambridge University Press, 2002), pp. 230–55.

——, 'Le parlément et la regulation du travail des enfants dans les fabriques en Grande-Bretagne 1783–1819', in *La société civile. Savoirs, enjeux et acteurs en France et en Grande-Bretagne 1780–1914*, ed. C. Charle and J. Vincent (Rennes: n.p., 2011).

Ireson, A., 'Reminiscences' (1929–30), in *Destiny Obscure: Autobiographies of Childhood, Education and Family from the 1820s to the 1920s*, ed. J. Burnett (London: Allen Lane), 1982), pp. 70–7.

Jordanova, L. J., 'Conceptualising Childhood in the Eighteenth Century: The Problem of Child Labour', *British Journal for Eighteenth-Century Studies*, 10 (1987), 189–99.

Joyce, P. (ed.), *The Historical Meanings of Work* (Cambridge: Cambridge University Press, 1987).

——, 'Work', in *Cambridge Social History of Britain*, ed. F. M. L. Thompson (Cambridge: Cambridge University Press, 1990), vol. 2, pp. 131–94.

Kay, J. P., *The Moral and Physical Condition of the Working Classes Employed in the Cotton Manufacture in Manchester* (London: James Ridgway, 1832.

——, 'Observations and Experience concerning Molecular Consumption and on Spinners' Phthisis', *North of England Medical and Surgical Journal*, 1 (August 1830–May 1831), 348–63.

Keating, J., 'Struggle for Identity: Issues Underlying the Enactment of the 1926 Adoption of Children Act', *University of Sussex Journal of Contemporary History*, 3 (2001), 1–9.

Keeling, F., *Child Labour in the United Kingdom: A Study of the*

Development and Administration of the Law Relating to the Employment of Children (London: International Association for Labour Legislation, 1914).

Kerridge, E., *Textile Manufacturers in Early Modern England* (Manchester: Manchester University Press, 1985).

King, H., *The Disease of Virgins: Green Sickness, Chlorosis and the Problems of Puberty* (London: Routledge, 2004).

King, P., 'Punishing Assault: The Transformation of Attitudes in the English Courts', *Journal of Interdisciplinary History*, 27 (Summer 1996), 43–74.

Kirby, P., *Anthropometric Data Relating to working-class children, 1841* (database), UK Data Archive, University of Essex (1993), http://www.esds.ac.uk/findingData/snDescription.asp?sn=3108.

——, 'Attendance and Work Effort in the Great Northern Coalfield, 1775–1864', *Economic History Review*, 65 (2012), 961–83.

——, 'A Brief Statistical Sketch of the Child Labour Market in Mid-Nineteenth Century London', *Continuity and Change*, 20 (2005), 229–45.

——, 'Causes of Short Stature among Coalmining Children, 1823–1850', *Economic History Review*, 48 (1995), 687–99.

——, *Child Labour in Britain, 1750–1870* (Basingstoke: Palgrave, 2003).

——, *Evidence to the Children's Employment Commission, 1842* (database), UK Data Archive, University of Essex (2009), http://www.esds.ac.uk/findingData/snDescription.asp?sn=6128.

——, 'The Historic Viability of Child Labour and the Mines Act of 1842', in *A Thing of the Past? Child Labour in Britain in the Nineteenth and Twentieth Centuries*, ed. M. Lavalette (Liverpool: Liverpool University Press, 1999), pp. 101–17.

——, 'How many Children were "Unemployed" in Eighteenth- and Nineteenth-Century England?', *Past & Present*, 187 (May 2005), 187–202.

——, *The Physical Stature of 16,402 Children in Northern English Factory Districts, 1837* (database), UK Data Archive, University of Essex (2010), http://www.esds.ac.uk/findingData/snDescription.asp?sn=6426.

——, 'Short Stature among Coalmining Children: A Rejoinder', *Economic History Review*, 50 (1997), 538–42.

——, 'The Transition to Working Life in Eighteenth and Nineteenth-Century England and Wales', in *Child Labour's Global Past: 1650–2000*, ed. K. Lieten and E. van Nederveen Meerkerk (Amsterdam: International Institute for Social History, 2011), pp. 119–36.

Kirby, R. G. and A. E. Musson, *The Voice of the People: John Doherty, 1798–1854* (Manchester: Manchester University Press, 1975).

Knight, A., 'On the Grinders' Asthma', *North of England Medical and Surgical Journal*, 1 (1 August 1830), 85–91 and 2 (1 November 1830), 167–79.

Knight, B., 'History of Child Abuse', in *Child Care Through the Centuries: An Historical Survey from Papers Given at the Tenth British Congress on the History of Medicine*, ed. J. Cule and T. Turner (Cardiff: British Society for the Social History of Medicine, 1986), pp. 109–19.

Knowles, L. C. A., *Industrial and Commercial Revolutions in Great Britain During the Nineteenth Century* (London: Routledge, 1921).

Kovačević, I. and S. B. Kanner, 'Blue Book into Novel: The Forgotten Industrial Fiction of Charlotte Elizabeth Tonna', *Nineteenth Century Fiction*, 25 (1970), 152–73.

Kunitz, S. J., 'Speculations on the European Mortality Decline', *Economic History Review*, 36 (1983), 349–64.

Kussmaul, A., 'The Ambiguous Mobility of Farm Servants', *Economic History Review*, 34 (1981), 222–35.

La Berge, A. E. F., *Mission and Method: The Early Nineteenth-Century French Public Health Movement* (Cambridge: Cambridge University Press, 2002).

Labriola, M., T. Lund and J. Andersen, 'Work Environment, Health and Wellbeing among Children and Adolescents in Denmark: Results from a Study of 545 13–17 Year Olds', *Occupational and Environmental Medicine*, 68, Supplement 1 (2011), Abstract 24.

Laforce, F. M., 'Woolsorters' Disease in England', *Bulletin of the New York Academy of Medicine*, 54 (1978), 956–63.

Landau, N. (ed.), *Law, Crime and English Society, 1660–1830* (Cambridge: Cambridge University Press, 2002).

Landers, J., 'Mortality and Metropolis: the Case of London, 1675–1825', *Population Studies*, 41, 1 (1987), 59–76.

Lane, J., *Apprenticeship in England, 1600–1914* (London: University College Press, 1996).

——, 'Apprenticeship in Warwickshire cotton mills, 1790–1830', *Textile History*, 10 (1979), 161–74.

——, *A Social History of Medicine: Health, Healing and Disease in England, 1750–1950* (London: Routledge, 2001).

Lane, S. R. and R. D. E. Sewell, 'Correlative Measurement of Four Biological Contaminants on Cotton lint, and their Implications for

Occupational Health', *International Journal of Occupational and Environmental Health*, 12 (2006), 120–5.

Laslett, P., *Family Life and Illicit Love in Earlier Generations* (Cambridge: Cambridge University Press, 1977).

——, *The World we have Lost* (London: Methuen, 1965).

Lavalette, M. (ed.), *A Thing of the Past? Child Labour in Britain in the Nineteenth and Twentieth Centuries* (Liverpool: Liverpool University Press, 1999).

Lawton, R., 'Regional Population Trends in England and Wales, 1750–1971', in *Regional Demographic Development*, ed. J. Hobcraft and P. Rees (London: Croom Helm, 1977), pp. 29–70.

Leach, J., 'Surat Cotton, as It Bodily Affects Operatives in Cotton Mills', *The Lancet*, 2, 5 December 1863, 648–9.

Lee, C. H., *A Cotton Enterprise, 1795–1840: a History of M'Connel and Kennedy, Fine Cotton Spinners* (Manchester: Manchester University Press, 1972).

Lee, W. R., 'Emergence of Occupational Medicine in Victorian Times', *British Journal of Industrial Medicine*, 30 (1973), 118–24.

——, 'Occupational Medicine', in *Medicine and Science in the 1860s: proceedings of the sixth British Congress on the History of Medicine, University of Sussex, 6–9 September, 1967*, ed. F. N. L. Poynter (London: Wellcome Institute of the History of Medicine, 1968), pp. 151–81.

——, 'Robert Baker: the First Doctor in the Factory Department, Part 1. 1803–1858', *British Journal of Industrial Medicine*, 21 (1964), 85–93.

Leifchild, J. R., 'Life and Labour in the Coal Fields', *Cornhill Magazine*, 5 (1862), 343–53.

——, 'Life, Enterprise and Peril in Coal Mines', *Quarterly Review*, 110 (1861), 329–67.

Lieten, K. and E. van Nederveen Meerkerk (eds), *Child Labour's Global Past: 1650–2000* (Amsterdam: International Institute for Social History, 2011).

Levene, A., *Childcare, Health and Mortality at the London Foundling Hospital, 1741–1800: 'Left to the Mercy of the World'* (Manchester: Manchester University Press, 2007).

——, *The Childhood of the Poor: Welfare in Eighteenth-Century London* (Basingstoke: Palgrave, 2012).

——, '"Honesty, Sobriety and Diligence": Master–Apprentice Relations in Eighteenth- and Nineteenth-Century England', *Social History*, 33 (2008), 183–200.

Lever, J. H., 'Paget's Disease of Bone in Lancashire and Arsenic Pesticide in Cotton Mill Wastewater: a Speculative Hypothesis', *Bone*, 31 (2002), 434–6.

Levine, D., *Family Formation in an Age of Nascent Capitalism* (New York: Academic Press, 1977).

Leyser, H., 'Corporal Punishment and the Two Christianities', in *Childhood and Violence in the Western Tradition*, ed. L. Brockliss and H. Montgomery (Oxford: Oxbow Press, 2010), pp. 113–22.

Lieten, K. and E. Van Nederveen Meerkerk (eds), *Child Labour's Global Past, 1650–2000* (Bern: Peter Lang, 2011).

Lind, J., *A Treatise on the Scurvy* (Edinburgh: A. Millar, 1753).

Lindert, P. H. and J. G. Williamson, 'English Workers' Living Standards during the Industrial Revolution: a New Look', *Economic History Review*, 36 (1983), 1–25.

Locke, J., *Some Thoughts Concerning Education*, intro. and notes R. H. Quick (Cambridge: Cambridge University Press, 1889).

Lomax, E., 'Hereditary or Acquired Disease? Early Nineteenth Century Debates on the Cause of Infantile Scrofula and Tuberculosis', *Journal of the History of Medicine and Allied Science*, 32 (1977), 356–74.

Long, V., *The Rise and Fall of the Healthy Factory: The Politics of Industrial Health in Britain, 1914–60* (Basingstoke: Palgrave, 2010).

Loomis, W. F., 'Rickets', *Scientific American*, 223(6) (1970), 76–91.

Luckin, W., 'Evaluating the Sanitary Revolution: Typhus and Typhoid in London', in *Urban Disease and Mortality in Nineteenth-Century England*, ed. R. I. Woods and J. H. Woodward (London: Batsford Academic, 1984), pp. 102–19.

Lugol, J. G. A., *Researches and Observations of the Causes of Scrofulous Disease* (London: Churchill, 1844).

Lyons, J., 'Family Response to Economic Decline: Handloom Weavers in Early Nineteenth-Century Lancashire', *Research in Economic History*, 12 (1989), 45–91.

MacDonagh, O., *Early Victorian Government* (London: Weidenfeld & Nicolson, 1977).

Mackenzie, M. H., 'Cressbrook and Litton Mills, 1779–1835', *Derbyshire Archaeological Journal*, 88 (1968), 1–15.

——, 'Cressbrook and Litton Mills: A Reply', *Derbyshire Archaeological Journal*, 90 (1970), 56–9.

——, 'Cressbrook Mill, 1810–1835, *Derbyshire Archaeological Journal*, 90 (1970), 60–71.

Malcolm, L. A., 'Protein-Energy Malnutrition and Growth', in *Human growth*, ed. F. Falkner and J. M. Tanner (London: Plenum Press, 1979), vol. 3, pp. 361–72.

Malone, C., *Women's Bodies and Dangerous Trades in England, 1880–1914* (Woodbridge: Boydell Press, 2003).

Marland, H., *Medicine and Society in Wakefield and Huddersfield, 1780–1870* (Cambridge: Cambridge University Press, 1987).

Marmot, M. G., M. J. Shipley and G. Rose, 'Inequalities in Death – Specific Explanations of a General Pattern', *Lancet*, 1 (1984), pp. 1003–6.

Martin, B., 'Leonard Horner: a Portrait of an Inspector of Factories', *International Review of Social History*, 14 (1969), 412–43.

Marvel, H. P., 'Factory Regulation: A Reinterpretation of Early English Experience', *Journal of Law and Economics*, 20 (1977), 379–402.

Marx, K., *Capital: A Critical Analysis of Capitalist Production*, vol. 1, trans. S. Moore and E. Aveling (New York: International Publishers, 1947).

Mathisen, A., 'Treating the Children of the Poor: Institutions and the Construction of Medical Authority in Eighteenth-Century London' (D.Phil. thesis, Oxford University, 2011).

McBride, T. M., *The Domestic Revolution: The Modernisation of Household Service in England and France, 1820–1920* (London: Croom Helm, 1976).

McEvoy, A. F., 'Working Environments: an Ecological Approach to Industrial Health and Safety', in *Accidents in History*, ed. R. Cooter and W. Luckin (Atlanta: Rodopi, 1997), pp. 59–89.

McIvor, A., 'Health and Safety in the Cotton Industry: A Literature Survey', *Manchester Region History Review*, 9 (1995), 50–7.

——, *Lethal Work: A History of the Asbestos Tragedy in Scotland* (Glasgow: Tuckwell, 2000).

—— and R. Johnston, *Miners' Lung: A History of Dust Disease in British Coal Mining* (Aldershot: Ashgate, 2007).

McKechnie, J., 'A Peculiarly British Phenomenon? Child Labour in the USA' in *A Thing of the Past? Child Labour in Britain in the Nineteenth and Twentieth Centuries*, ed. M. Lavalette (Liverpool: Liverpool University Press, 1999), pp. 193–215.

McLaren, A., 'The Early Birth Control Movement: an Example of Medical Self-Help', in *Health Care and Popular Medicine in Nineteenth-Century England*, ed. J. Woodward and D. Richards (London: Croom Helm, 1977), pp. 89–104.

McNay, K., J. Humphries and S. Klasen, 'Excess Female Mortality in

Nineteenth-Century England and Wales: A Regional Analysis', *Social Science History*, 29 (Winter 2005), 649–81.

Meiklejohn, A., 'Industrial Health – Meeting the Challenge', *British Journal of Industrial Medicine*, 16, 1 (1959), 1–10.

——, 'Outbreak of Fever in Cotton Mills at Radcliffe, 1784', *British Journal of Industrial Medicine*, 16, 1 (1959), 68–70.

Mercer, A., *Death, Disease and Mortality in the Demographic Transition: Epidemiological-Demographic Change in England since the Eighteenth Century as part of a Global Phenomenon* (Leicester: Leicester University Press, 1993).

Middleton, J., 'Thomas Hopley and Mid-Victorian Attitudes to Corporal Punishment', *History of Education*, 34 (November 2005), 599–615.

Mill, J. S., *On Liberty* (1859), in *Utilitarianism and On Liberty*, ed. M. Warnock (Oxford: Blackwell, 2003), pp. 88–180.

Mills, C., *Regulating Health and Safety in the British Mining Industries, 1800–1914* (Aldershot: Ashgate, 2010).

Mitchell, B. R., *British Historical Statistics* (Cambridge: Cambridge University Press, 1988).

Mitchell, J., 'Burden of Industrial Accidents', *Annals of the American Academy of Political and Social Science*, 38 (1911), 76–82.

Montgomery, J., *The Theory and Practice of Cotton Spinning; or the Carding and Spinning Master's Assistant* (2nd edn, Glasgow: J. Niven, 1833).

Morgan, P. and A. D. M. Phillips (eds), *Staffordshire Histories: Essays in Honour of Michael Greenslade* (Stafford: Staffordshire Record Society, 1999).

Mottram, J., 'The Life and Work of John Roberton (1797–1876) of Manchester, Obstetrician and Social Reformer' (MSc thesis, University of Manchester, 1986).

Muldrew, C., '"Th'ancient Distaff" and "Whirling Spindle": measuring the contribution of spinning to household earnings and the national economy of England, 1550–1770', *Economic History Review*, 65 (2012), 498–526.

Murlidhar, V., V. J. Murlidhar and V. Kanhere, 'Byssinosis in a Bombay Textile Mill', *National Medical Journal of India*, 8 (1995), 204–7.

Musson, A. E., 'Robert Blincoe and the Early Factory System', in *Trade Union and Social History*, ed. A. E. Musson (London: Frank Cass, 1974), pp. 195–206.

Nardinelli, C., 'Child Labor and the Factory Acts', *Journal of Economic History*, 40 (1980), 739–55.

——, *Child Labor and the Industrial Revolution* (Bloomington and Indianapolis: Indiana University Press, 1990).

——, 'Corporal Punishment and Children's Wages in Nineteenth-Century Britain', *Explorations in Economic History*, 19 (1982), 283–95.

——, 'The Successful Prosecution of the Factory Acts: A Suggested Explanation', *Economic History Review*, 38 (1985), 428–30.

Newton, H., *The Sick Child in Early-Modern England, 1580–1720* (Oxford: Oxford University Press, 2012).

Nicholas, S. and R. H. Steckel, *Tall but Poor: Nutrition, Health and Living Standards in Pre-Famine Ireland*, NBER Historical Paper 39 (Cambridge, MA: National Bureau of Economic Research, 1992).

Nissel, M., *People Count: A History of the General Register Office* (London: HMSO, 1987).

Oddy, D. J. and D. S. Miller (eds), *Diet and Health in Modern Britain* (Beckenham: Croom Helm, 1985).

Oliver, T. (ed.), *The Dangerous Trades: the Historical, Social and Legal Aspects of Industrial Occupations as Affecting Health* (London: John Murray, 1902).

O'Malley, A., *The Making of the Modern Child: Children's Literature and Childhood in the Late Eighteenth Century* (London: Routledge, 2003).

Osborn, L. M., T. G. DeWitt, L. R. First and J. A. Zenel (eds), *Pediatrics* (Philadelphia: Elsevier Mosby, 2005).

Owen, I., 'Geographical Distribution of Rickets, Acute and Subacute Rheumatism, Chorea, Cancer, and Urinary Calculus in the British Islands', *British Medical Journal*, 1 (1889), 113–16.

Owen, R. D., *Threading my Way: An Autobiography* (New York: G. W. Carleton, 1874).

Parkinson, G., *True Stories of Durham Pit-Life* (2nd edn, London: Charles Kelly, 1912).

Passey, R. D., 'Experimental Soot Cancer', *British Medical Journal*, 2 (1922), 1112–13.

Paterson, C. S., 'From Fever to Digestive Disease: Approaches to the Problem of Factory Ill-Health in Britain, 1784–1833' (Ph.D. thesis, University of British Columbia, 1995).

Peacock, A. E., 'The Justices of the Peace and the Prosecution of the Factory Acts, 1833–1855' (D.Phil. thesis, University of York, 1982).

——, 'The Successful Prosecution of the Factory Acts, 1833–55', *Economic History Review*, 37 (1984), 197–210.

Peers, S., 'Power, Paternalism, Panopticism and Protest: Geographies of

Power and Resistance in a Cotton Mill Community, Quarry Bank Mill, Styal, Cheshire, 1784–1860' (D.Phil. thesis, Oxford University, 2008).

Pelling, M., 'Apprenticeship, Health and Social Cohesion in Early Modern London', *History Workshop*, 37, 1 (1994), 33–56.

——, 'Child Health as a Social Value in Early Modern England', *Social History of Medicine*, 1 (1988), 135–64.

——, *Cholera, Fever and English Medicine, 1825–1865* (Oxford: Oxford University Press, 1978).

Percival, T., 'Observations on the Medicinal Uses of the Oleum Jecoris Aselli, or Cod Liver Oil, in the Chronic Rhumatism, and Other Painful Disorders', in *Essays Medical, Philosophical, and Experimental* (Warrington: J. Johnson, 1789), pp. 354–62.

——, 'Observations on the State of Population in Manchester, and Other Adjacent Places', *Philosophical Transactions*, 64 (1774), 54–66.

Phillips, B., *Scrofula; its Nature, its Causes, its Prevalence, and the Principles of Treatment* (Philadelphia: Lea & Blanchard, 1846).

Phillips, G. L., *England's Climbing-Boys: a History of the Long Struggle to Abolish Child Labor in Chimney-Sweeping* (Boston, MA: Baker Library, 1949).

Pickstone, J. V., 'Dearth, Dirt and Fever Epidemics: Rewriting the History of British "Public Health", 1780–1850', in *Epidemics and Ideas: Essays in the Historical Perception of Pestilence*, ed. T. Ranger and P. Slack (Cambridge: Cambridge University Press, 1995), pp. 125–48.

——, 'Ferriar's Fever to Kay's Cholera: Disease and Social Structure in Cottonopolis', *History of Science*, 22 (1984), 401–19.

——, *Medicine and Industrial Society* (Manchester: Manchester University Press, 1985).

Piecková, E. and Z. Jesenská, 'Filamentous Microfungi in Raw Flax and Cotton for the Textile Industry and their Ciliostatic Activity on Tracheal Organ Cultures in Vitro', *Mycopathologia*, 134 (1996), 91–6.

Pinchbeck, I., *Women Workers and the Industrial Revolution, 1750–1850* (London: Routledge, 1930).

—— and M. Hewitt, *Children in English Society, vol. 2, From the eighteenth century to the Children Act 1948* (London: Routledge, 1973).

Pollard, S., 'Factory Discipline in the Industrial Revolution', *Economic History Review*, 16 (1963/4), 254–71.

Pooley, M. E. and C. G. Pooley, 'Health, Society and Environment in Nineteenth-Century Manchester', in *Urban Disease and Mortality in Nineteenth-Century England*, ed. R. Woods and J. H. Woodward (London: Batsford Academic, 1984), pp. 148–75.

Pope, W., 'On the mines of mercury in Friuli', *The Philosophical Transactions of the Royal Society of London* (1672–83; abridged, London: C. & R. Baldwin, 1809), vol. 1, pp. 10–12.

Pott, P., *Chirurgical Observations Relative to the Cataract, the Polypus of the Nose, the Cancer of the Scrotum, the Different Kinds of Ruptures, and the Mortification of the Toes and Feet*, vol. 3 (London: T. J. Carnegy, 1775).

Poynter, F. N. L. (ed.), *Medicine and Science in the 1860s: proceedings of the sixth British Congress on the History of Medicine, University of Sussex, 6–9 September, 1967* (London: Wellcome Institute of the History of Medicine, 1968).

Pressley, J., 'Childhood, Education and Labour: Moral Pressure and the end of the Half-Time System' (Ph.D. thesis, Lancaster University, 2000).

Prothero, I. J., *Artisans and Politics in Early Nineteenth-Century London* (Folkestone: Dawson, 1979).

Pryce, W., *Mineralogia Cornubiensis* (London: J. Phillips, 1778)

Ramazzini, B., *Treatise of the Diseases of Tradesmen* (English edn, London: Andrew Bell, 1705).

Ranger, T. and P. Slack (eds), *Epidemics and Ideas: Essays in the Historical Perception of Pestilence* (Cambridge: Cambridge University Press, 1995).

Rathbone, W. R., *The Life of Kitty Wilkinson: A Lancashire Heroine* (Liverpool: H. Young, 1910).

Reading, R., 'Poverty and the Health of Children and Adolescents', *Archives of Disease in Childhood*, 76 (1997), 463–7.

Reid, D. A., 'The Decline of Saint Monday, 1766–1876', *Past & Present*, 71 (May 1976), 76–101.

——, 'Weddings, Weekdays, Work and Leisure in Urban England, 1791–1911: The Decline of Saint Monday Revisited', *Past & Present*, 153 (November 1996), 135–63.

Riley, J. C., *Sick, Not Dead: the Health of British Workingmen during the Mortality Decline* (Baltimore: Johns Hopkins University Press, 1997).

Rimmer, W. G., *Marshalls of Leeds: Flax Spinners, 1788–1886* (Cambridge: Cambridge University Press, 1960).

Roberton, J., *General Remarks on the Health of English Manufacturers; and on the Need for Convelescent Retreats as subservient to the medical charities of our large towns* (London: J. Ridgway, 1831).

——, 'An Inquiry into the Natural History of the Menstrual Function', *Edinburgh Medical and Surgical Journal*, 38 (1 October 1832), 227–54.

——, 'On Infant Mortality in Manchester and some other Parts of

Lancashire', *London Medical Gazette: or, Journal of Practical Medicine*, 15 (12 February 1835), 733–5.

——, 'Remarks on the axiom of political economists, that a general improvement in the duration of life indicates a corresponding improvement in public health', *Manchester Guardian*, 18 June 1831, p. 3.

Robson, A. H., *The Education of Children Engaged in Industry in England, 1833–1876* (London: Kegan Paul, 1931).

Rodger, R., *Housing in Urban Britain, 1780–1914* (Cambridge: Cambridge University Press, 1995).

Rom, W. N. and S. B. Markowitz (eds), *Environmental and Occupational Medicine* (Philadelphia: Lippincott, Williams & Wilkins, 2007).

Rooke, P. J., 'A Study of Rewards and Punishments in the Elementary Schools of England and Wales, 1800–1893' (MA thesis, University of London, 1962).

Rose, M. B., 'Social Policy and Business: Parish Apprenticeship and the Early Factory System, 1750–1834', *Business History*, 31 (1989), 5–32.

Rose, M. E., 'The Doctor in the Industrial Revolution', *British Journal of Industrial Medicine*, 28 (1971), 22–6.

Rosen, G., *The History of Miners' Diseases: A Medical and Social Interpretation* (New York: Schuman's, 1943).

——, 'On the Historical Investigation of Occupational Diseases: An Aperçu', *Bulletin of the History of Medicine*, 5 (1937), 941–6.

Rosenberg, C. E., 'The Bitter Fruit: Heredity, Disease, and Social Thought', in *No Other Gods: On Science and American Social Thought* (Baltimore: Johns Hopkins University Press, 1997), pp. 25–53.

Rule, J., *The Experience of Labour in Eighteenth-Century Industry* (London: Croom Helm, 1981).

Rylander, R., P. Haglind and M. Lundholm, 'Endotoxin in Cotton Dust and Respiratory Function Decrement among Cotton Workers in an Experimental Cardroom', *American Review of Respiratory Disease*, 131, 2 (1985), 209–13.

Saito, O., 'Children's Work, Industrialism, and the Family Economy in Japan, 1872–1926', in *Child Labour's Global Past, 1650–2000*, ed. K. Lieten and E. Van Nederveen Meerkerk (Bern: Peter Lang, 2011), pp. 457–78.

——, 'Labour Supply Behaviour of the Poor in the English Industrial Revolution', *Journal of European Economic History*, 10 (1981), 633–52.

Sambrook, P. A., 'Childhood and Sudden Death in Staffordshire, 1851 and 1860', in *Staffordshire Histories: Essays in Honour of Michael Greenslade*, ed. P. Morgan and A. D. M. Phillips (Stafford: Staffordshire Record Society, 1999), pp. 216–52.

Sanders, W., *Rules and Tables for Provident and Independent Institutions* (Birmingham: T. Knott, 1834).

Saunders, E., 'The Teeth A Test of Age', *The Lancet*, 2 (30 June 1838), 492–96.

——, *The Teeth, a Test of Age, Considered with Reference to the Factory Children* (London: H. Renshaw, 1837).

Scola, R., *Feeding the Victorian City: The Food Supply of Manchester, 1770–1870* (Manchester: Manchester University Press, 1992).

Seaman, E., *Osteoporosis in Men* (Nyon, Switzerland: International Osteoporosis Foundation, 2004).

Shahar, S., *Childhood in the Middle Ages* (London: Routledge, 1990).

Shaw, A., 'Upon Distortion of the Spine and Pelvis, from Rickets; with illustrations of a peculiar Conformation of the Skeleton produced by that disease, a paper read to the Medico-Chirurgical Society, 22 May 1832', *London Medical Gazette*, 10 (1832), 397–8.

Sigerist, H. E., 'Historical Background of Industrial and Occupational Diseases', *Bulletin of the New York Academy of Medicine*, 12 (1936), 597–609.

Simmons, J. R. (ed.), *Factory Lives: Four Nineteenth-Century Working-Class Autobiographies*, intro. J. Carlisle (Toronto: Broadview Editions, 2007).

Singer, C., *A Short History of Medicine* (Oxford: Oxford University Press, 1928).

Smelser, N. J., *Social Change in the Industrial Revolution: An application of theory to the Lancashire Cotton Industry, 1770–1840* (London: Routledge & Kegan Paul, 1959).

Smiley, J. A., 'Background to Byssinosis in Ulster', *British Journal of Industrial Medicine*, 18, 1 (1961), 1–9.

Smith, A., *An Inquiry into the Nature and Causes of the Wealth of Nations*, ed. R. H. Campbell, A. S. Skinner and W. B. Todd (Oxford: Clarendon Press, 1976).

Smith, A. M., S. Chinn and R. J. Rona, 'Social factors and Height Gain of Primary Schoolchildren in England and Scotland', *Annals of Human Biology*, 7 (1980), 115–24.

Smith, F. B., *The People's Health, 1830–1910* (London: Weidenfeld & Nicholson, 1979).

Smith, G., 'Expanding the Compass of Domestic violence in the Hanoverian Metropolis', *Journal of Social History*, 41 (2007), 31–54.

Smith, R. A., 'On the Air and Rain of Manchester', *Memoirs of the Proceedings of the Manchester Literary and Philosophical Society*, 10 (1852), 207–17.

Snell, K. D. M., 'Agricultural Seasonal Unemployment, the Standard of Living, and Women's Work in the South and East, 1690–1860', *Economic History Review*, 34 (1981), 407–37.

——, *Annals of the Labouring Poor: Social Change and Agrarian England, 1660–1900* (Cambridge: Cambridge University Press, 1985).

——, 'The Apprenticeship System in British History: The Fragmentation of a Cultural Institution', *History of Education*, 25 (1996), 303–21.

Spence, C., 'Accidentally Killed by a Cart: Workplace Hazard, and Risk in Late Seventeenth Century London', *European Review of History*, 3 (1996), 9–26.

Stark, J., 'Bacteriology in the Service of Sanitation: The Factory Environment and the Regulation of Industrial Anthrax in Late-Victorian Britain', *Social History of Medicine*, 25 (2012), 343–61.

Statistical Society of London, 'Report on the Eleventh Meeting of the British Association for the Advancement of Science', *Journal of the Statistical Society of London*, 4 (October 1841), 181–2.

Steckel, R. H., 'Heights and Human Welfare: Recent Developments and New Directions', *Explorations in Economic History*, 46 (2009), 1–23.

Stevenson, T. H. C., 'The Fertility of Various Social Classes in England and Wales from the Middle of the Nineteenth Century to 1911', *Journal of the Royal Statistical Society*, 83, 3 (1920), 401–44.

Struve, C. A., *A Familiar View of the Domestic Education of Children during the early period of their lives: being a compendium addressed to all mothers, who are seriously concerned for the welfare of their offspring* (London: Murray & Highley, 1802).

Szreter, S. and G. Mooney, 'Urbanisation, Mortality, and the Standard of Living Debate: New Estimates of the Expectation of Life at Birth in Nineteenth-Century British Cities', *Economic History Review*, 51 (1998), 84–112.

Tann, J., *The Development of the Factory* (London: Cornmarket, 1970).

Tanner, J. M., *A History of the Study of Human Growth* (Cambridge: Cambridge University Press, 1981).

Teleky, L., *History of Factory and Mine Hygiene* (New York: Columbia University Press, 1948).

Tennant, H. J., 'Infant Mortality and Factory Labour (I)', in *The*

Dangerous Trades: the Historical, Social and Legal Aspects of Industrial Occupations as Affecting Health, ed. T. Oliver (London: John Murray, 1902), pp. 73–84.

Thackrah, C. T., *The Effects of Arts, Trades, and Professions ... on Health and Longevity* (London: Longman, Orme, Brown & Green, 1831; 1832).

Thiselton-Dyer, T. F., *Old English Social Life as told by the Parish Registers* (London: Elliot Stock, 1898).

Thomas, M. W., *The Early Factory Legislation: A Study in Legislative and Administrative Evolution* (Leigh-on-Sea: Thames Bank Publishing, 1948).

——, *Young People in Industry, 1750–1945* (London: T. Nelson, 1945).

Thompson, E. P., *The Making of the English Working Class* (1963; London: Penguin, 1980).

——, 'Time, Work-Discipline and Industrial Capitalism', *Past & Present*, 38 (December 1967), 56–97.

Thompson, F. M. L. (ed.), *Cambridge Social History of Britain, 1750–1950* (Cambridge: Cambridge University Press, 1990).

Timmins, G., *Made in Lancashire: a History of Regional Industrialisation* (Manchester: Manchester University Press, 1998).

Tomes, N., 'A "Torrent of Abuse": Crimes of Violence between Working-Class Men and Women in London, 1840–1875', *Journal of Social History*, 11 (Spring 1978), 328–45.

Tonna, C. E., *Helen Fleetwood* (London: R. B. Seeley & W. Burnside, 1841).

Trollope, F., *The Life and Adventures of Michael Armstrong the Factory Boy* (London: Henry Colburn, 1840).

Tropp, A., *The School Teachers: The Growth of the Teaching Profession in England and Wales from 1800 to the Present Day* (London: Heinemann, 1957).

Tweedale, G., *Magic Mineral to Killer Dust: Turner & Newall and the Asbestos Hazard* (2nd edn; Oxford: Oxford University Press, 2001).

Unwin, G., *Samuel Oldknow and the Arkwrights: The Industrial Revolution at Stockport and Marple* (Manchester: Manchester University Press, 1924).

Ure, A., *Philosophy of Manufactures: or, an exposition of the scientific, moral, and commercial economy of the Factory System of Great Britain* (London: Charles Knight, 1835).

Van Manen, N., 'The Climbing Boy Campaigns in Britain, c.1770–1840:

Cultures of Reform, Languages of Health and Experiences of Childhood' (Ph.D. thesis, University of York, 2010).

Verdon, N., *Rural Women Workers in Nineteenth-Century England: gender, work and wages* (Woodbridge: Boydell Press, 2002).

Vernati, P., 'The Method of Making Cerusse', *The Philosophical Transactions of the Royal Society of London* (1672–83; abridged, London: C. & R. Baldwin, 1809), vol. 2, pp. 421–2.

Villermé, L. R., *Sur la population de la Grande-Bretagne: considérée principalement et comparativement dans les districts agricoles, dans les districts manufacturiers et dans les grandes villes* (Paris: n.p., 1834).

Vincent, D., *Bread, Knowledge and Freedom: A Study of Nineteenth-Century Working-Class Autobiography* (London: Methuen, 1981).

Voth, H-J., *Time and work in England, 1750–1830* (Oxford: Oxford University Press, 2000).

—— and T. Leunig, 'Did Smallpox Reduce Height? Stature and the Standard of Living in London, 1770–1873', *Economic History Review*, 49 (1996), 541–60.

Wakley, T., 'The Factory-Slave Bill', *A Voice from the Commons*, 15 May 1836, 1–16.

Waldron, H. A., 'A Brief History of Scrotal Cancer', *British Journal of Industrial Medicine*, 40 (1983), 390–401.

Walker, J. E. M., 'John Ferriar of Manchester. M.D.: His Life and Work' (MSc thesis, University of Manchester, 1973).

Wall, R., 'The Age at Leaving Home', *Journal of Family History*, 3 (1978), 181–202.

Waller, J., *The Real Oliver Twist. Robert Blincoe: A Life that Illuminates a Violent Age* (Thriplow: Icon Books, 2006).

Walvin, J., *A Child's World: A Social History of English Childhood, 1800–1914* (Harmondsworth: Penguin, 1982).

Ward, J. T., *The Factory Movement, 1830–1855* (London: Macmillan, 1962).

——, 'New Introduction', in J. Fielden, *The curse of the factory system* (1836), ed. J. T. Ward (London: Kelley, 1969), pp. v–xlix.

Ward, L., 'Effect of British Statutory Regulations Directed to the Improvement of Hygienic Conditions of Industrial Occupations', *Journal of the Royal Statistical Society*, 68 (1905), 435–525.

Ware, N., *The Industrial Worker, 1840–1860* (1924; Chicago: Quadrangle Books, 1964).

Warner, J. and R. Griller, '"My Pappa is out, and my Mamma is asleep." Minors, their Routine Activities, and Interpersonal Violence in an

Early Modern Town, 1653–1781', *Journal of Social History*, 36 (Spring 2003), 561–84.

Warnock, M. (ed.), *Utilitarianism* (London: Fontana, 1986).

Watterson, P. A., 'Infant Mortality by Father's Occupation from the 1911 Census of England and Wales', *Demography*, 25 (1988), 289–306.

Weindling, P., 'Linking Self Help and Medical Science: The Social History of Occupational Health', in *The Social History of Occupational Health*, ed. P. Weindling (London: Croom Helm, 1985), pp. 2–31.

Weinstein, S. L., L. A. Dolan, J. C. Cheng, A. Danielsson and J. A. Morcuende, 'Adolescent Idiopathic Scoliosis', *The Lancet*, 371, 3 May 2008, 1527–37.

Welton, T. A., 'On the Effect of Migrations in Disturbing Local Rates of Mortality, as Exemplified in the Statistics of London and the Surrounding Country, for the years 1851–1860', *Journal of the Institute of Actuaries and Assurance Magazine*, 16 (1870–2), 153–86.

White, G. S., *Memoir of Samuel Slater, the Father of American Manufactures, connected with a History of the Rise and Progress of the Cotton Manufacture in England and America* (Philadelphia: n.p., 1836).

Wilkinson, R. G., 'Income and Mortality', in *Class and Health: Research and Longitudinal Data*, ed. R. G. Wilkinson (London: Tavistock, 1986), pp. 88–114.

Willan, R., *Reports on the Diseases in London* (London: Phillips, 1801).

Williams, J. C., J. M. Phillips and J. Wilson, letters, 4–9 June 1833, *London Medical Gazette*, 2, 12 (1833), 365–6.

Williams, S., 'Practitioners' Income and Provision for the Poor: Parish Doctors in the Late Eighteenth and Early Nineteenth Centuries', *Social History of Medicine*, 18 (2005), 159–86.

Williamson, J. G., *Did British capitalism breed inequality?* (Winchester, MA: Allen & Unwin, 1985).

——, 'Earnings Inequality in Nineteenth-Century Britain', *Journal of Economic History*, 40 (1980), 457–76.

Wilson, J., *Memories of a Labour Leader* (London: T. Fisher Unwin, 1910).

Wilson, R., 'On the Coal-Miners of Durham and Northumberland, their Habits and Diseases', *Transactions of the British Association for the Advancement of Science*, 33 (1863), 126.

Wing, C., 'Dr Harrison's Treatment of Spinal Deformity', *The Lancet*, 1, 22 October 1836, 166–8.

——, *The Evils of the Factory System Demonstrated by Parliamentary Evidence* (1837; London: Frank Cass, 1967).

——, 'Pathology of Curvature of the Spine', *The Lancet*, 1, 24 December 1836, 463–4.

Wohl, A. S., *Endangered Lives: Public Health in Victorian Britain* (1983; London: Methuen, 1984).

——, 'Sex and the Single Room: Incest among the Victorian Working Classes', in *The Victorian Family: Structure and Stresses*, ed. A. S. Wohl (London: Croom Helm, 1978), pp. 197–216.

Woods, R. I. and J. H. Woodward (eds), *Urban Disease and Mortality in Nineteenth-Century England* (London: Batsford Academic, 1984).

——, P. A. Watterson and J. H. Woodward, 'The Causes of Rapid Infant Mortality Decline in England and Wales, 1861–1921, Part I', *Population Studies*, 42 (1988), 343–66.

Woodward, J. and D. Richards (eds.), *Health Care and Popular Medicine in Nineteenth-Century England* (London: Croom Helm, 1977).

Wrigley, E. A. and R. Schofield, *The Population History of England, 1541–1871* (Cambridge: Cambridge University Press, 1989).

——, R. S. Davies, J. E. Oeppen and R. S. Schofield, *English Population History from Family Reconstitution, 1580–1837* (Cambridge: Cambridge University Press, 1997).

Wyke, T., 'Mule Spinners' Cancer', in *The Barefoot Aristocrats: A History of the Amalgamated Association of Operative Cotton Spinners*, ed. A. Fowler and T. Wyke (Littleborough: George Kelsall, 1987), pp. 184–96.

Zuberer, D. A. and C. M. Kenerley, 'Seasonal Dynamics of Bacterial Colonization of Cotton Fiber and Effects of Moisture on Growth of Bacteria within the Cotton Boll', *Applied and Environmental Microbiology*, 59, 4 (1993), 974–80.

Index

Printed and bound by CPI Group (UK) Ltd, Croydon, CR0 4YY

13/04/2025

14656514-0003